T0355854

Come On Over!
Northeastern Ontario
A to Z
2nd Edition

By Dieter K. Buse
with Graeme S. Mount

Library and Archives Canada Cataloguing in Publication

Title: Come on over! : Northeastern Ontario A to Z / by Dieter K. Buse with Graeme S. Mount.
Names: Buse, Dieter K., author. | Mount, Graeme S. (Graeme Stewart), 1939- author.
Description: 2nd edition. | Includes bibliographical references.
Identifiers: Canadiana (print) 2023057226X | Canadiana (ebook) 20230572308 | ISBN 9781988989648 (softcover) | ISBN 9781988989808 (EPUB)
Subjects: LCSH: Ontario, Northern—History. | LCSH: Ontario, Northern—Miscellanea.
Classification: LCC FC3094.4 .B87 2024 | DDC 971.3/13—dc23

Book design: Matthew Foti
Cover design: Alfred Boyd
Interior cartoons: Jennifer Rouse Barbeau

Published by Latitude46 Publishing
229 Elm Street Suite 3D,
Sudbury, Ontario, Canada, P3C 1T8
info@latitude46publishing.com
https://latitude46publishing.com

We acknowledge the financial support of the Ontario Arts Council.

Come on Over!
Northeastern Ontario
A to Z
2nd Edition

**By Dieter K. Buse
with Graeme S. Mount**

Dedicated to Judith M. Buse with much gratitude.

Through hiking and kayaking she came to identify with the region's highlights such as Killarney Provincial Park.

TABLE OF CONTENTS

INTRODUCTION —————————————————————————— 9
Algoma, District of —————————————————————— 16
Anishinaabek & Mushkegowuk:
The Indigenous Peoples of Northeastern Ontario ———————— 23
Arctic-Atlantic Watershed ——————————————————— 27
Birds and Birding ————————————————————————— 30
Blind River ———————————————————————————— 32
Bruce Mines ———————————————————————————— 34
Chapleau ————————————————————————————— 36
Cobalt ——————————————————————————————— 39
Cochrane, District of ——————————————————————— 42
Cochrane, Town of ———————————————————————— 49
Early European Explorers of James Bay ——————————————— 53
Elliot Lake ————————————————————————————— 55
Espanola ————————————————————————————— 58
Fires ——————————————————————————————— 65
Food ——————————————————————————————— 67
Forests and Forestry ——————————————————————— 69
Fort St. Joseph —————————————————————————— 73
French Legacies and Realities —————————————————— 75
French River ———————————————————————————— 81
Geology or Moving Rocks ————————————————————— 84
Hearst —————————————————————————————— 88
Kapuskasing ———————————————————————————— 92
Killarney ————————————————————————————— 96
Kirkland Lake and Swastika ———————————————————— 98
Manitoulin District and the Islands ———————————————— 104
Mattawa ————————————————————————————— 116
Moose Factory ——————————————————————————— 119
Moosonee ————————————————————————————— 123
Nipissing, District of ——————————————————————— 127
North Bay ————————————————————————————— 132
Parks, National and Provincial——————————————————— 141
Railways, Budd Cars, Train Troubles, and the Spanish River Train Wreck— 152
1910 Spanish River Train Wreck —————————————————— 155
Recreation ———————————————————————————— 157

Rivers ——————————160
Sables-Spanish Rivers Township ——————164
Sault Ste. Marie ——————————168
Steamers ——————————175
St. Joseph Island ——————————179
Sudbury, City of Greater ——————————181
Communities Surrounding the Sudbury Core   199
The Myths of Sudbury ——————— 205
Sudbury, District of ——————————— 208
Temiskaming, District of ——————— 214
Temiskaming Shores ——————— 219
Thessalon ——————————— 223
Timmins ——————————— 225
Waterfalls ——————————— 231
Wawa ——————————— 234
West Nipissing ——————————— 237
Zinger Lake ——————————— 241
 Afterword:
Thoughts on National Historic Sites ——————— 242
Acknowledgements ——————————— 246

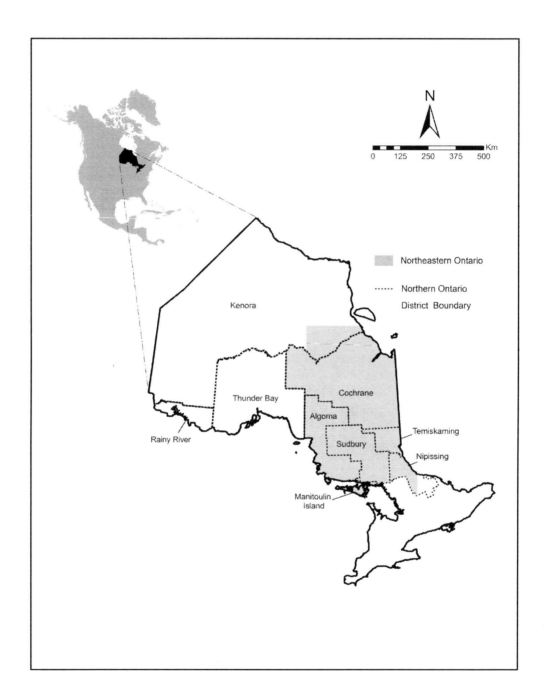

Map of Northeastern Ontario

INTRODUCTION

Where can we see statues of some of the most significant North American explorers, the people who blazed the trails into the interior of North America? Where can we walk in the footsteps of the soldiers who achieved one of the significant British victories at the outbreak of the War of 1812? What was the world's most exciting mining town in the first decade of the twentieth century? Where can we be photographed swimming with polar bears? Where can we experience Cree culture firsthand? Where were the homes of Winnie the Pooh and Shania Twain? The general answer to all these questions is "Northeastern Ontario," an area that extends from the Ontario-Quebec border in the east to the western limits of the District of Algoma on the shores of Lake Superior, and from Lake Nipissing, the French River and Manitoulin Island in the south to the shores of James Bay in the north. (The specific answers are, respectively, Mattawa, Fort St. Joseph on St. Joseph Island, Cobalt, Cochrane, Moosonee and Moose Factory, White River and Timmins; the details are in this book).

Shania Twain, Northeastern Ontario's most prominent singer, tells us if we want to "Get a life—get a grip" we need to "Come on over"! Her 1997 album by the same name sold 40 million copies and is among the top-selling albums in music history. Who are we to argue with such success by a Northeasterner? We too want you to come on over . . . to the region and to this book.

North of Parry Sound in central Ontario is where the special combination of lakes, rocks and trees is everywhere as depicted by the Group of Seven. Those artists recognized and rendered beauty when they saw it. That is where the voyageurs had to travel to expand the fur trade, which was, after fish, Canada's long-time reason for existence, in European eyes. That is where the entrepreneurs found forests after exhausting those in the Maritimes, Quebec and southern Ontario. That is where most of Canada's minerals came and come from. Further, that is among the best landscape and recreational territory in the country, though perhaps not in the vast expanse of the Hudson Bay Lowlands, especially during mid-winter or bug season.

Northeastern Ontario is central to Canadian history, to its economic development and to its image. It contains about 500,000 people, as many as Newfoundland and Labrador. In terms of territory, the most northerly of the six districts of Northeastern Ontario is bigger than Newfoundland. Northeastern Ontario has rightly been termed "a vast and magnificent land."

Yet it has modern cities, some of which were the first in Canada to go fibre optic; some have high tech firms and movie or TV productions, but none are so big as to submerge people. Few people will be surprised that Northeastern Ontario has exported hundreds of hockey players to the National Hockey League (NHL). Many, however, will be surprised to learn of the multitude of other sport attainments—including numerous Olympians and the invention of ringette. Most will be taken aback at the area's contributions to high and pop culture: directors of the National Gallery and Stratford Festival, international cartoonists, opera singers and country music artists.

The area's communities have been and remain a mix of the founding peoples: Indigenous, Métis, French and English. Additionally, many European ethnic groups contributed to the hard labour of lumbering, mining and construction. During the past two decades, minorities from other continents have joined the mix. Less populated places are often seen as backward, yet Northeasterners elected the first woman and the first Black mayor in Canada demonstrating that it sometimes had modern and progressive attitudes. By presenting such facts and stories we seek to explore both the communities and the shared characteristics of the Northeast.

The six districts presented in this book are Algoma, Cochrane, Manitoulin, Nipissing, Sudbury and Temiskaming. The boundaries of these political and judicial administrative areas are as artificial as most such lines across traditional and natural territories. However, they have a unity, tied together by the history of furs, forests, minerals, rail and road, by many Indigenous and Francophone inhabitants. The latter is one of the traits which, like the extent of mining, sets the region off from Northwestern Ontario.

Northeastern Ontario is not a geological unit but comprises distinct formations or provinces as geologists define it. From South to North are six physiographic (the way that the land appears) regions: The Laurentian highlands southeast of Sudbury, St. Lawrence Lowlands of Manitoulin Island, Penokian Hills along the North Shore of Lake Huron, the Cobalt Plain northeast of Sudbury and the Abitibi Uplands north of Sudbury, which extends north to the Moose River Basin.

The physiography of the region is controlled by two major geological components. The first is the recent sediments (sand, silt, clay and till) left behind during the melting of the glaciers that covered most of the area up to 9,000 years ago. Silt and clay, deposited under ancient lakes that formed as the glaciers retreated, created the farmland that is seen from Verner to St. Charles, Blind River to Echo Bay, Temiskaming Shores to Englehart and Matheson to Iroquois Falls. North of the Arctic-Atlantic watershed the meltwater rivers dropped sands and till quickly, which covered more of the landscape than south of the watershed giving rise to extensive coniferous forests. The second component is the underlying older, 360 million to 3.2-billion-year-old, pre-Cambrian Shield and post-Cambrian (Paleozoic) bedrocks which were eroded by the glaciers to form the recent sediments.

The geography of Northeastern Ontario is defined by the height of land dividing the north, which has rivers draining into James Bay, from the south from where they drain into the St. Lawrence (though many flow west and southwest via lakes Superior, Huron and Erie). Water has determined much of the human usage of a region of lakes and many rivers. The Indigenous utilized rivers as highways and lakes for food. In the southeast, the Mattawa-Ottawa basin was crucial to Canada's pattern of exploration and exploitation. The Hudson Bay lowlands are dissected by many large rivers that served as highways. In the southwest lakes, especially the two great lakes of Huron and Superior delimit the edge of the region. Boreal forest covers much of the area aside from Manitoulin, though the south is more varied. Farmland exists between the rocks and lakes but is limited to the area of tillable soils.

How to read and use this book: We describe the places and provide a glimpse into their histories, demographics and economic situations. We outline attractions and special aspects. Some stories offered by CBC listeners during a series of interviews in fall 2010, for the first edition, have been included and photos illustrate noteworthy aspects. The reader can simply look alphabetically for what is of interest. Smaller places without a stand-alone article can be found under their district.

Making this book involved much research and travel. Information gathered on trips to archives, museums, libraries, welcome centres and economic development offices, were checked against internet websites and often vetted by persons familiar with a place. Most enjoyable and worthwhile was meeting people on trips to Cobalt, Haileybury, Kirkland Lake, to Sault Ste. Marie via Blind River and Bruce Mines, to Mattawa, to provincial parks, to Elliot Lake, to Cochrane, to Moose Factory and Moosonee via the Polar Bear Express, to Marten River, Earlton, Englehart, Matheson, to waterfalls, to Chapleau, Wawa, White River, Hornepayne, Hearst, Kapuskasing, Moonbeam, Smooth Rock Falls, to Timmins, Iroquois Falls, to West Nipissing, to North Bay for the NORAD bunker, to Manitoulin Island and Espanola, plus a multitude of places in between.

To understand and to travel the Northeast, the following are useful:

- *Northeastern Ontario Backroad Mapbook* (very thorough for hiking, snowmobile trails, fishing and hunting, though it omits a part of the French River, and its city maps are inconsistent).
- Though too big to take anywhere, Matt Bray and Ernie Epp, eds., *A Vast and Magnificent Land: An Illustrated History of Northern Ontario* (Toronto: Ministry of Northern Development, 1984) contains wonderful photos and researched historical essays.
- Community profiles collated by the Province of Ontario, available at http://www.sse.gov.on.ca/medt/investinontario/_en/Pages/communities.aspx (to be used with caution as some parts contain factual errors).
- Heritage Ontario offers overviews of the seven sites recognized in Northeastern Ontario https://www.northeasternontario.com/attractions-culture/historic-sites/
- The provincial parks of the whole province are detailed, including access points for hiking and canoeing at https://www.ontarioparks.com/en

- Historical recreations for Manitoulin and Sudbury are available in cd format from libraries and from the Ontario Visual Heritage project at http://www.visualheritage.ca/

- For a profound and reflective study examining the interaction of Indigenous, settlers, mining firms and ethnic groups see Kerry M. Abel, *Changing Places: History, Community and Identity in Northeastern Ontario* (Montreal: McGill-Queen's, 2006).

- Doug Bennet and Tim Tiner, *The Complete Up North: A Guide to Ontario's Wilderness from Black Flies to the Northern Lights* (Toronto: McClelland and Stewart, 2010) which describes the "creepy crawlies" we avoid.

- For a light-hearted, virtual tour of one road corridor, see http://www.highway11.ca.

- The many books by Michael Barnes range from fires to mining, from places to people. His readable accounts have done much to publicize the Northeast.

- This book's maps provide overviews of the whole region, of each district and their communities and of the main parks and rivers. On the maps only a few places of interest have been identified since most places are of interest.

- The first edition of *Come on Over* won the Louise de Kiriline Lawrence Award for best Northern Ontario non-fiction in 2012.

- Though not an expert on all issues regarding the region, I have researched and written about diverse aspects of Northeastern Ontario's history, especially labour in Mercedes Steedman, Peter Suschnigg and Dieter K. Buse, eds., *Hard Lessons: The Mine Mill Union in the Canadian Labour Movement* (Toronto: Dundurn, 1995) and numerous historical essays offered in Sudbury.com (searchable under Buse). Regarding the military involvements of its people, I co-authored a large social history: *Untold: Northeastern Ontario's Military Past*, 2 volumes (Sudbury: Latitude 46 Publishing, 2018 and 2019) which won the prize of the Ontario Historical Society for best regional study of the past three years in 2020. The two volumes are crucial to understanding the contributions (mostly unrecognized) to Canada's wars by people from the Northeast, their experiences on the military and home fronts (often contrasting with other regions), as well as illustrating the way participation in warfare is commemorated throughout the region (often different than elsewhere). Creating those volumes was inspired by the travels undertaken to research this book and the discovery of the huge hole in Canada's military history as all the sacrifices of Northeasterners, acknowledged in local monuments, went unnoticed by so-called national narratives.

The limits of my knowledge appeared in the first edition, as the history of First Nations received too little consideration. The basic question of who existed before settlement by Europeans was mostly left unanswered. I hope part of that hole has been filled here. The history of Indigenous peoples has been one of encroachment and displacement by settlers, as previously they had lived all over Northeastern Ontario. What is known and increasingly been shown is that they hunted, fished, had agriculture and craft skills so that they used the forests and resources to build a culture rather than merely surviving. Often, they met and utilized the places later favoured by settlers, so what had been their meeting and trading places such as Sault Ste. Marie, or Temiskaming or North Bay became European settlers' meeting and trading places.

The Arctic-Atlantic watershed served as the general dividing line for land sharing treaties signed with the Indigenous. In 1850 the Robinson-Huron treaties with the Ojibwes (though more groups were involved) covered most of the peoples living south of the watershed and east of Lake Superior and north of Lake Huron. In 1905/06 treaties were signed with the Kashechewan First Nation (Fort Albany), Moose Cree First Nation (Moose Factory), Taykwa Tagmou First Nation (New Post), Abitiwinni and Wahgoshig First Nation, Matachewan First Nation, Mattagami First Nation, Flying Post First Nation and New Brunswick House First Nation. After lengthy court cases in 2023 a twelve-billion-dollar settlement was reached regarding compensation for nonpayment of promised treaty terms and utilization of resources from land reserved for Indigenous groups in the Robinson-Huron area.

For the late nineteenth and much of the twentieth century, First Nations' history includes attempted assimilation by limiting land holdings through broken treaties and by cultural reformation through Indian Act regulations and residential schools. Such schools existed at Moose Factory, Fort Albany, Sault Ste. Marie, Spanish and Chapleau. Shingwauk, at the Sault, has become a centre for research and education about the system. The report of the Truth and Reconciliation Commission (2008 to 2015) revealed that this horrid Canadian story includes a lengthy chapter from our area.

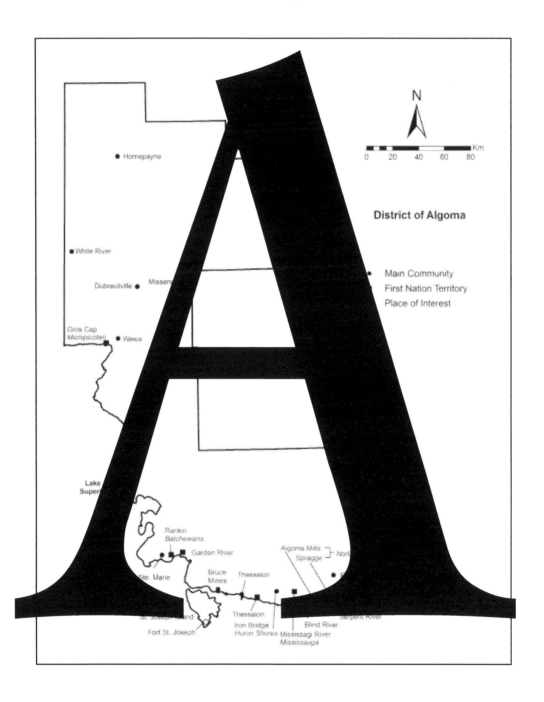

Map - District of Algoma

Algoma, District of

Real estate is about location, location and location. The concept also applies to regions. This geographically large district (population 117,500 in 2006; 114,100 in 2016; 113,800 in 2021) covers the area east of Lake Superior and north of Lake Huron and the St. Mary's River. Sudbury District is to the east, Cochrane to the north and Thunder Bay to the west. Sault Ste. Marie and Elliot Lake are its cities; Blind River, Bruce Mines, Thessalon and Wawa its towns. The villages and townships encompass Hornepayne, the North Shore, Huron Shores (including Iron Bridge), Dubreuilville, White River and St. Joseph Island.

Canada's National Historic sites are special and important places. This region has three with interpretive centres (detailed later): Fort St. Joseph, the Sault Ste. Marie ship canal and Ermatinger/Clergue buildings in Sault Ste. Marie. Villages mostly dot the southern and western boundaries on Highway 17, but many are on secondary roads north and east of that corridor. Below, after outlining the district's history, the smaller communities are described from north to south, starting with White River.

Indigenous people lived or moved throughout the District of Algoma for centuries. Most identified with specific areas for hunting and fishing seasons. The area was home to the Michipicoten First Nation in the northwest, the Batchawana and Garden River (Ketegaunseebee) in the southwest and Thessalon, Serpent River, Mississauga and Sagamok in the southeast. Missanabie and Horn Payne are in the northeast.

The first European to explore and begin to map the area was Étienne Brûlé, sent by the governor of New France in the early seventeenth century to gather information about a route west up the Ottawa River. He reached the falls at Sault Ste. Marie and in 1622 probably became the first European to see impressive Lake Superior. In all his travels, going west on the Mattawa River, then across Lake Nipissing, along the French River, and the North Shore of Lake Huron, he had the help of the First Nation's peoples.

The area is rich in ores (copper, iron, uranium, plus recent gold discoveries in the Wawa area) and wonderful scenery, and was once crucial to the fur trade, followed by logging as the primary industry. The judicial district was organized in 1858, but

Lake Superior Overview

major economic development came only after the Canadian Pacific Railway (CPR) from Sudbury sliced across the northeast corner in the 1880s and after the railway bridge to the U.S opened that area to timber from the north. Lumbering, and later pulp and paper and tourism remain main economic enterprises. Some agriculture, mostly poultry and dairy farming, exists in the south along Highway 17. The logging shore of Lake Huron has become the yachting shore as marinas replaced mills.

Highway 17 from Sault Ste. Marie to Wawa is one of the most spectacular drives in Ontario. Until 1960, this stretch with its rocks and hills remained a gap in the Trans-Canada Highway system, but travellers could take the Algoma Central Railway north to Hearst and connect to the CPR or go the northerly route via Highway 11. Lake Superior, often visible from the highway, truly is an inland sea. Beside the lake are campsites and picnic tables, but only the hardiest souls swim in the water, which is frigid even in August. Many moose live in the woods between Sault Ste. Marie and Wawa, making it risky to travel after dark.

White River (population 645 in 2016; 557 in 2021; almost 90% claim English as a first language, 12% French), located on the Canadian Pacific Railway (CPR) and Highway 17 near the northwestern limits of the District of Algoma, makes three claims to fame. First, from the arrival of the CPR in 1885, White River provided a base for CPR employees, and until the arrival of Highway 17 in 1961, the CPR provided the only land transportation to and from White River. The town is also at the southern end of Highway 631, which links Highway 17 with Highway 11. Second, White River has developed a reputation as the coldest community in any of the provinces. On the south side of the Trans-Canada Highway (Highway 17) stands an enormous thermometer that indicates a temperature of -72 degrees Fahrenheit (-58 Celsius). Cold as that is, on 3 January 1935 Iroquois Falls logged a temperature of -58.3 Celsius, and Snag Yukon on 3 February 1947 recorded -62.8 Celsius but as residents of Iroquois Falls and Snag do not regard that as

17

an attractive feature of their communities, they maintain silence on the matter. Hence, White River's claim usually goes unchallenged.

Most significantly perhaps is the third claim to fame: White River was home to the bear who inspired A.A. Milne's endearing story, *Winnie the Pooh*. In August 1914, Harry Colebourn was travelling from his home in Winnipeg to the battlefields of Europe. A hunter had shot Winnie's mother, and in those days residents of White River frequently adopted orphan bears as pets. During World War I, trains transported horses as well as troops, as horses still had military uses, and trains would stop in White River for several hours so that the horses could drink water and exercise. During one such stop, someone sold Winnie to Colebourn, who named her for the city where he had lived. Later that year, Colebourn was ordered to France. As he could not take Winnie, he lent her to the London Zoo, where she became a feature attraction. Whenever Colebourn had leave from the front he would visit Winnie, but when the war ended and he saw how popular she was, he donated her to the zoo. She lived until 12 May 1934. During the 1920s, author A.A. Milne visited the zoo with his son Christopher Robin, who called the bear by the name "Pooh," the name of his pet swan. Subsequently, Milne wrote the famous children's books about Christopher Robin and Winnie the Pooh. In 1961, Disney Corporation bought the rights to the story and took legal action when White River first advertised itself as Winnie's birthplace. The problem has since been resolved, and since 1992 a statue of Winnie stands near White River's Visitor Centre, on the south side of Highway 17. The community promotes Winnie as a tourist attraction which it has combined with a small railway museum.

One First Nations community, Missanabie, is close to the northern Algoma-Sudbury District border, on the river and lake of the same name. The Indigenous lived primarily from fishing, hunting and the fur trade before the latter declined. In 1905, Indian Affairs drafted the James Bay Treaty (also known as Treaty 9), which arranged for the surrender by Cree and Ojibwe of 130,000 square miles (340,000

Harry Colebourn and Winnie   White River Station / Museum

square kilometres) of land. Treaty 9 did not include the Missanabie Cree, and in 1915 the Department of Indian Affairs and Northern Development specifically rejected a request from the Missanabie Cree for the return of their own territory. In 1919, the Department again rejected a request for land, and the huge Chapleau Crown Game Preserve, established in 1925, further eroded opportunities to subsist on hunting and fishing. Not until 1951 did the department recognize the Missanabie as an "Indian band". In 2011, 39 square kilometres were handed to the band and in 2018 it was recognized as a reserve. To compensate for previous years the fiscal terms included the largest per capita settlement in Canada. The Hornepayne First Nation, just south of Hornepayne, faces similar issues of land ownership and compensation for non-fulfillment of treaty terms.

Hornepayne, with a population of 980 in 2016, and 968 in 2021, is located where Highway 631 crosses the Canadian National Railway tracks. It dates from the arrival of the Canadian Northern Railway (now part of Canadian National) in 1915, when its name was "Fitzpatrick." Subsequently a divisional point (where railway crews changed), in 1920 it was renamed Hornepayne, in honour of British financier Robert Horne-Payne. The old, unused railway roundhouse, a large square brick and glass building, needs repair but remains an impressive sight. It takes little imagination to envision the era when trains were turned and repaired at this then busy junction. In Hornpayne, hockey is clearly an important local tradition; NHL player Mike McEwen was born there, and Kris King, who became senior vice-president of the National Hockey League, spent his formative years in Hornepayne. Hunting and fishing are other popular activities.

Dubreuilville is on Highway 519, 32 kilometres east of Highway 17. The two highways meet almost midway between Wawa and White River. Dubreuilville (population in 2021: 576, down from 967 in 2001, more than 80% French-speaking) takes its name from the four Dubreuil brothers (Augustin, Joachim, Marcel and Napoleon), who established it as a lumber town in 1961. A company town with only a company-controlled access road until 1977, Dubreuilville was then incorporated as a municipality. Most of the town's businesses are housed in one central building. Its residents emphasize the availability of hunting, fishing, hiking, cross-country skiing and snowmobiling. The Alouettes Club has existed since 1969 and offers 800 kilometres of snowmobile trails.

Employment and development in Dubreuilville are shifting from forestry to mining, with two large gold mines. Island Gold Mine may become one of Canada's most productive while Alamos Gold has invested in a long-term underground operation.

The Municipality of Huron Shores (population 1,700) extends 50 kilometres along Highway 17 on the north shore of Lake Huron from Thessalon to Blind River. The largest community is Iron Bridge (formerly called Tally-Ho for the call used by lumberjacks). Agriculture, lumbering, tourism, hunting and fishing, provide the main occupations. Agricultural settlements developed after the CPR line came through the area.

Huron Shores is the site of a large, enclosed deer yard; deer can often be seen along the roadside on the edges of the town. Also in the region is the Kirkwood Forest, with its large red pines. Huron Shores has two of Canada's three 12-sided barns. One just east of Thessalon off Highway 17 (near Sowerby) was built in 1928 and is known as the Round Barn. Unfortunately, the eclectic craft collection is no longer available in the unusual three-storey building. Tours, entitled Art and Farm, offer many local products, such as honey or vegetables, and identify the private art galleries of the region. This lakeshore area is part of the Great Lakes Heritage Coastline, with fine views over Lake Huron.

The Township of the North Shore (Algoma Mills, Spragge, Serpent River; amalgamated 1973 to 1985), stretching along Highway 17 east of Blind River, is historically and aesthetically more important than its declining population would indicate (about 830 in 1986; around 550 in 2006, under 500 in 2016; though 531 in 2021). Agriculture and tourism dominate the economy, but who would guess that steamers, railways and lumbering once made Algoma Mills a busy harbour? Who would guess that the beautiful vistas along the highway are only a small part of the many First Nations territories (Serpent River, Mississagi River, Sagamok) stretching along the North Shore from the Bay of Islands to Blind River (with another smaller one at Thessalon)? None of those territories is part of the township, but they share its terrain.

Lake Huron's inland seacoast is the place where canoes of the fur trade were replaced by steamers, and the latter were challenged by railways and highways, and eventually replaced by small fishing and large sailing craft. The rolling hills of La Cloche in the east give way to gentler terrain in the west, but endless islands continue to dot the bays. Inland from the highway are numerous lakes, including large Lauzon Lake near Algoma Mills from which float planes take fishermen to secret interior spots.

The Voyageur Hiking Trail (Penewobikong Section) traverses Iron Bridge. That trail, started in 1973 but still incomplete in places, also passes through the hinterland, while shorter trails start near the communities: Kennebec Trail in Serpent River, Wagoosh Tral in Spragge and the Little Lake Bog Trail in Algoma Mills. Swimming, boating, fishing, sailing and snowmobiling are the main leisure activities that draw tourists to the numerous camps and resorts. The Deer Trail triangular driving route that passes through Elliot Lake has its southern base along this part of Highway 17. The later trail is home to an annual studio tour, which features local artists and their work at various locations along a 184-kilometre circle tour in mid-September.

Algoma Mills, originally called Ullin, has a rich history. First Nations fished the seashore though evidence of their encampments is limited. The first sawmill on Lauzon Creek between Lake Lauzon and the North Channel appeared in 1870, but by 1881 the mill and timber rights were sold to the CPR. Another sawmill opened at Bootlegger's Bay in 1882, when the CPR acquired land and started a rail line from Algoma Mills to Sudbury. Perhaps it reflected the beauty of the region, with its lake vistas and fishing opportunities, that plans were afoot for a 300-room hotel. A new dock was constructed for moving rails, materials and workers to the CPR's railroad construction. Even a grain elevator was started. By 1884 the line from Lake Nipissing to Algoma Mills was complete. Algoma Mills became the CPR's main coal depot supplying the railway and communities from North Bay to Sault Ste. Marie. About

200,000 tons of coal was moved per season by barges, through the docks and over the rails, with lumber forming the main load on return trips. But work on the grain elevator stopped as it was less expensive to ship by water than rail. Hotel construction ended in 1886, and the funds were used for the Banff Springs Hotel instead. Algoma Mills' boom ended as Britt became the main northern coal depot in 1910, Webbwood became the CPR's crew change site, and Sudbury the locomotive depot. However, lumbering continued until the main mill burned in 1918; it was not rebuilt because timber supplies had declined. Exemplifying the demise of a once busy entrepôt, the railway station was closed in 1927.

The development of Spragge (formerly Cook's Mill) centred on lumbering after the first sawmill appeared in 1882. That business ended in 1932, due to a fire that destroyed the mill, its lumber and much of the town. With the uranium boom at Elliot Lake after 1953, Spragge expanded with auto sales, garages, motels, transport firms and service depots. Further, copper discoveries led to a large mine and harbour. Shipments of lime, sulphuric acid and road salt, as well as slag cement used in the mining industry, are shipped to southern ports from the docks on nearby Lake Huron. However, mine closures at Elliot Lake during the 1990s undercut the local economy, as reflected in the slightly declining population (530 in 2006; 497 in 2016), but revival (531 in 2021) due to the steady employment of transport.

Serpent River village—really a collection of houses, garages, restaurants—developed due to the uranium boom at Elliot Lake. Its pub, the Mayflower, served as a well-known stopping point for single males (wild entertainers and topless dancers) during the 1960s. An appropriately named Atomic Drive-In shared the boom and the bust by the 1970s. By the 1980s all these service industries were gone.

All the villages and trading posts on the Highway 17 corridor provide services primarily to passing tourists, as do the First Nations communities. At Serpent River, the latter has a particularly attractive log building north of the highway and a business selling Woodland School-style art and crafts. By contrast, at the hamlet of Echo Bay stands a large statue of a Canadian dollar, the Loonie. It honours the designer, Robert Carmichael, who came from here. Just east of Sault Ste. Marie, the Garden River First Nations territory extends to Echo Bay. Highway 17 passes east-west through this Indigenous territory and for decades narrowed to two lanes with reduced speed limits. A bypass around the populated area has resolved the traffic problem and provided road maintenance employment for the Indigenous of Garden River First Nation. The band has a large community and administrative centre and administers its own police and other services.

Resources
Barbara Chrisholm and Andrea Gutsche, *Superior: Under the Shadow of the Gods* (Toronto: Lynx, 1999).
Dan Douglas, *Northern Algoma: A People's History* (Toronto: Dundurn Press, 1995).
Ted Weatherhead, "In Which Pooh joins the Army and lands in the Zoo," *The Beaver* (Oct/Nov 1989), 35-38.
Andrea Gutsche et al., *The North Channel and St. Mary's River* (Toronto: Lynx, 1997).

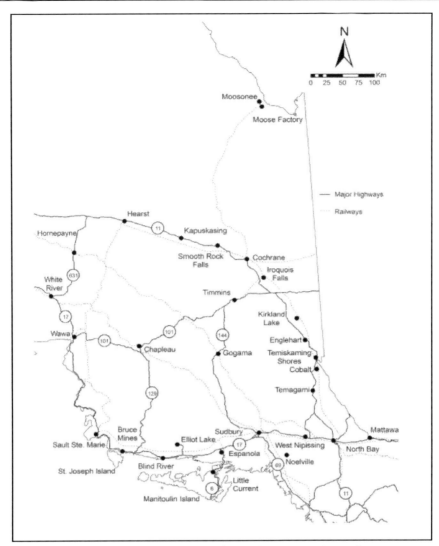

Highways and Railways of Northeastern Ontario

Railway roundhouse, Hornepayne

Anishinaabek & Mushkegowuk: The Indigenous Peoples of Northeastern Ontario

By Darrel Manitowabi and Alan Corbiere

Northeastern Ontario is home to two Indigenous groups with similar languages and cultures. Early Jesuit missionaries first referred to the southerly groups as "Outchibouec," in reference to their "puckered-up" style of moccasin footwear. Over time this word was rendered in various spellings: Ojibwe, Ojibwa, Chippewa or Ojibway. From the perspective of these Indigenous peoples, they have always been and continue to be the "Anishinaabe" (singular) or "Anishinaabek" (plural), translated as "original people." North of the Anishinaabek, the Jesuits met another group of people they referred to as "Kiristinon," a corruption of the Anishinaabe word "Kinishtino." Eventually, this word became "Cree," though they refer to themselves as "Mushkego" (singular) or "Mushkegowuk" (plural), meaning "people of the muskeg." Since the time of treaties, the Anishinaabek and Mushkegowuk have been threatened by colonial policies designed to assimilate. Despite this, these people have survived and are a vibrant and resilient presence in this part of North America. The following provides a brief background of these original peoples, some elements of their cultural and political history, and the contemporary issues they face.

The oral traditions of the Indigenous peoples of Northeastern Ontario are rich in history and culture. One of the central characters of these traditions is the mythical non-human being known as the trickster. For the Anishinaabek, "Nenaboozhoo," variously spelled as "Nanabush" or "Waynaboozhoo," meaning "Great Hare," served as the medium by which the Anishinaabek learned through stories about their history, values and way of being in the world. For the Mushkegowuk, this being is "Wisakaychak." To give insight into the central role played by these figures, the following story relates the connection between the land, the history and the culture of Northeastern Ontario: Nenaboozhoo, the Anishinaabek's great uncle, was half spirit and half-human, and travelled all over Mishiikenmnising (Turtle Island or North America) and his exploits have resulted in a change in the appearance or attributes of plants, animals, fish, birds and the land.

Nenaboozhoo heard of Mishi-amik or "giant beaver" who was menacing the Anishinaabek, so he sought to kill it. This giant beaver made a dam at Sault Ste. Marie and created a pond that is now called Lake Superior, or Ojibwe-gichi-gamiing (Great Lake of the Ojibwe). Nenaboozhoo went to the dam and erected stakes where he intended to break the dam. These stakes would allow the water to rush out but would trap an escaping beaver. Nenaboozhoo broke the dam, but Mishi-amik escaped by breaking through the stakes. The remnants of these stakes now cause the rapids, and all the debris from the beaver's dam became the many islands along the north shore of Lake Huron.

Nenaboozhoo continued causing trouble down by Lake Erie and was chased up to Manitoulin. There, he picked up his grandmother and ran with her on his back, but he soon tired. About to be descended upon, he dumped his grandmother in Lake Mindemoya (inland lake on Manitoulin Island). She became Mndimoowenh Mnis (Old Lady Island), now called Treasure Island. He continued but dropped his michigiw (spearhead) and spear handle. As a result, the Anishinaabek call this place "Michigiwadinong," meaning "bluff in the shape of a spear." Eventually, this word became "M'Chigeeng." This land formation comprises part of the Cup-and-Saucer north of the M'Chigeeng First Nation, Manitoulin Island.

Various Indigenous histories, such as the above, reveal a deeply embedded connection with the land of Northeastern Ontario and beyond. One significant event that altered this typical land use and sense of place occurred with the arrival of newcomers. In Northeastern Ontario, this process was marked by the signing of treaties. From the Indigenous perspective, these historic events were nation-to-nation agreements exchanging land title for rights such as hunting, fishing and annual gifts. In 1836, the Manitoulin Island Treaty was signed with the intention of removing Indigenous people from Upper Canada, now southern Ontario, to Manitoulin Island, to facilitate newcomer settlement. In 1850, the Anishinaabek on the north shore of Lake Huron signed the Robinson-Huron Treaty to accommodate newcomer demand to extract natural resources and occupy the land. The Anishinaabek on Manitoulin Island were faced with yet another treaty in 1862 due to expanded newcomer demand for land. The Mushkegowuk experienced the same fate with Treaty Number 9 in 1905 due to road and railway expansion to the west and future resource extraction. The significance of reserve settlement is evident in the Anishinaabek language as the word for reserves is "Shkonganing," meaning "place that is left over."

Through treaties, the Anishinaabek and Mushkegowuk were relegated to reserves and entered a period of colonization. The Indian Act of Canada of 1876 and subsequent revisions introduced the legal and political measures that remain today. Policies of assimilation were introduced, such as education at residential schools, municipal-style government and the imposition of paternalistic Indian Agents.

Following World War II, a new era emerged. Parts of the Indian Act were repealed, such as the stipulation making Indigenous ceremony a crime. One by one, residential schools started to close. The Anishinaabek of Walpole Island in Southwestern Ontario rejected their Indian Agent in 1965, and other groups soon did the same. Generations of Anishinaabek and Mushkegowuk united to voice various social, political and educational reforms and focused public attention on colonial

Fort Albany 1956 (Credit: Latchford Museum)

policies. Elders and traditional knowledge holders began to share ceremonies and teachings and to relate oral histories once again. Indigenous peoples began to refer to themselves as First Nations to remind all about the historic nation-to-nation treaties.

Despite positive change, the legacy of political and economic marginalization remains a challenge for the Anishinaabek and Mushkegowuk. Many have disputed the terms of earlier treaties and are now engaged in land claims. Current-day natural resource economic activities, from mining on the Wahnapitae First Nation (Anishinaabek outside of Sudbury) to diamond extraction near the Attawapiskat First Nation (Mushkegowuk) on coastal James Bay, have introduced new players First Nations must deal with—private and public corporations, including their legal and social privileges (for example, operating without consulting or employing Indigenous).

Despite these historical and contemporary challenges, the persistent spirit of the Anishinaabek and Mushkegowuk remains. The Anishinaabek of Northeastern Ontario are united under the Anishinaabek Nation (formerly Union of Ontario Indians) while the Mushkegowuk are under the Mushkegowuk Council. Both are political organizations that formed to meet their First Nations interests at regional, provincial and national levels. Non-profit organizations such as the Ojibway and Cree Cultural Centre in Timmins; the Cree Culture Interpretive Centre on the Moose Cree First Nation; and the Ojibwe Cultural Foundation on the M'Chigeeng First Nation promote, preserve, and in some cases, revitalize Anishinaabek and Mushkegowuk culture.

The Indigenous people have persisted against the forces of colonization and assimilation. They remain resilient actors contributing to the cultural fabric of Canada and beyond.

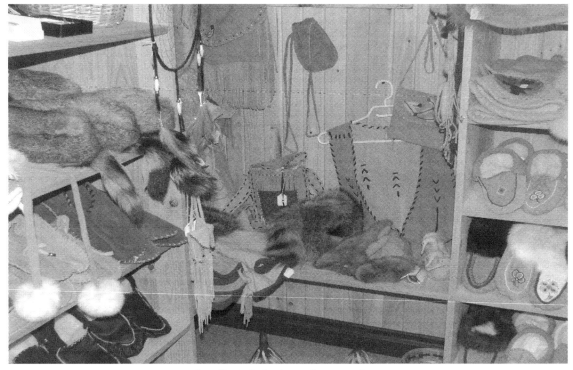

Crafts: Nipissing First Nation

Resources

Louis Bird, *Telling Our Stories: Omushkego Legends and Histories from Hudson Bay* (Peterborough, ON: Broadview Press, 2005).

Basil Johnston, *Ojibwe Heritage* (Toronto: McClelland and Stewart, 1976).

Edward S. Rogers and Donald B. Smith, eds., *Aboriginal Ontario: Historical Perspectives on the First Nations* (Toronto: Dundurn Press, 1994)

Reuben G. Thwaites, ed, *The Jesuit Relations and Allied Documents*, 73 Volumes (Cleveland: Burrows Brothers Co, 1896-1901).

Arctic-Atlantic Watershed

The Arctic-Atlantic Watershed in Northeastern Ontario separates the waters that flow into the Great Lakes and the Atlantic Ocean from those that flow into James and Hudson bays. It is not high: 318 metres on Highway 11 south of Matheson, 395 metres on Highway 144 south of Gogama, and 466 metres on both Highway 120 south of Chapleau and Highway 101 west of Chapleau. Signs mark the locations on all four highways.

For centuries, the watershed has had historical as well as geographical significance. For First Nations, people of the muskeg or Cree lived to the north while the Ojibwe lived to the south. Indeed, it served as the Iron Curtain of the eighteenth century, delineating the territories claimed by the competing states, Great Britain and France.

In 1670, King Charles II of England (1660-1685) chartered the Hudson's Bay Company (HBC), whose first governor was his uncle through marriage, Prince Rupert. The charter awarded the HBC jurisdiction over all lands that drained into Hudson Bay and James Bay, subsequently known as Rupert's Land. Of course, the Indigenous, mostly Cree in Northeastern Ontario, living on and using that land were not consulted. That territory included Ontario north of the Arctic-Atlantic Watershed, as well as parts of present-day Alberta, Manitoba, Minnesota, North Dakota, Nunavut, Quebec and Saskatchewan. The HBC, a fur-trading company, established a post at Moose Factory in 1673, the first British outpost in what is now Ontario. French forces challenged the claim and occupied the region. In 1713, by the terms of the Treaty of Utrecht (which ended the War of the Spanish Succession), France dropped any claims to Rupert's Land. Until the termination of French sovereignty on the North American mainland exactly 50 years later, the watershed was the official border between the (usually hostile) British and French empires. Until 1869, when the Hudson's Bay Company lands became Canadian territory, the watershed marked the northern limits of Quebec until 1791, Upper Canada (until 1841), Canada West (until 1867) and Ontario. In 1850, the Ojibwe First Nation ceded lands south of the divide to British colonial authorities through the Robinson-Huron Treaties. North of the line, the Ojibwe maintained their rights until 1905/06 when both Cree and Ojibwe signed treaties with the crown roughly defining the territories reserved for First Nations.

Both the Roman Catholic and Anglican churches still use the watershed to separate their respective dioceses of Hearst (Roman Catholic) and Moosonee (Roman Catholic and Anglican) to the north from the dioceses of Sault Ste. Marie (Roman Catholic) and Algoma (Anglican) to the south. Another aspect of the divide is differentiation in the type of forest on either side, which is mostly boreal (jack pine, spruce, tamarack, some poplar and white birch) to the north and transitional mix of conifers (pines, cedars) and deciduous (yellow birch, maple, oak, poplar, hemlock) to the south.

Arctic-Atlantic Watershed, Highway 144, south of Gogama

The Northern Hawk-Owl is a highly sought-after species of the boreal forest.
(Credit: Photo ©2009 David Bell)

Birds and Birding

By David Bell

When compared with many other areas of the world—the Amazon in Brazil, the Sunshine Coast of Australia, or even places closer to home, such as South Texas or Point Pelee—Northeastern Ontario is not generally considered a hot spot for birders. It does, however, support a surprising number of birds, with over 350 species recorded.

From mixed wood forests and farmlands in the south, to boreal forests in the centre and the subarctic tundra of the Hudson Bay lowlands in the north, Northeastern Ontario boasts a variety of habitats. The wetlands and mudflats along the James Bay coast provide an important staging area for waterfowl and shorebirds in fall, when tens of thousands of birds can be found congregating near Moosonee. The boreal forests, nearly uninhabited in winter, teem with life during summer as many species of songbirds, waterfowl and raptors breed among the spruces. The mixed wood forests farther south support many species more typical of southern climes, some of them at the northern limit of their range here. Farm fields around Sault Ste. Marie and on Manitoulin Island provide habitat for prairie and grassland specialists. All these habitats bring species from the north, south and west together.

Winter can be unpleasant for some, but it brings the birds of the high Arctic and boreal forests farther south. Highly sought-after species such as Great Gray, Boreal and Northern Hawk-Owls, Gyrfalcon, Pine Grosbeak, Hoary Redpoll, American Three-toed Woodpecker and Boreal Chickadee irrupt south every now and then, providing birders an opportunity to view birds that are rarely seen on breeding grounds.

Summer is breeding season and Northeastern Ontario provides a great place to look for breeding birds if one does not mind bugs such as black flies and mosquitos. Twenty-six warblers make up about one eighth of the total number of species that breed here and are perhaps the birds that get the most attention from birders. They join species such as Olive-sided Flycatcher, Spruce and Sharp-tailed

Grouse, Le Conte's Sparrow, Brewer's Blackbird and Black-backed Woodpecker, as well as many other species of songbirds, shorebirds, waterfowl and raptors.

Spring and fall migrations are the time when the largest numbers of birders are out looking for breeding species either arriving or departing depending on the time of year. Many birds that breed in the High Arctic pass through Northeastern Ontario on their way to and from their breeding grounds. In Northeastern Ontario, spring migration begins in mid-March, with the first waterfowl and raptors arriving in the southern portion. It ends in about mid-June, with the last of the shorebirds and passerines making their way to breeding grounds. Fall migration starts, surprisingly, in about mid-June, with the first shorebirds heading south, and ends in mid-December when the last of the waterfowl head south. A special sight is the Sandhill Cranes gathering by the thousands and milling in farmers' fields on Manitoulin Island before they majestically sweep south. Migration is also a time for vagrants; birds that are not normally found in the area, indeed, some that live as far away as Europe! They can get blown off course by storms or they are young birds whose internal compass is a bit off. Regardless of how they get here, the variety is quite extensive, and includes Anhinga, Painted Bunting, Yellow-billed Loon, Rock Wren, Sooty Shearwater, Dovekie, Tricolored Heron, Northern Wheatear and Tufted Duck.

Resources:

The Atlas of the Breeding Birds of Ontario is available from the Ontario Field Ornithologists and provides detailed species accounts and up-to-date range maps for each species found breeding in the province.

Dieter Buse comment: If one has not seen loons do their mating dance, frequently visible on Northeastern Ontario's tranquil lakes, one has yet to discover Canada.

The Wood Duck is a common breeder among the deciduous forests in the south.
(Credit: Photo ©2009 David Bell)

Blind River

> **Did you know?**
> - During the 1930s Blind River had the largest sawmill in Canada east of the Rockies
> - Neil Young's hearse—Mortimer Hearseburg—briefly "died" there; in other words, stopped functioning and sat by the roadside for a decade
> - A large marina serving watercraft of all sizes is tucked away off the highway

Half-way between Sudbury and Sault Ste. Marie on Highway 17, Blind River has become a major coffee stop for travellers on the Trans-Canada Highway. Ironically it has long been a meeting place as the Indigenous met there for trade and gatherings since the 1600s. The population of 3,422 (in 2021; 3,600 in 2016) makes a living from tourism and fishing, and the town serves as a distribution centre, whereas earlier its mainstay was logging and timber processing.

The river mouth was hidden from the Lake Huron side, and hence the name Blind River signified how difficult it was to find. However, the river has a large estuary with a deep-water access that proved convenient for sawmills, as timber could be brought out of the hinterland, then cut and shipped via Lake Huron. The mouth of the Mississagi River is just west of town, providing further log supplies from its watershed. The J. J. McFadden sawmill was once Canada's largest. At first much of the production went to Bruce Mines for mine shafts; later, lumber was shipped to Canadian and American markets by water and rail. Huge booms held logs in the harbour and sometimes as much as 15 kilometres of lumber stacks were drying behind the mill.

The harbour, with a protective sea wall and travel centre (free wi-fi, hot showers), is now a pleasure craft anchorage, though the lumbering industry's historical importance is registered in two ways. First, the Timber Village Museum shows the history of local timber production and pioneer life, especially in the lumber camps. A remarkable video documents a lumber drive of the early 1950s, including a stove used to cook for 65 men being loaded with its hot embers onto a boat and run down the river to the next camp. The museum's collection of photographs is extensive and of high quality. It is located next to the Northern Ontario Logging Memorial on Highway 17 (east of the main town) and shows local artwork at a small gallery that sometimes has special exhibits. Annual festivities include Voyageur Days Living History Re-enactment and Lumberjack Dinner the Saturday before the Thanksgiving holiday.

A second way logging is remembered is through the Boom Camp Interpretive Park, which provides well-marked hiking and cross-country ski trails west of town. The 12-kilometre loop trails are part of the North Channel History Trails project along Lake Huron. They illustrate the heritage of the First Nations (including lifestyle, plant usage and trade patterns), forestry, geology and industry at the mouth of the Mississagi River. One hundred years old in 2006, Blind River has become a regional supply centre. Nearby is the world's largest commercial uranium refinery (Cameco), processing ores from around the world. The town has a large fountain, parks and suburbs with vistas over the North Shore. The shoreline of Lake Huron offers excellent beaches, fishing and boating. The modern marina includes a large community building. A championship golf course, Huron Pines, is just west of town.

Northern Ontario Logging Memorial

Bruce Mines

The town of Bruce Mines (population 548 in 2006; 582 in 2016 and identical in 2021), is situated 65 kilometres east of Sault Ste. Marie on Highway 17 beside the shores of Lake Huron. The town is named in honour of James Bruce, 8th Earl of Elgin and Kincardine, who was governor general of Canada from 1847 to 1854.

With the establishment of copper mines during the 1840s, Bruce Mines became the first mining centre in Northeastern Ontario. Tin miners came from Cornwall, England, bringing with them skills and traditions going back hundreds of years.

In 1846 James Cuthbertson filed a copper claim. The following year, the Cornish miners—now employees of the Montreal Mining Company—reached Bruce Mines by water, more than a generation before railways were available to link Northeastern Ontario's other mining centres to the outside world. For many years the mining companies controlled the wharf and docks to limit access by outside merchants.

Copper from Bruce Mines had a ready market in the United States during the Civil War (1861-1865), but with peace demand dropped, and in 1876 the mine closed. Since then, residents have found employment in agriculture, lumbering and later tourism. By 1905, the town was able to build a full-sized, covered arena that is still available for skating, hockey and curling.

Today, attractions include a marina with a park and short walking path (offering an attractive view towards Lake Huron), a historical museum showing pioneer life (housed in a former Presbyterian church) and the Simpson Copper Mine Shaft Museum. The reconstructed mine includes a display of mining tools from various eras. The short boardwalk from the museum to the mine site is through a majestic pine forest. Tourism is supported by the usual infrastructure of motels and restaurants that benefit from Trans-Canada Highway traffic. The town has an interesting, if odd, assortment of family businesses, including one specializing in homemade foods, and is particularly famous for pies.

United Church, Iroquis Falls

Chapleau

Demographically Chapleau has been declining. In 2021 Chapleau had a population of 1,945, less than a third of that at its height in 1950, when the town, which sits at the junctions of highways 129 and 101, first gained road connections to the outside world. Even today, it takes more than two hours to drive to the nearest cities. Over 10% of Chapleau's residents are Cree or Ojibwe with three First Nations groups (Chapleau Cree, Chapleau Ojibwe, Brunswick House Ojibwe) represented in the area. In 1879, John Sanders was ordained as the first Ojibwe Anglican priest. About one third of the population is French Canadian.

Chapleau was incorporated as a township in 1901. The town is spread out, with some neighbourhoods resembling the suburbia of much larger communities. The downtown offers basic services, and the Kebsquasheshing River, which meanders through the western part, provides a beach and adjacent sports park. The library and town hall, built in more prosperous times, contrast with other buildings though now have accessibility options. Notable is the public art, with at least eleven large murals and monuments depicting town history and attractions (https://chapleau.ca/visitors/attractions/chapleau-murals/). One is at the historic Smith and Chapple general store, which was incorporated in July 1914. Larger centres could emulate this attempt to foster local pride. The Michael Levesque Trail (partly accessible) starts at the Peace Park—dedicated during 1992 in honour of Canada's Peacekeeping efforts.

Chapleau Railway Monument

Although the Hudson's Bay Company had a post nearby as early as 1870, Chapleau owes its existence to the Canadian Pacific Railway (CPR). Tracks from Montreal reached Chapleau in 1885, and it became a CPR divisional supply point. The wife of Noel de Tilly, the first CPR engineer to live there, named the community in honour of Sir Joseph-Adolphe Chapleau, who was Quebec's Conservative premier from 1879 until 1882. The CPR remains vital to Chapleau, both as an employer and as the sole provider of interurban public transportation via a self-propelled "Budd" car operated by Via Rail and offering flag-stop service three times a week between Sudbury and White River.

The lumber company, Tembec, producer mainly of 2x4s and 2x6s, remains the primary employer though part of its mill is not operating. The company has been acquired by GreenFirst Forest Products of Vancouver, which has also acquired mills in Cochrane, Hearst and Kapuskasing. First Nations people hope that a cedar-plank mill, initiated by an Indigenous group, will also be a source of jobs. Domtar offers walking tours of its local sawmill.

Once Chapleau had obtained rail connections to the Canadian heartland, the forest industry developed, but those same forests have provided some frightening experiences. Indeed, the history of Chapleau has been a history of fires. The museum at the welcome centre highlights the blazes of 1944, 1948, 1967 and 1969. The fire of 1948 darkened the skies as far away as North Bay. For days, the people of Chapleau lived with their suitcases packed, and the CPR had a train ready to evacuate the town on short notice. In 1967, the CPR evacuated some 3,000 residents, who boarded boxcars for the trip. Also, devastating fires of major buildings, including the Biglow Lumber Company's mill in 1969, have affected the town's economy.

Chapleau's major attractions are fishing, hunting and camping. Its museum reinforces that with displays of various fish (after a trip to the taxidermist), local pottery, and pioneer living conditions. Outside, a metal triangle made of railway ties surrounds a totem pole, erected in 1992 to celebrate Canada's 125th anniversary. The combination of wood and metal symbolizes the union of Chapleau with the train tracks and the rest of Canada.

Chapleau is the gateway to the Crown Game Preserve, which dates from 1925 when the then-provincial Department of Game and Fisheries feared the extinction of certain fur-bearing animals. Reportedly the world's largest animal preserve, it now provides a safe habitat for bears, moose and beaver to survive and multiply. The preserve promotes ecotourism and provides a place to raise wildlife both for reintroduction into other areas and for research opportunities. Visitors should nevertheless be patient as many kilometres of gravel road can be travelled through the preserve without seeing animals. The season, time of day, and luck all affect opportunities for sightings—as does the traveller's vigilance. The best approach is to stay at one of the resorts in or near the preserve and seek advice about viewing from locals. Numerous provincial parks offering fishing, canoeing and hiking are nearby, including Ivanhoe, Chapleau, Shoals, Misinnabi and Wakami Lake.

Chapleau has the usual social organizations and clubs found elsewhere, and in 2010, the Volunteer Fire Department—a vital institution in an area of forest fires—celebrated its centennial. The town also has the Centre Culturel Louis-Hémon, a French-Canadian club named for an author born in France in 1880 and whose novels about the fictitious Chapdelaine family and French-Canadian life sold more than one million copies. In 1913, Hémon was travelling west in search of material for a new book but was struck by a train and died near Chapleau. He is buried in a local cemetery.

Although Chapleau is a peaceful community where most people know each other, there have been tensions. Until 2006, one common secondary school served English and French students. Now they are housed in separate buildings: an English-language public school and a French-language Roman Catholic school, each controlled by a different school board. The establishment of the French-language school was met by protests, but tensions between linguistic groups—and between settlers and First Nation residents—have diminished. The community enjoys a three-day Cree festival with powwow-style dancing, a public barbecue on the main street, and medicine walks on tribal territory. The revival of these activities, some of which had antecedents in pre-settlement times, underscores the emergence of a younger generation intent on demonstrating its heritage. Part of that heritage is the cemetery of the residential schools that lasted until 1948. William McLeod has exposed the horrid conditions of the residential system at Chapleau with its attendant racism.

Chapleau has produced players for the NHL: Floyd Curry (1925–2006), a member of the Montreal Canadiens when they won the Stanley Cup in 1953, 1956, 1957 and 1958; and Jason Ward, who has played for the Canadiens, among others. In addition to hockey facilities, the town has a nine-hole golf course. In recognition of the Arctic-Atlantic watershed, Chapleau also has the Arctic Watershed Snowmobile Club. From Chapleau, snowmobilers can travel along trails for hundreds of kilometres, some going to Elliot Lake, some as far as the Quebec border.

Resources

Vincent Crichton, *Pioneering in Northern Ontario* (Belleville: Mika, 1975).

William E. McLeod, *Chapleau Game Preserve: History, Murder, and Other Tales* (Sudbury: n.p., 2004).

William E. McLeod, *Chapleau: Retrospective on Life in an Isolated Northern Community* (Sudbury: n.p., 2010).

William E. McLeod, *St. John's Anglican Residential School, Chapleau, Ontario, 1907 to 1948* (Sudbury, n.p., 2018).

Cobalt

Some locals and even historians claim that Cobalt, in the District of Temiskaming, about 100 kilometres north of North Bay, is the town that "saved Ontario." In 1903 during the building of the railway (Temiskaming and Northern Ontario, now Ontario Northland) to the agricultural settlement of New Liskeard in an economic downturn, nuggets of the precious metal for which the town is named were found. Then silver was discovered. By 1910, a prospecting frenzy and mining boom made Cobalt the world's fourth largest producer of silver. Eventually more than 100 mining operations were being worked. These finds spurred further exploration of the pre-Cambrian shield to expose its mineral wealth and to fill the province's coffers. Locals claim that many of the skills and much of the technology of hard-rock mining were developed here before being applied elsewhere in Northern Ontario. Sudburians make the same claim because its mines developed at the same time with similar technology. Before the great rush of the early twentieth century, Indigenous Algonquin people knew of and used silver from Cobalt. For hundreds of years, they made jewelry and musical instruments and traded it. Though the trade routes are not clear, Cobalt silver has been identified as far away as Ohio and Michigan.

After 1903 many ambitious people raced to Cobalt to make their fortunes. Between 1903 and 1911, when the supply of silver started to decline, Cobalt enjoyed amenities from street cars to blind pigs (a means for dispensing illegal liquor so seller and buyer would not see each other); and from theatres to stock markets. Illustrative of the town's short-term importance, the *North Bay Nugget* newspaper began as the *Cobalt Nugget*. In 1915 the *Northern Miner* began in Cobalt and continues today as the world's main digest for mining information. When established these papers reported daily on the silver prices and company shares on the New York and later Toronto stock exchanges.

Profits from the Cobalt silver mines led to increased prospecting and financed development of the Porcupine gold fields after 1909 and led to the Kirkland Lake gold rush of 1912. As a result, the provincial government decided to extend the railway to the gold fields. The original intent had been to build the railway to link North Bay with the farms of the Clay Belt on the shores of Lake Temiskaming. Some think that settlement outside that agricultural area of Northeastern Ontario owes its existence to the Cobalt rush.

The mining frenzy resulted in a special townscape running up and down the rocky hills. While mining and refining operated, an aerial trolley ran buckets of ore from the town's mines up to the refinery on the hill across the lake; a net protected those passing underneath. Headframes popped up everywhere, including some that were later surrounded by commercial buildings.

Other headframes, on the edge or outside town, stand as rusting, aesthetic monuments to an industrial past that now serves amateur artists who use the town's narrow, old streets and stately buildings for backdrops.

In addition to mining, the town is known for a fire in 1909 that nearly eradicated it. Typhoid struck later that year, affecting more than 1,000 people because they were living in tents and drinking contaminated water from the lake. According to *The New York Times* on 3 July 1909, anti-foreign attitudes blamed the fire on Chinese residents: "COBALT FIRE SWEPT; 3,000 HOMELESS; Half Million Dollars' Damage in Mining Town—One Dead and Six Injured. ANGRY AT THE ORIENTALS: Third Blaze in Last Three Months Due to the Chinese, and They May be Driven from District!" The article claimed the fire started in a Chinese restaurant.

The town is also known for one of the most bitter strikes in Ontario's history just after World War I. Already in 1916, the workers threatened action and by war's end the workers' response to low pay and atrocious working and living conditions led to a government inquiry. Eventually the whole town took sides in the two-month struggle during 1919. The Ontario Workmen's Compensation Act in aid of injured workers is credited to the Cobalt miners' efforts.

The town has a rich sports and cultural history, with the Silver Kings winning the National Hockey Association playoffs in 1909. Within two years of its founding, the town had numerous hotels and taverns, an opera hall and a stock exchange, and by the 1920s many large vaudeville theatres—of which some, such as the Crystal Palace, still exist—provided risqué entertainment. A streetcar system ran some eight kilometres to Haileybury where managers and mine owners preferred to live. During the 1930s, however, as the silver veins ran out, most of the mines closed, including those at outlying places such as Silver Centre and Silverton.

Cobalt's population has slowly declined, from 7,000 in 1908 to 1,640 in 1986, 1,220 in 2006, 1,118 in 2016 and 989 in 2021. The region now depends on tourism and some lumbering. Its old mine infrastructure has been designated the Cobalt Mining District National Historic Site (but not provided with funds for an interpretive centre; similar to Timmins and Sudbury). A possible economic revival may reverse the population decline, as some metals used in electric vehicles might be mined here.

A special attraction is the Cobalt Mining Museum with extensive and well-organized displays, showing a silver mining camp at work. Artifacts and photographs explain the social as well as the technological side of the town's history. Labourers' difficult and dangerous conditions are well illustrated. A second well-organized museum, the Bunker Military Museum of Cobalt, opened during 2012 in an appropriately renovated building up the street from the mining museum. The collection had previously existed in cramped quarters with conditions not up to museum standards, but now has one of the largest display galleries in Northern Ontario. Its collection of artifacts has items from the late nineteenth century to the present. It includes original war paintings, uniforms from all military services, and examples of personnel records. The life trajectories of men and women who served can be followed in case studies. Much military equipment with informative signage is on display. Aside from the many local monuments, it is one of few institutions to recognize Northeastern Ontario's many contributions to Canada's military past.

The headframe of the first mine shaft can still be viewed, and many important aspects of the town's mining and refining history can be seen on its Heritage Silver Trail drive, including headframes, glory holes and refinery ruins looking like mini-Mayan monuments, as can the cuts into the rock faces where the silver veins were followed. An annual miner's festival draws tourists as did a major Northeastern Ontario landmark: the former Highway Book Shop—one of the largest in Ontario. The store published a series of books on local history, giving representation to events and people that mainstream publishers overlook or avoid. It is closed but many books remain in the building and White Mountain Publishing is trying to emulate the Highway Book Shop. A specialty tea shop is located in a former mine head frame. The Grievous Angels, a band known for its socially conscious lyrics, often performed here, since one of its leading members, Charlie (Chuck) Angus, lives near Cobalt. Angus, a respected author and founding editor of *High Grader Magazine*, is the well-spoken Member of Parliament for Timmins-James Bay. Walking-tour guides make Cobalt, designated Ontario's most historic town, very accessible.

Resources

Charlie Angus and Brit Griffin, *We Lived a Life and Then Some: The Life, Death, and Life of a Mining Town* (Toronto: Between the Lines, 1996).
Charlie Angus, *Cobalt, Cradle of the Demon Metals: Birth of a Mining Superpower* (Toronto: House of Anansi Press, 2022).
Cobalt Walking Trail Guide (Cobalt: High Grader, n.d.).
Peter Fancy, *A Guide to Historic Cobalt* (Cobalt: Highway Book Shop, 2003).
The Heritage Silver Trail Guide (Cobalt: Highway Book Shop, 2000).

Cobalt refinery ruins   Cobalt mine in town

Cochrane, District of

Did you know?
Three schools share one building in Iroquois Falls:
- École Secondaire Catholique L'Alliance
- École Secondaire Publique L'Alliance
- Iroquois Falls Secondary School

The districts of Northeastern Ontario are relatively large. The District of Cochrane (pop. 82,500 in 2011, 78,000 in 2023) slightly smaller than the state of Michigan, remains the second largest district in Ontario. It includes Cochrane, Fauquier, Hearst, Iroquois Falls, Kapuskasing, Mattice, Matheson, Moonbeam, Moose Factory, Moosonee, Smooth Rock Falls and Timmins. In 1921, the Government of Ontario carved the district out of the districts of Temiskaming and Thunder Bay. The Town of Cochrane (incorporated 1910), which sits on the forty-ninth parallel at the elbow of Highway 11, is the judicial seat.

An aside: On the research trip north from Cochrane to Moosonee on the Polar Bear Express, I talked to a Cree family. Since they had lots of fishing gear on the train, we chatted about how the fishing went and then asked where they had been. The father answered, "Far south." When I asked where, he said, "Fraserdale." Since Fraserdale is well north of Cochrane and seemed "far north" to us, his reply reinforced the vastness of the land, and that perspective always depends on from where you come.

Fort Albany (pop. 750 in 2016; 770 in 2021), an Indigenous community at the mouth of the Albany River on James Bay, about 130 kilometres northwest from Moosonee, is in the district, but larger Attawapiskat, just further northwest, is not. The people are mostly Cree and Cree-speaking and have hunted and fished the area for centuries. Presently, supplies are brought in by air or by barge from Moosonee. Apart from government services, its economy is largely reliant on state support and traditional occupations such as hunting and trapping.

The residential school, St. Anne's run by the Roman Catholic church from 1906

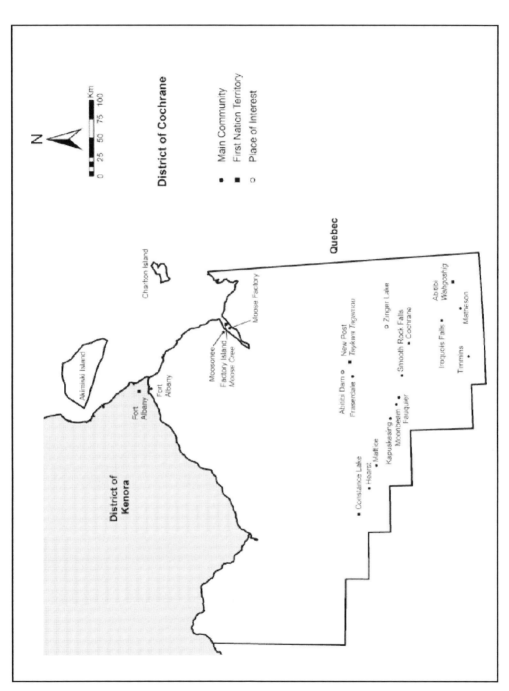

District of Cochrane

to 1972, has become infamous for its treatment of children and for court cases about obtaining records and justice. Many mysteries remain about children who ran away and others who died at the school. In 1965 the federal government took over the management of the school and in 1970 of the residence. The school was transferred to the Fort Albany First Nation. Some former staff members have been convicted of assault and indecent assault. Edmund Metatawabin, as a survivor, penned an autobiography, *Up Ghost River*, in which he detailed abuses such as punishment by electric shock (electric chair) and whippings. The Ontario Provincial Police interviewed 700 victims and survivors between 1992 and 1998. At least 156 former students sued the federal government and received compensation for abuses in 2004.

Other Cochrane District First Nations communities include Constance Lake First Nation, Taykwa Tagamou First Nation and Wahgoshig First Nation (formerly Abitibi). About 820 people live on the Constance Lake reserve, although the community claims 1,470 members, both Cree and Ojibwe. The 2016 census gave the population as about 590, dependent on seasonal fluctuations. The Eagle's Earth resort with multimedia centre, cabins, restaurant and symbolic dream catcher opened in 2007 northwest of Constance Lake; in 2017 it became an addiction treatment centre. Since 1984, the Taykwa Tagamou has occupied a site 20 kilometres west of the town of Cochrane on Highway 574, not far from the Abitibi Hydro Generation Station. The Wahgoshig First Nation on Highway 101 near Matheson had substantial population gains and losses: a decline of 10.2% between the censuses of 2001 and 2006, but an estimated increase from 114 in 2006 to 250 in 2009, yet stood at 145 in the census of 2016. The James Bay Treaty, signed 7 June 1906, provided for a reserve of 30 square miles (78 square kilometres) on the shores of Lake Abitibi. At that point, problems of provincial jurisdiction created complications. The Abitibi, who thought that they would benefit, signed the Treaty at a Hudson's Bay Company post in the Province of Quebec, but the territory itself was (and remains) in Ontario. However, they hunted in Quebec, and Quebec authorities refused to co-operate. In 1908, the different levels of government agreed to provide money on an annual per capita basis, but not land.

South of Cochrane and to the east of Highway 11 is Iroquois Falls (pop. 4,729 in 2011; 4,418 in 2021). The name is strange, as the community has neither Iroquois (self-identify as Haudonosaunee) nor waterfalls. The possible origins of the name vary among sources, but one version, repeated locally, is that the Iroquois—a First Nation from southern Ontario—once attacked the local Ojibwe and Cree near the falls on the Abitibi River. According to legend, the Iroquois massacred the men, and after celebrating fell asleep in their canoes. Local women loosened the canoes, and the Iroquois, sound asleep, drifted downstream to what were then the falls and their death. Ontario Heritage notes that the Indigenous fished and hunted the area for hundreds of years and utilized the interlinked water routes. In the twentieth century, the Abitibi Power and Paper Company replaced the falls with a dam.

Present-day Iroquois Falls dates from 1912. A Montreal businessman and visionary, Frank Harris Anson, saw the potential of the area as a supplier of pulpwood for paper production, and that year, he and Shirley Ogilvie received a timber concession of more than one million acres (400,000 hectares). Soon, Abitibi was

North America's largest supplier of newsprint. Abitibi's daily output of newsprint, 225 tons by 1915, doubled by 1920. To reach beyond the depleted neighbouring forests, in 1922 Abitibi began construction of its own railway, which transported logs until the mid-1950s, when trucks proved more economical.

Iroquois Falls began as a company town, owned by the Abitibi power company directed by Frank Harris Anson, but was incorporated in 1915. A fire the next year was devastating, but the community rebuilt, this time incorporating some elements of Garden City planning ideals, based on a movement in Britain. Anson hired a Chicago architect, A.P. Melton, to apply Garden City principles in laying out the town. Those principles promoted planned, self-sufficient, architecturally attractive communities with separate residential and industrial areas. Today, Iroquois Falls advertises itself as both the "Garden Town of the North" and a "Snowmobile Paradise." Flowers and maintained yards are notable. Abitibi once owned the land and the houses, which it rented to employees. Those—mainly French Canadians—who disliked the arrangement relocated to nearby Ansonville. Their English-speaking bosses lived in a section of Iroquois Falls where streets had British names like Cambridge, Essex and Devonshire, and with Anglican and United Church churches. Such segregation by ethnicity and class reflected the power structure of many northern communities. Until the 1960s, a small Jewish community had its own house of worship, which is now a private house on Synagogue Avenue.

Today, the town's economic backbone remains AbitibiBowater, successor to Abitibi Power and Paper Company, although another employer is the nearby prison, the Monteith Correctional Complex.

For residents and tourists, Iroquois Falls offers four beaches and the nine-hole Abitibi Golf Course, as well as the Iroquois Falls Pioneer Museum. The museum includes exhibits about Pierre de Troyes, a captain in the French army who passed through the region in 1686 as head of a successful military expedition from Montreal to James Bay, where he captured Moose Factory and Rupert House from the English. The museum also shows Abitibi's activities in Iroquois Falls and the lifestyle of residents. Photo exhibits illustrate the community's people and buildings, such as the magnificent hotel from the 1920s. A display on the Truman Gibbens and Davis boats, transported by rail from Owen Sound to Iroquois Falls in 1947 and 1951 respectively,

Abitibi engine the *Shay*, Iroquois Falls

notes that those steel vessels (85 x 18 feet) had shallow drafts so that they could transport logs around Lake Abitibi, which is not very deep. They served until 1972 when they were replaced by trucks. The Pioneer Museum has a model of the tugboat *F.H. Anson*, which with 360 horsepower was the company's most powerful vessel. It hauled logs to Iroquois Falls until 1974. Outside the museum is the actual steam engine, *the Shay*. It hauled logs from 1947 until 1955, and even after Abitibi terminated its railway in favour of trucks, *the Shay* shunted rail cars around the company's yard until 1972.

South of Iroquois Falls, Matheson, in the Black River-Matheson township, is a distribution centre formerly based on gold mining and lumbering. Matheson is a declining community, and the population of 3,222 in 1996, fell to 2,912 in 2001 and 2,619 in 2006. In 2021 it had 2,572. The Thelma Mines Museum houses a twentieth-century hospital room, displays on farming, mining and trapping, and a simulated underground mining tunnel. West of Highway 11 at Matheson is the nine-hole Black River Golf and Country Club. Destructive fires were major events in Matheson's history, especially those in 1910, 1911 and 1916.

Smooth Rock Falls, 50 kilometres northwest of Cochrane, has a population of 1,200 in 2021 and is declining (from 2,043 in 1991 to 1,982 in 1996 and 1,830 in 2001). Overwhelmingly Roman Catholic, the population includes many French Canadians.

In 1917, the Mattagami Pulp and Paper Company built a dam, powerhouse and pulp mill at the place where the gushing waters had smoothed a huge rock. In 1929, Smooth Rock Falls was incorporated as a town. However, the closure of the Tembec Malette pulp mill in 2006 eliminated some 210 jobs. Smooth Rock Falls survives because some of its residents commute to work in Kapuskasing, Cochrane, Timmins and even to towns in Quebec. Real estate is inexpensive, and some retirees from elsewhere have bought homes in Smooth Rock Falls. It

remains a supply centre for Clay Belt farmers.

From 1952 until 1957, the Honourable Philip Kelly from Smooth Rock Falls, Member of the Provincial Parliament for Cochrane North, became Minister of Mines in the Progressive Conservative government of Ontario Premier Leslie Frost. Another prominent resident was Duncan Chisholm (1861-1939), founder of the Mattagami Pulp and Paper Company, who moved to Smooth Rock Falls around 1916 and remained there until 1927. Byron Norman Frederick Rawson (1922-1945) was born in Smooth Rock Falls when his father, the Reverend Norman Rawson, was Methodist minister. He reportedly became the "youngest Wing Commander in the British Empire." Actress Louise Pitre, star of the musical Mamma Mia, once lived in Smooth Rock Falls, as have distinguished hockey players, such as Carl Hudson, Jean-Paul Parisé and Brandon Lamothe.

The museum at Smooth Rock Falls occupies what was previously Trinity United Church, and it is well worth a visit (drive from Highway 11 along 3rd Avenue to 4th Street and turn left). It features information and superb photos of building the Abitibi Canyon Dam, accessed via Highway 634 due north of Smooth Rock Falls. The dam, begun in 1930, created employment during the depression. Unfortunately, now that the system is in place, few workers are needed. The eclectic town museum, which has limited opening hours, has exhibits about local celebrities, as well as the clothing styles, technology and furniture of past generations.

Travelling west from Smooth Rock Falls, the next community on Highway 11 is Fauquier, on the Groundhog River and identifiable by a statue of a formidable groundhog. Fauquier's population fell from 678 to 568 between 2001 and 2006, and to 536 in 2016 and only had 427 in 2021. About three quarters of the population has French as mother tongue.

Continuing west, the Township of Moonbeam is next, with a population of 1,157 in 2021 overwhelmingly French Canadian. What was then the National Transcontinental Railway arrived in 1912, and settlers from Quebec followed. With the incorporation of the Canadian National Railway in 1919, the National Transcontinental became part of CN, and remained so until 1994. That year, Ontario Northland purchased the tracks between Cochrane and Hearst, and offered rail passenger service. Agriculture and lumber provide the economic base.

Early settlers named the community for flashing lights, moonbeams, which they claimed to have seen. The community's local symbol is a flying saucer, located outside the Welcome Centre on the north side of Highway 11. A local son, René Brunelle, held various portfolios in the Ontario government of Progressive Conservative premiers John Robarts and William Davis: Minister of Lands and Forest, 1966-1971; Minister of Mines, 1967-1968; Minister of Social and Family Services, 1972; Minister of Community and Social Services, 1972-1975; Minister without Portfolio, 1975-1977; and Provincial Secretary for Resource Development, 1977-1981. A nearby provincial park and a ski resort bear his name. A special hiking/biking trail runs 34 kilometres north to the provincial park from Highway 11; bikes can be borrowed and the first part of the trail from the highway is wheelchair accessible for about two kilometres.

From Moonbeam, Highway 11 leads to Kapuskasing, then to Mattice on the Missinaibi River, 70 kilometres to the west. Mattice, roughly midway between

Winnipeg and Toronto, began as a Hudson's Bay Company post in 1905, but at present its 542 (2021) people depend largely on the lumber industry. In 1911, a bridge across the Missinaibi River made it possible for travellers to go from points in Central Canada to Winnipeg. With the paving of Highway 11 in 1961, cars became more popular than trains, and the railway station at Mattice was demolished in 1971.

The Missinaibi River has long been part of a trade waterway for the Indigenous and then fur traders from Michipicoten on the north shore of Lake Superior to James Bay; Missinaibi Provincial Park straddles much of the route. In addition to evidence of Indigenous occupation, archeologists have discovered more than 20 sites associated with the two main fur-trading companies, the Hudson's Bay Company and the Northwest Company.

Resources

Michael d'Armours, *Moonbeam, 1913–1945 : la colonisations, la vie économique et social* (Sudbury : Société historique du nouvel Ontario, 1980).

Mark Kuhlberg, *In the Power of the Government: The Rise and Fall of Newsprint in Ontario*, 1894–1932 (Toronto: University of Toronto Press, 2015).

Edmund Metatawabin, *Up Ghost River: A Chief's Journey Through the Turbulent Waters of Native History* (Toronto: Alfred A. Knopf, 2014). A difficult but significant read.

Ontario Heritage Trust, *The Founding of Iroquois Falls* (Toronto, 2009).

Eddie O'Donnell, ed., *Loose Canon[sic]: A Collection of Recollections of Early Days in Iroquois Falls* (Matheson: O'Donnell Expeditions, 1995).

Cochrane, Town of

The Town of Cochrane (incorporated 1910) sits on the forty-ninth parallel at the elbow of Highway 11, 725 kilometres east of Thunder Bay and 700 kilometres north of Toronto. With a steady population (about 5,300 in 2021), half of them French speaking, it serves as headquarters for the District of Cochrane. Most residents can speak English, with some able to speak Cree. The area is in Treaty 9 territory. Lumber, paper, electrical production, transportation (railway, trucking), tourism (hunting, fishing, sight-seeing) and provincial government services are the bases of its economy. It has received a boost from the Kirkland Lake Gold (formerly Detour Lake) mine development to the northeast (past the end of Highway 652).

Before European settlement the Indigenous used the place as a summer camping ground. During the fur trade area, it served as a stopping place for traders going to Moose Factory. During World War I many of the Indigenous recruits from James Bay passed through here and some families stayed for the war's duration. The Ininew Friendship Centre, founded in 1974, serves a large area with mental health and children's programs, among other social supports.

Cochrane bears the name of Frank Cochrane, a successful Sudbury hardware merchant who served as Minister of Lands and Forests from 1905 to 1911. In 1909, Ontario extended the Temiskaming and Northern Ontario Railway (T&NO, now Ontario Northland) to Cochrane and named the temporary northern terminus in honour of Northern Ontario's cabinet minister. There, the T&NO intersected with the newly constructed National Transcontinental Railway (part of CN since 1919 and Ontario Northland since 1993). Historical highlights include fires in 1911 and 1916, a bitter labour dispute in 1963 and amalgamation with the villages of Glackmeyer and Lamarche in 2000. Since 2001, the population has declined but remained steady since 2016 at about 5,300, increasing to 5,390 in 2021.

Cochrane resembles a small town on the prairies. Located north of the rugged Laurentian Shield, it is flat with wide streets. The area around Commando Lake Park is especially picturesque, and the park offers a sandy beach and trails near the town centre. The level of the lake is controlled by a small dam.

Despite Cochrane's location at the junction of CNR and Ontario Northland, most tourists nowadays arrive by car or bus—though in the past Québecois arrived by rail from the east and some settled there. Transcontinental passenger service through Cochrane ended in 1931. Nevertheless, the town remains a supply centre for points north and east. Six days a week, mixed passenger/freight trains link Cochrane with Ontario Northland's northern terminus at Moosonee.

Since 1923, provision of provincial government services has been increasingly important to Cochrane's economy. Until 1923, residents of Cochrane had to travel to Haileybury even to register a real-estate transaction. Civil and criminal trials also took place in Haileybury, 200 kilometres to the south. Cochrane's courthouse dates from 1923, and a land titles office opened shortly thereafter. The OPP established a post and the Department of Lands and Forests (now Ministry of Natural Resources and Forestry) followed.

Cochrane's principal tourist attraction must be the Polar Bear Rehabilitation Centre, a shelter for abused, orphaned, or injured polar bears established in 2004. Custodians do not capture wild polar bears; they provide a home for polar bears rescued from substandard zoos, as well as wild bears unable to fend for themselves. For example, the Rehabilitation Centre provided temporary shelter for two bears from the Toronto Zoo, whose permanent residence was being refurbished in the summer of 2010. Then the only polar bear in residence was Nanook, a well-known 27-year-old who died in 2017. According to an official at the shelter, polar bears are solitary animals and Nanook seemed rather pleased when the other two bears returned to Toronto and left him with extra space. In 2022, three bears resided in the large compound. To see the bears being rehabilitated, it is imperative to visit the centre during feeding times, 10 a.m. and 1:30 p.m. on Sundays, Mondays, Wednesdays, Fridays; 11:30 a.m. and 2:45 p.m. Tuesdays, Thursdays and Saturdays. Arrive half an hour early to hear a presentation about polar bears in general and the bears in residence. Failure to arrive at feeding time may well mean no polar bear sighting, for they have a vast pen in which to amuse themselves. When bears are in residence, they appear on top of a rock near the glass partition that separates them from the spectators, and it is highly rewarding to watch them eat the carrots, lettuce and watermelon provided by the keepers. They receive and eat much of their food in a swimming pool, and viewers can observe them through the glass both above and below the water level. Outside the building, tourists can pose in front of the glass that separates them from the bear, but they are so close that with little imagination it can appear as though they are feeding or swimming with them (a change house on site allows visitors to slip into bathing suits). People of all ages will find the visit a memorable experience.

An admission ticket to the Polar Bear Rehabilitation Centre also grants access to the Hunta Museum Heritage Village (a pioneer village), with simulated trapper's cabin and a snowmobile museum. Other Cochrane attractions include 650 kilometres of snowmobile trails, radiating out from the town.

One of the immense forest fires of Northeastern Ontario, in 1916, which took many lives and destroyed part of the community is memorialized by a monument erected in 2016. Less known is the typhoid epidemic which seemed to have been spread by the movements of one person, known as Typhoid Mary, just before World War I. The disease was normal in the early twentieth century due to unfiltered water. In Cochrane during 1923 some 500 cases, or one out of four inhabitants, had symptoms with at least eight deaths.

Hockey player and hockey hall of fame member, Tim Horton, son of a mechanic with CN Rail, was born in Cochrane in 1930. He spent the first 15 years of his life there before moving to North Bay, Sudbury, and ultimately to an NHL career of 24 years. Before his death in a 1974 car accident, he co-founded the chain of coffee houses/donut shops that bear his name. In 2023 there were 3,580 Tim Horton's outlets in Canada and more than 800 in the United States; over 5,000 worldwide. The Tim Horton Events Centre, about 10 blocks east of Commando Lake Park, includes a museum with Tim Horton memorabilia, but the multimillion-dollar complex also includes an NHL-size ice rink, an indoor swimming pool and "lazy river" simulated to resemble a place in the tropics, a space with the latest equipment for physical workouts and a meeting hall. Check at the Welcome Centre for hours of operation as at times some or all of it is closed. The Tim Horton Events Centre receives its heat free of charge from Northern Power Inc., whose electricity-producing equipment burns sawdust (co-generation) drawn from huge piles clearly visible across the street.

Cochrane also boasts a nine-hole golf course, the Gardiner Ferry across the Abitibi River, walking trails, (some accessible) and a ski club. Its winter carnival, staged during the first full week of February, includes a Polar Bear dip performed by hardy souls who cut a hole in the ice of Lake Commando and jump into the icy water. Other annual events include the Polar Bear Riders Annual Major Bear Snofest, held for snowmobilers late each January; Pioneer Days at the Hunta Museum Heritage Village on the second weekend of August; the summer fest of food and activities held at the same time; and the Cochrane Fall Fair, which began in 1913 and takes place a week before Labour Day weekend.

Resources

Dick Bourgeois-Doyle, *Stubborn: Big Ed Caswell and the Line from the Valley to the Northland* (Renfrew: General Store, 2010).

W. f. Begley, *Cochrane d'hier à demain* (Cobalt: Highway Book Shop, 1977).

Commando Lake Park

Denison doors, Elliot Lake

Early European Explorers of James Bay

X

Henry Hudson, the seventeenth-century explorer, led three of his four expeditions into Arctic waters in search of routes to China and India. His fourth (1610-1611) took him to the James Bay shore of what is now Northern Ontario, where he vanished. The Indigenous Cree simply termed it the land, Eeyou, though some identified the area by the main transport routes, the rivers, such as Moose and Abitibi. During the first contact by Europeans, Northeastern Ontario was seen from the north, whereas today the perspective is primarily from the south.

Henry Hudson

European governments were more interested in trade with China and India than the Americas, and largely regarded the latter as an obstacle. The Virginia Company of London and the East India Company sponsored Hudson's final voyage. His ship, the *Discovery*, sailed through the Hudson Strait and entered Hudson Bay, which Hudson mistook for the Pacific Ocean. The first European ship ever to enter the bay, the *Discovery* headed south until the land barrier (the south coast of James Bay) appeared. Hudson and his crew headed west, along what today would be the Ontario shore of James Bay, in search of the passage to the Pacific. On 10 November 1610, the *Discovery* became stuck in the ice. There it remained until the following June.

Thomas James

When spring arrived, Hudson wanted to continue the search for the Northwest Passage, but his crew correctly feared that no navigable outlet existed from Hudson Bay to the Pacific and that everyone might die of exposure or starvation. When Hudson insisted, the crew mutinied and placed Hudson, his teenage son John, six other crew members, and some supplies into a lifeboat. Their fate remains unknown. When the *Discovery* returned to England, the mutineers faced criminal charges, but the court found them "not guilty," and two of the mutineers subsequently found employment with the Muscovy Company, one of Hudson's earlier sponsors.

Thomas James, after whom James Bay is named, continued the search for the Northwest Passage in 1631-1632. After a horrendous winter on Charlton Island, in what is now Nunavut in the southernmost part of James Bay, James decided that if there was a Northwest Passage, it was too icebound to be useful. A generation later, when Europeans next returned to James Bay, they were looking not for the Northwest Passage but for furs.

Resources

William J. Mills, *Exploring Polar Frontiers: A Historical Encyclopedia* (www.abc.clio.com, 2003).

Samuel Eliot Morison, *The European Discovery of America: The Northern Voyages* (New York: Oxford University Press, 1971).

Elliot Lake

Age is trump in this small retirement city. Founded in the 1950s as a planned mining community, during the 1990s Elliot Lake was decaying much faster than the uranium it once mined. After the city replaced that product by selling itself as a retirement community with modern facilities and services, it survived the mine closures. By 2005, it attained a stable population of about 12,000, after highs of 25,000 and lows of 6,000; 11,372 in 2021. The town is in the territory of the Serpent River First Nation and part of Huron Robinson Treaty lands.

Elliot Lake's fortunes have gone up and down, even more extremely than the boom-and-bust pattern typical of mining communities. Uranium ore discoveries in the late 1940s led to building several mines and mills by 1955. In 1954, a 20-kilometre road (Highway 108) linking the townsite to Highway 17 provided access from Sudbury or Sault Ste. Marie, about 170 kilometres to the east and west, respectively. Many suppliers and some miners lived in Spragge and Blind River. The first mine, Pronto, was rushed into production in 1953 when Eldorado Mining obtained a government contract to supply uranium based on a deposit found in 1952. By 1956, at least nine mines were active. In 1960, the population peaked at 24,887 with some 7,000 working for the mining companies, which by this time were mostly amalgamated as Rio Algom and Denison. By 1961, with demand for uranium down, houses were boarded and some feared that Elliot Lake would soon become a ghost town. Despite federal and provincial attempts to stockpile uranium and open educational facilities, by 1966 the population dropped to 6,664. During the 1970s, as more countries turned to nuclear electric power, some mines reopened, and the population slowly rebounded. In 1978, Ontario Hydro's long-term contract for uranium oxide led to renewed mining and refining. Suddenly predictions indicated that Rio Algom and Denison could have 8,000 workers by 1988 and the city could grow to some 31,000. However, those predictions proved to be illusions as the price of uranium oxides dropped during the mid-1980s. Between 1990 and 1996 all the major mines closed.

During the 1950s, when the uranium mines represented a bright future, an integrated community of suburbs surrounding shopping and recreational facilities was planned for up to 30,000 residents. However, uranium finds with much higher yields, especially in Northern Saskatchewan, undercut Elliot Lake, and the closures of nearly all the mines operated by Denison and Rio Algom led to two important consequences. First, employment plummeted. Second, the city diversified its economy, capitalizing on its beautiful northern setting. Some laid-off miners were employed as part of a longitudinal study conducted by Laurentian University to document the lives of the workers, who were repeatedly surveyed regarding employment and lifestyles. Research centres (one measuring radioactivity), an art academy, and emphasis on tourism helped maintain some employment. The main revival, however, came with marketing the town for retirement: diverse recreational facilities (hiking, canoeing, fishing, snowmobiling, a small ski hill and recently a championship golf course), cheap housing, attractive lake landscape and solid health services were all on offer. The city administers apartments, townhouses and houses through Elliot Lake Retirement Living. The arts, including performing arts, provide a vibrant contribution to the emphasis on community living close to nature. Allegedly, the city has the highest number per capita of social clubs in the province.

Among other attractions, the Arts on the Trail goes through the city and the District of Algoma. It is organized as a triangle that heads north from Highway 17 along Highway 108 to Elliot Lake, continues north on Highway 639 to Mississagi Provincial Park, next turns south-west on Highway 546, and rejoins Highway 17 at Iron Bridge. The 120 kilometres offer unspoiled wilderness including pockets of majestic white pine trees, waterfalls and stops for canoeing, biking, hiking and nature study. Part of the route follows alongside the Mississagi River. Some lodges and resorts offer fishing as well as many lake views. During the fall colours in mid-to-late September, this annual studio tour offers visits with local artisans at many locations along the route. Shut down during the pandemic, it restarted in 2023. In Elliot Lake, the Fire Tower Lookout and Heritage Centre provide an overview of the city and its environs. A wildlife sanctuary at nearby Sheriff Creek offers birding opportunities.

The Nuclear and Mining Museum, temporarily housed in the old city cinema, is awaiting the building of a new arts and culture centre. In addition to mining, the museum displays local wildlife and aspects of the trapping life that was prevalent before the mining industry developed. Its focus, though, is the history of finding uranium, the city's difficult boom-and-bust past, the process of mining and refining, and the advantages of nuclear power over coal. Tours of the reclaimed and restored mine sites commence here (sign up at the welcome centre) and show the sustained efforts to restore nature. Just a bit further along the highway is the Miners' Memorial Park, honouring over 260 men and women who died in the mining process. Their names are inscribed on the back of the monument and on bricks in the walkway.

In addition to the mining museum and monument, arts and cultural festivals, Elliot Lake is worth visiting to see its setting. The city proclaims itself "a jewel in the wilderness." Partly that claim can be made because its many parks and trails have lakes as backdrops. Partly the claim can be made because its mine sites have been closed, industrial buildings removed and shafts capped. Further, the tailings—refuse from processing ore—have either been covered by water with huge dams to hold in and control effluent or covered with grasses and clover to make them appear as large meadows. Legislated monitoring and testing indicate that radiation is at acceptable levels, so nearly all the mined areas are open to pedestrian traffic, but ATVs and snowmobiles are prohibited to prevent dumping of garbage or removal of materials.

Though not always acknowledged, the novel by Alistair MacLeod, *No Great Mischief*, is partly set in Elliot Lake's uranium mining industry. The conflicts and tensions between Anglophones and Francophones are central to the novel's larger themes. The account also provides insight into the harsh social and working conditions in the uranium mines.

A major tragedy occurred on 23 June 2012 when the Algo Centre mall roof collapsed. Many were injured and two were killed; the mall had been the main shopping complex including meeting places such as the public library.

Mostly, Elliot Lake should be viewed as a modern town living an experiment in coming to terms with economic problems by serving an ageing population.

Resources
Anne-Marie Mawhinney, ed., *Boom Town Blues: Elliot Lake—Collapse and Revival in a Single-Industry Community* (Toronto: Dundurn Press, 1999).

Miners' Monument

Espanola

ℵ

By Eileen Goltz

The "Espanola turn" is about 75 kilometres west of Sudbury, where Highway 17 and Highway 6 intersect. The northern boundary of Espanola is one kilometre south of Highway 6. The main Town of Espanola, with a population of 4,500 in 2021, appears after the bridge over the Spanish River. To the east is the pulp and paper mill powered by the dammed river, the reason for the town's existence, while to the west is the Espanola Golf and Country Club, one of the town's many recreational resources. With the sudden closure of the mill in 2023, the town's population will probably decline.

The name Espanola derives from an early North Shore legend that tells of an Ojibwe raiding party that returned from a foray south accompanied by a Spanish woman captive. The woman became a member of the tribe and taught her children to speak Spanish. French voyageurs travelling in the area were amazed to hear a European language spoken in the wilds of Georgian Bay and exclaimed "Espagnole!" Some evidence suggests that this is more than a romantic story, since an Ojibwe family, surnamed Espaniel, has long lived on the Sagamok-Anishnawbek territory, along the Spanish River. In addition, just before World War I an Ojibwe trapper named Alex Espaniel taught the art of trapping to Grey Owl in Biscotasing.

Espanola, a company-owned town from 1903 until 1958, was part of a tradition of company-owned towns built in sparsely populated areas of resource development to ensure the presence of a stable workforce. Company towns ranged from the extremely well-planned and well-cared for (Iroquois Falls, Kapuskasing), to the laissez-faire type (Creighton), where planning might be absent and care non-existent. Pulp and paper towns were among the best planned and tended of company towns, and Espanola benefitted from the largesse of the initial company, the Spanish River Pulp and Paper Company. Although most population nodes along the North Shore of Georgian Bay grew adjacent to the railway line, Espanola did not. The company needed electrical power for its mill operations, and to generate that power it situated operations at Webbwood Falls on the Spanish River. It built a spur line to the nearest junction of the Canadian Pacific Railway line at McKerrow (then called Stanley). Thus began the first of four distinct phases in the town's history: the early company town, followed by the ghost town, the later company town, and finally, the incorporated town.

The Spanish River Company began building houses and other structures in 1903 in Merritt Township, an under-populated farming and lumbering area that in 1901 had a population of only 73. The company supplied electrical power from its generating station and was responsible for police and fire protection. Planning was evident from the beginning, with the usual grid pattern of streets being modified by the addition of curved avenues and the careful placement of living and business structures. Company housing was available for those employees who were considered necessary for company operations, while other employees provided their own. They did this in a fringe development that burgeoned to the south after the 1911 construction of a paper mill and the extension of the Manitoulin North Shore Railway to connect the mainland to Manitoulin Island. This fringe development was known locally as Frenchtown, because a French-Canadian farmer had divided his field into lots. The area included English and French Canadians plus immigrants from Europe and the Middle East, who built houses, established businesses, and continued their cultural traditions, such as Ukrainian choirs and theatre. For example: in 1928, the Ukrainians of Espanola, despite their small community, had a language school teaching Ukrainian with over 50 pupils. They had built their own hall and had church services with a choir. Further, a retail district grew, in competition with the company-sanctioned one in Espanola. As residents became aware that the term Frenchtown might be considered derogatory the name changed to Espanola South, and the area continued to provide homes for pulp and paper mill employees and others for whom no houses were available in the company-owned town.

In 1928, the Abitibi Power and Paper Company purchased the company and the town, and it continued production at the mills. Following the stock market crash of 1929, Abitibi suffered economic reverses, and by 1932 was in receivership and had closed its Espanola operations. The town was left without a major employer and many people moved away resulting in the ghost town phase, when 85% of those remaining lived on government assistance. By 1934, the population in the company town was only 597, while that in the fringe development, where people owned homes, was 1,925.

Little occurred to alleviate the economic difficulties of this phase until 1941, when the Canadian government established a prisoner-of-war (POW) camp in the old pulp and paper mill buildings. Camp 21, as this facility was known, was capable of housing 1,400 men, although usually fewer were interned in Espanola. Most of the prisoners were German, but since Espanola provided the only treatment centre in Canada for POWs suffering from tuberculosis, occasionally Japanese and Italian prisoners were on site. The camp provided a focus for bored, unemployed townspeople. The guards, who numbered about 400, provided entertainment in the form of concerts, bingos, singsongs and dances, thereby stimulating social life in the town.

Espanola Prisoner of War camp

The POW camp existed only until 1943, but it has loomed large in the memory of townspeople, and in the minds of the POWs, some of whom have returned to visit the scene of their incarceration. One very permanent remembrance is the very detailed map of the world that prisoners drew on an interior wall of the mill building that had been used as a dormitory. It is generally believed that one prisoner was responsible for creating the map over the period of a year, although some have suggested that several prisoners were involved.

The purchase of the mill buildings and the town in 1943, by the Kalamazoo Vegetable Parchment Company (KVP) of Kalamazoo and Parchment, Michigan, initiated the later company town phase and ushered in an era of growth and prosperity. Because the mills had been idle since 1930, KVP spent three years modernizing before being able to turn its attention to the town. More streets, housing and services were provided, including steam heat piped from the mill to apartments, stores, and offices in the company town. In 1948, the company established the Espanola Development Company (EDC), a wholly owned, privately incorporated subsidiary, to administer the town and moved town administration from the mill to a newly constructed town hall. Both Espanola and the fringe development, Espanola South, benefitted.

In 1947, a group of tourist operators sued KVP for polluting the Spanish River. The plaintiffs won their suit, but the company appealed the decision all the way to the Privy Council, where it continued to be upheld. With doom facing the town, the Ontario government passed the KVP Act, which allowed the company to continue polluting the river to assure production. Thus, at the expense of pollution, prosperity had been ensured by government intervention, and building in the town continued. All construction was virtually completed by 1951, and by 1953, with 1,000 employees at the mill, Espanola was an attractive, planned town.

The road approach to the Town of Espanola had long included a one-lane bridge across the Spanish River at the north end of the town. This two-span bridge was supported in the middle by a concrete pier anchored in the river and had a load limit of six tons, a limit that was frequently exceeded. In August 1952, a tractor trailer carrying a bulldozer was navigating the bridge when one of the spans came loose and the truck and its load landed in the river. Although the driver and his partner were uninjured, the bridge was a complete loss, and was replaced by a single-lane Bailey bridge. This bridge was in use until 1960 when a modern, two-lane bridge was built—a bridge that still serves the town and traffic to Manitoulin Island.

In 1958 the provincial government passed legislation to incorporate both the town and the fringe development. Although earlier viewed as necessary to ensure a stable workforce, company-owned towns were now considered to be anachronistic, and the company was pleased to be relieved of its administrative burdens. The company sold its housing to the inhabitants, and an elected mayor and council replaced the company administrators. As a company town, Espanola had depended on the paternalism of a succession of companies. They owned all the land and restricted the establishment of businesses and the building of private homes. Most provided a selection of recreational facilities for the employees and encouraged participation in recreational activities. Long-time residents praised the various companies, with the understandable exception of the Abitibi Company, and considered subtle interference in their leisure time by the company as benevolence. Company officials were regarded as friends who were truly interested in the development of the town, and many townspeople mourned the passing of the company town days.

During its time as a company-owned town, Espanola attracted a varied workforce, the population rose and fell according to the fortunes of the company. In 1921, during a period of expansion, the population of Merritt Township, most of whom lived in Espanola and its fringe development, numbered 2,750. However, in 1931, during the ghost town phase, the population fell to 1,915. By 1951, reflecting the prosperity instituted by KVP, the population rose to 3,860, and the first census (1961) taken of the newly incorporated town indicated a population of 5,535. All figures include Espanola and Espanola South. The national origin of the population in 1961 was overwhelmingly English and French Canadian, with fewer than 500 people originating from Continental Europe or Asia. By 2006, 3,870 spoke only English, while 1,320 spoke both English and French, and 50 spoke only French; 475 were First Nations. In 2016 the population stood at 4,996 but declining to 4,682 in 2023.

Espanola has always been a service centre for a large area to the east, west and south. People from the small towns, villages and townships in its orbit, a catchment area of 30,000, travel to Espanola for shopping, recreation, employment, and medical and legal assistance and to access government offices. This service centre factor has allowed the Town of Espanola to provide a number, variety, and depth of services not normally found in towns of this size. It has become a centre for business, retail, medical, legal and government facilities, as well as transportation and distribution.

Present-day Espanola is a modern town in the foothills of the La Cloche Mountains. It is a family-oriented community, the motto of which is Advance en

Avant (move forward), a viewpoint threatened by the mill's closure.

Heritage Park, at the extreme north end of the town, just south of the bridge, welcomes visitors to the town. In this park, the Espanola Historical Society has provided an informative mural depicting the history of Espanola. Across the street is the town hall, where the Provincial Offences Act Office provides court services. The court service area begins in Elliot Lake and continues east to Nairn Centre.

Recreational facilities include baseball fields, soccer fields, an athletic track, parks and playgrounds, tennis courts, golf and country club, curling club, snowmobile club and ski hill. The jewel in this mass of recreational facilities is the Espanola Regional Recreational Complex, open to people living outside the Town of Espanola. The complex boasts a 5-lane, 25-metre-long swimming pool, the first municipal pool in Northern Ontario to use a saltwater purification system. In the aquatic section of the complex are a wading pool, a double loop slide, a whirlpool and a sauna. Elsewhere in the complex is an arena with a 200 x 85-foot ice surface with seating for 450 spectators, and an auditorium complete with seating for 350. Meeting rooms, public display areas, administrative offices, a fitness centre and two squash courts, complete the centre. A door from the recreation centre leads to the Espanola Public Library. In 1958, recreation director Red McCarthy, involved also in the creation of ringette as a sport, organized the Espanola Little Theatre, which has performed nationally and internationally.

Espanola enjoys proximity to lakes, beaches and wilderness areas. Clear Lake is at the south end of town, along Highway 6, with a sandy beach, swimming and picnic facilities, a beach volleyball area and public washrooms. Additionally, a fitness trail (partly accessible) wends its way from the mall area at the south end of town to Clear Lake. The Espanola and District Snowmobile Club, allied with the Ontario Federation of Snowmobile Clubs, is responsible for the maintenance of 253 kilometres of trails.

As with many Ontario towns, the major business and shopping section of Espanola has left the old downtown area and has re-established itself south of the town, straddling Highway 6 with a large mall, fast-food franchises and a nearby industrial park. Financial institutions have not followed the trend to relocate to the southern part of town but have remained in the central part of the old company town near the Espanola campus of Sudbury-based Cambrian College.

The provision of health services has always been of prime importance in Espanola. Doctors, nurses and a hospital of some type have been present from the town's earliest days. In 1954, during the KVP company town days, an inadequate hospital was replaced by a modern, well-equipped facility with medical, surgical and obstetrical services. This facility was replaced during the 1980s with a multi-care institution, anchored by the Espanola Regional Hospital, at the southern end of the town. With the move to amalgamate hospital services in Northeastern Ontario, the Espanola hospital no longer provides obstetrical and major surgical services which have been deferred to the Sudbury Regional Hospital (Health Sciences North).

The Espanola Regional Health Care Centre has 15 acute-care beds, 62 nursing-home beds, 18 seniors' supportive housing units and 30 seniors' apartments. Another part of the multicare facility is the Espanola Family Medicine Centre, which through the efforts of the Espanola and Area Family Health Team provides access for area patients to doctors, nurses, nurse practitioners, dietitian, social workers, diabetes counsellor, pharmacist, visiting doctors and a variety of other medically related services. These three facilities are physically and administratively connected.

Espanola boasted two weekly newspapers, now offered via the internet. The *Midnorth Monitor* reports area events, including marriages, births and deaths and is read by most area residents. *Around & About* is a smaller pamphlet-type paper that is circulated free of charge. There are five local radio stations and a repeater station for the CBC from Sudbury. Cable service and a community news channel are available.

Espanola has had interesting people and events. Lois Maxwell, the Miss Moneypenny of the early James Bond films, is an Espanola personality who owned a home on Faraway Road, north of the bridge over the Spanish River. Another is Al Secord, who had a twelve-year (1978–1990) NHL career with four different teams, most notably with the Chicago Blackhawks. Body-builder Conrad Laframboise won the Mr. Canada title in 1963, 1965 and 1967 and Mr. World in 1967 and 1968. He started with primitive, homemade equipment.

Also, Guinness World Records awarded Espanola a certificate (posted in the Recreation Centre), that reads: "The longest duration for a game of ice hockey is 103 hours and was played at the Espanola Recreation Complex... on 21-25 April 2003." That record is now held in Alberta.

Resources
Eileen Goltz, "Espanola: The History of a Pulp and Paper Town," *Laurentian University Review* (June 1974), 75-105.

Conrad Laframboise, Mr World (Credit: Jimmy Caruso)

French River, looking west from the snowmobile bridge, at Highway 69
(Credit: Laurence Stevens)

Fires

Where there are forests, there are fires. Northeastern Ontario has had many, but it may not want to boast about having the world's seventh largest in terms of loss of life. In July and August 1916 that fire, identified by the main town it burned at Matheson, killed 224 people. It covered parts of 49 townships and burned 20 completely. The villages of Kelso, Muska (renamed Val Gagné after a priest who saved numerous lives) and parts of Porquis Junction and Iroquois Falls were severely burned. That was only the worst of periodic catastrophes caused by lightning, human carelessness, or deliberate attempts to control nature. For instance, in September 1932 Spragge (in Algoma District) lost three quarters of its buildings. The following year the sawmill burned. Listed below are the most noteworthy fires, though five particular years are usually cited for their destructive blazes: 1911, 1916, 1922, 1948 and 1977.

Many smaller fires have gone unrecorded.

- 1901 from Kabinakagami to Little Abitibi; parts of Cochrane

- 1909 Cobalt—3,000 homeless; 1,000 later had typhoid from drinking contaminated water

- 1911 Porcupine and Cobalt—73 deaths; parts of Timmins, South Porcupine and Cochrane

- 1916 Matheson—224 deaths; extensive swath from east of Timmins

- 1922 Haileybury—43 deaths (after which people lived in 87 street cars shipped from Toronto). Sharon E. Cornett recounted a family story about this fire: "In 1904, my grandmother's family, the Robbs, moved to Haileybury by steamer. They built a log cabin and worked in lumbering and prospecting before moving back to Toronto. After World War I, during which her first husband died, my grandmother Sarah Ellen Robb returned to Haileybury with a new husband. The 1922 fire burned their house and they moved into her parents' home. My mother was very upset because she wanted to live in a streetcar like many of her friends."

- 1948 Chapleau—sometimes considered the largest Ontario fire, with 200,00 hectares destroyed. It started north of Blind River apparently from a camper's fire. Firefighter Edmond Duhaime, age 19, reportedly went for a walk while fighting the 1948 Chapleau fire and completely disappeared. His distraught family thought officials were not doing much to find him, organized their own search and left food in the forest. As no body was ever found, Edmond's mother refused to believe that he had perished, so there was no funeral or obituary. (Story by Gary Duhaime; see *Sudbury Star* 6-12 July 1948)

- 1977 Cobalt—burned nearly half of the northern part of the town. The fire started from a casually dropped cigarette.

When looking at old photos of mining camps and towns denuded of trees, usually the correct assumption is made that the lumber was used for railways, mine-supporting timbers or shipped away to build elsewhere. But memoirs of individuals living in such places include the happiness at having a huge treeless space around their buildings because it served as a firebreak. Dry summers or winters with relatively little snowfall usually set the scene for large fires, some of which merged to create cataclysms. Control attempts have included watchtowers, cut or ploughed fire breaks, and even setting counter fires. Since the 1920s, aerial surveillance has operated from Ontario's main fire-fighting base at Sault Ste. Marie (see Bushplane Heritage Centre). Airplanes slowly replaced spotters living during summer in high watchtowers. Ground crews with hoses, axes and pumps try to control the spread of large fires. Since the 1950s water bombers have been used to douse and thereby slow or redirect fires.

Resources
Michael Barnes, *Killer in the Bush: The Great Fires of Northeastern Ontario* (Erin: Boston Mills, 1987).
Don Curry, *Fire Cobalt: May 23, 1977* (Cobalt: Highway Book Shop, 1978).

Main St. and Ferguson Ave., Haileybury, after the fire of October, 1922.

Haileybury fire, 1922 (Credit: Haileybury Museum)

Food

Northeastern Ontario has enough farmland on Manitoulin and in the Clay Belt and flat areas of the Canadian Shield to provide fresh food for half the year. It has more than enough rivers and lakes to provide fresh fish all year but few commercial fishing outfits exist. The region offers delicacies, such as speckled trout from many lakes and rivers.

Are there any special foods or recipes in this region? Great fish and chips made from Lake Huron whitefish are offered at the Killarney marina, at several places on Manitoulin Island and along Highway 17. Some Sudburians fly float planes to Killarney for fish and chips at the dock. Others drive 45 minutes to combine a big fish and chips lunch with hiking in Killarney or on George Island to work it off. Smoked fish—trout, salmon and whitefish—sold at many small stands or shops continue a regional First Nations tradition. Pickerel dinners are a favourite throughout the northeast, mostly offered by non-franchise local restaurants, as at Alban, Espanola or Little Current. Smelt fishing has declined because of smaller spring runs but the small fish remains a beloved delicate taste. Bass, perch and pike are the other main varieties of fish. Fishermen especially relish bass for its fighting spirit.

Moose and bear meat is not for sale, but locals often invite guests, especially after hunting season. If you have not tasted moose sausage or steak, you have missed a treat. Bison farms sell their products near St. Joseph Island and Noelville. Northern hare meat is rare near cities, but some farmers offer them, as do specialty meat stores, especially where Italians or Greeks have influenced the cuisine from Sault Ste. Marie to North Bay. Local farms raise beef, lamb, pork and chicken of high quality that is mostly found in local meat shops. When bought directly or through local butchers, the cuts have more flavour than those from the supermarket.

Otherwise, fast food at the franchise outlets is the same homogenized fare as elsewhere. Northern greasy spoons do exist, often frequented by the gnarled individuals who have survived logging, trucking, mining and many bars. A notable problem for many small towns is that restaurants are closing for lack of clientele, who stop only at the larger centres with international franchises. An exception is the Casey's chain, which started in Sudbury in 1980 and expanded to Timmins, Sault Ste. Marie, North Bay and Kapuskasing; many locals swear by their dishes and ambiance, similarly with Cortina pizza. Manitoulin has no franchise outlets, and its restaurants emphasize local products.

Those who want a unique dining experience need to look more carefully and ask knowledgeable locals: in Iron Bridge they used to tell you about the Red Top Inn and in Wawa about Caribbean curry at Kinni-wabi Pines, while in Sault Ste. Marie they will argue for a long time about which is the best Italian place. Those in Sudbury know that the prize winner in the latter category is Verdicchio's, while Bella Vita Cucina is a close second (author's opinion). Do the French Canadians make six pâtés (or six-part potato pies with moose, rabbit, deer, grouse, fish)? Likely, as well as sugar pie. Finns will know about pastries and pancakes, and Ukrainians will go on at length about perogies, while Germans and Poles can argue about sausages and sauerkraut. The larger communities have Japanese, Korean, East Indian and Mexican among other styles, but is there a real original northeastern dish? Is it blueberry soup (which Swedes make)? Is it stuffed moose heart? Is it beaver roasted in maple syrup? First Nations offer traditional fare such as corn soup or bread-on-a-stick (bannock) at pow wows. Some dishes are flavoured with maple syrup. The Indigenous eat hunted rabbit, grouse, moose and venison, and many newcomers of the last two centuries have joined them. Mostly the meats are now fried or barbecued whereas earlier they were dried or smoked. Not surprising is that the newcomers liked the wild game, given what a surveyor during the 1880s found offered for breakfast when stopping in hamlets near Lake Temiskaming: the North European staples of salt herring and boiled potatoes!

One specialty of the northeast is blueberries, which are far tastier than the cultivated variety. Many individuals earn substantial funds from picking and selling them at roadsides or to intermediaries who take them to southern markets. However, no special northeastern recipe using blueberries has emerged. Businesses that sell them have existed since the 1920s with markets as far away as Toronto and New York. Highways 11 and 17 near towns and cities are home to endless vendors from July to September.

A lesser-known specialty is the 300 varieties of mushrooms in the Northeast, but one must of course know the edible ones. Ethnic groups of European and Chinese background spend much time foraging and enjoying chanterelles, morels and boletus (mostly found in the southern part). Yellow boletus is especially plentiful during wet warm summers.

At least one Northeastern place remains free of the so dominant fast-food franchises with about eighty percent of restaurants offering Italian: the Sault. There is, however, Casey's, the chain that started in Sudbury, and more recently Montanas.

Forests and Forestry

Northeastern Ontario contains almost half of the province's managed forest area—some 13.5 million hectares of productive forests. From north to south, these forests range from the sparsely treed Hudson Bay Lowlands with stunted spruce, tamarack and willow, through boreal forests dominated by spruce, jack pine, poplar and birch, and into the Great Lakes-St. Lawrence transition forest, with white pine, maples, yellow birch and other hardwoods. Not only are the forests in Northeastern Ontario diverse and seemingly endless, but they were key in the area's development. Along with mining, they still provide much of its economic base. Until the late nineteenth century, most of Northeastern Ontario's forests were inaccessible to loggers. When continued demand for white and red pine for square timber and sawlogs caused surveyors to look beyond central Ontario, logging was initially concentrated near the lakes and navigable rivers that were used to access the area and to transport logs to mills and markets.

While water provided an inexpensive means of transport, its use was limited to the ice-free seasons. As well, the area's narrow rivers and shallow lakes made water transport a challenge, spawning the design of an amphibious, steam-powered tugboat, called the "alligator," that could portage itself from lake to lake to help move logs to mills. Conceived and built by West and Peachy of Simcoe, Ontario, alligators were scow-shaped, shallow draft boats, fitted with side mounted paddle wheels, powered by a 20-horsepower steam engine and provided with a cable winch and large anchor. On the water, logs were pulled slowly across lakes in booms using the boat's winch and more than 1,700 metres of steel cable—a costly, slow process that was soon replaced by a more efficient network of railways and later roads. A restored version of the alligator, the *Fairy Blonde*, can be viewed at Wakami Lake Provincial Park near Chapleau.

Though the Indigenous utilized the forest, their limited numbers and their belief to live with the land, not off it, meant that the landscape was not much changed by their activities. Making teepee poles, baskets and fish nets impacted little on the environment.

Where logging occurred, settlement and commerce usually followed, with settlers providing supplies and amenities to the loggers, farming the lands cleared of timber, and establishing small towns. By the 1890s, many small water-powered sawmills were producing lumber to support local demand from newly arrived settlers and the building of the railroad. During this period, new mills were established along the railway to exploit nearby forests, only to be shut down when the resources were depleted, or economic conditions changed. In the early twentieth century, up to 150 sawmills, many of which were processing pine harvested and transported from Northeastern Ontario, were operating on the North Shore of Lake Huron. Some 12 sawmills existed near the mouth of the Spanish River in 1915, with smaller mills operating in Biscotasing (1905–1927), Gogama (1917) and Westree (1924–1968) in Sudbury District.

Until the mid to late 1880s, paper was made from rags, but new developments provided the opportunity to make paper from wood fibre, with spruce—particularly black spruce—favoured, because its longer fibres made stronger paper. The first agreement for cutting pulp wood was signed in 1892 between the Ontario government and Francis H. Clergue, giving his company a 21-year license to access 50 square miles of forest along the rivers north of Sault Ste. Marie. In return, Clergue committed to building the first paper mill in Northern Ontario and employing people for at least 10 months of the year. Despite many ups and downs, that mill, which began production in 1895, continued to operate into the twenty-first century. Similar agreements for wood licenses soon followed at Sturgeon Falls (West Nipissing), Mattawa and Spanish. The Kapuskasing River Pulp and Timber limit, which included 4,500 square kilometres of timber, was awarded to speculators Saphrenous A. Mundy and Elihu Stewart in 1917, but no development occurred. The still unexploited timber limits were sold to Kimberly-Clark in 1920, and The Spruce Falls Company Limited operated a pulp mill under the direction of F.J. Sensenbrenner until a fire at the mill stopped production. In 1926, The Spruce Falls Power and Paper Company was incorporated under joint ownership of Kimberly-Clark and The New York Times. Work to build a 550 ton per day paper mill at Kapuskasing, a 75,000 HP hydro generating station at Smoky Falls, and 80 kilometres of railway and power line connecting the two, began in spring 1926. Since July 1928, *The New York Times* has been printed entirely on Spruce Falls paper. The mill has run continuously under various ownerships, including Tembec Inc and First Green Forest Products.

In the early twentieth century, much of the demand for forest products went to support the development of the rail lines and the mining industry. Timber was used to construct headframes and support mineshafts and tunnels. As an example, by 1935 Lake Shore Mine in Kirkland Lake alone was using 12 million board feet of timber annually in props and other underground construction.

As the forest industry developed, so too did community dependence on the industry. Following a series of large forest fires in the first decades of the twentieth century that decimated communities and resulted in numerous deaths, the Ontario government recognized the importance of forest protection. The fires precipitated the establishment, during 1924, of a provincial air service that by 1929 had 22 float planes operating out of its main base in Sault Ste. Marie. Fire suppression with water bombers began in 1957.

The development of aircraft also influenced the area's forests. During World War II, Ontario's Great Lakes-St. Lawrence forests were exploited for yellow birch, which was harvested and turned into veneers used for the skins of the deHavilland Mosquito combat aircraft. The Mosquito, also referred to as the "timber terror" and the "wooden wonder" because of its speed and agility, was a mid- or shoulder-wing aircraft built mostly from wood. Its fuselage was a frameless shell made of sheets of Ecuadorian balsa wood sandwiched between sheets of Canadian birch, much of which came from central and Northeastern Ontario. Many of the aircraft from this era are preserved at The Bushplane Heritage Centre in Sault Ste. Marie.

By the late 1940s, concerns about the sustainability of forest harvesting prompted government funded reforestation efforts. Initially, the funds went mainly to the development of tree nurseries. Edward Bonner, who was then with Spruce Falls Power and Paper Co., set up and operated the first commercial-scale tree nursery in Northern Ontario at Moonbeam.

A unique feature in Northeastern Ontario is the Clay Belt (Greater and Lesser). Formed by the draining of the Glacial Lake Ojibwe about 8,000 B.C., it is a 120,000 square kilometre area of fertile soil between Cochrane District, Ontario and Abitibi County, Quebec, surrounded by the Precambrian Shield. The Canadian government encouraged immigrants to settle there during and after World War I. Settlers received homesteads, grants and guaranteed loans and were paid for clearing their land. Although the soil was fertile, the short growing season made farming next to impossible; one farmer described the conditions as "seven months of snow, two months of rain, and all the rest is black flies and mosquitos." Much of the land cleared for agriculture is being returned to productive forest that forms the mainstay for mills in communities such as Kapuskasing, Cochrane and Iroquois Falls.

At least 13 of the major communities of the Northeast remain highly dependent on the forest industry for their survival. Further, the area's forests provide most of the recreation opportunities including camping in park areas, fishing on rivers and lakes, hunting, snowmobiling, cross country skiing, bird watching, photography and, for many, a sense of home.

In the last decades First Nation involvement in the forest industry has increased, both in conjunction with existing enterprises and in creating their own initiatives. The knowledge which the Indigenous had for living with, as opposed to off, the land has been recognized as the industry seeks to attain sustainability. An example is the Wahkohtowin Development which is an Indigenous social enterprise based in sustainable forestry. The three First Nations in the Chapleau area (Brunswick House, Chapleau Cree and Missanabie Cree) are cooperating with GreenFirst, a large forest products enterprise. Those three First Nations took the Ontario government to court in 2022 with regard to pesticide spraying and not upholding treaty rights; the outcome is pending. Another initiative is a timber harvesting company, First Nation Timber, owned by Moose Cree members in Kapuskasing.

The large question for all who live in Northeastern Ontario is how to utilize the forests without ruining them. Sustaining the forests interests all hunters, anglers and hikers as well as timber harvesters.

Resources

K. A. Armson, *Ontario Forests: A Historical Perspective* (Markham: Fitzhenry and Whiteside, 2001).

A. E. Epp, "Ontario forests and forest policy before the era of sustainable forestry," in A. H. Perera et al, eds, *Ecology of a Managed Terrestrial Landscape* (Vancouver: UBC, 2003), 237-275.

Mark Kuhlberg, *In the Power of the Government: The Rise and Fall of Newsprint in Ontario, 1894–1932* (Toronto: University of Toronto Press, 2015).

R. S. Lambert with P. Pross, *Renewing Nature's Wealth: A Centennial History of the Public Management of Lands, Forests and Wildlife in Ontario, 1763-1967* (Toronto: Department of Lands and Forests, 1967).

A logging tugboat

Fort St. Joseph

Located at the southernmost tip of St. Joseph Island in Lake Huron, Fort St. Joseph had a brief but illustrious history from 1796 until 1812. Parks Canada now operates its ruins as a National Historic Site with an interpretive centre (open from the Victoria Day weekend until Thanksgiving). Only the foundations of the buildings remain, but visitors can appreciate the logistics of maintaining such a remote outpost of empire. The most impressive remains are a chimney, but to stand where the soldiers stood and see United States territory as they would have seen it is to share their experience.

Metres from the fort along the east shore is the area where civilian fur traders once lived. On some summer evenings, students appear in period costume, assume the identities of the soldiers and fur traders, and speak to the spectators. A museum displays scenes and artifacts of military and civilian life, and it provides information on relations among Europeans, the First Nations and Métis. A special researched exhibit on the role of Métis at the fort and on the island is being prepared.

After France ceded mainland Nova Scotia to Great Britain by the Treaty of Utrecht in 1713, French authorities built a series of forts to maintain what land they still had. One such fort was Michilimackinac at the northern tip of Michigan's southern peninsula, where Lake Huron and Lake Michigan join. British soldiers acquired the fort through the Treaty of Paris in 1763, and during the U. S. War of Independence (1774–1783), British soldiers relocated it to the more defensible Mackinac Island in Lake Huron. Under the terms of Jay's Treaty (1794), the British had to withdraw from Fort Mackinac within two years, and they relocated to Fort St. Joseph.

During this time, Fort St. Joseph gained a reputation as the British Empire's Siberia. Its garrison had to depend upon shipping from Montreal via the Champlain Trail (Ottawa, Mattawa, French River, Lake Huron) or from what is now Ontario's Essex County. While soldiers could supplement their food rations by growing vegetables and hunting, they lacked most consumer goods.

The British garrison learned about the outbreak of the War of 1812 before word reached the Americans on Mackinac Island. They surprised and captured the Americans. They retained Mackinac Island for the duration of the war, and with it control of the Upper Great Lakes. However, on 20 July 1812, American raiders burned and destroyed Fort St. Joseph.

By the Treaty of Ghent, signed 24 December 1814, each side returned to its own territory. Rather than re-establish the army base on St. Joseph Island, British authorities relocated to Drummond Island. After arbitrators decided that Drummond Island was U.S. territory, the soldiers moved to Penetanguishene, where they remained until the eve of the U.S. Civil War (1861–1865). The remains of the fort on St. Joseph's Island fell into ruins and received little attention, despite its importance during the War of 1812, until the 1960s when archeological excavations provided the informational basis for the national historic site. Often forgotten is the role the fort played in keeping a lifeline open to what became the Canadian west.

Resources

John Abbott and Graeme S. Mount, *A History of Fort St. Joseph* (Toronto: Dundurn Press, 2000).

William Newbigging, *Northern Soldiers: The History of the 49th Field Artillery Regiment, RCA* (Sault Ste. Marie: Regimental Senate of the 49th, 2021).

French Legacies and Realities

French-speaking people have had a connection with Ontario since 1610. That year, the French coureur de bois Étienne Brûlé (c.1592-c.1633) and, five years later, Samuel de Champlain (1567-1635), founder of New France, paddled up the Ottawa River from Montreal to its junction with the Mattawa. Then they went up the Mattawa to the south shore of Trout Lake, portaged across what is now Highway 17 east of North Bay to the headwaters of the LaVase Creek, and descended into Lake Nipissing. Crossing Lake Nipissing, they followed the French River into Lake Huron. Jean Nicolet followed the same route on his way to Lake Michigan fifteen years later. As hostile Iroquois dominated what is now southern Ontario, this more northern route became the main highway for fur-trading and other commerce between Montreal and the Upper Great Lakes from the seventeenth to the nineteenth century.

With the building of railways westward from Montreal in the 1880s, Northeastern Ontario attracted a substantial French-speaking population. By the late nineteenth century, virgin agricultural land was no longer available in Quebec, but the Canadian Pacific Railway provided transportation to Mattawa, North Bay, Sturgeon Falls, Verner (now part of West Nipissing) and Hearst. As gold mines in the Porcupine area became operational, French-speaking people moved to Timmins. From their vegetable and berry farms in the Sudbury Basin around Chelmsford and Val Caron, as well as in the Nipissing Lowlands and the more northerly Clay Belt areas, the new arrivals could provide fresh food to those who worked in the mining industry. Some French Canadians became miners and loggers, although with the passage of time, their sons and daughters have joined the professions and become prominent members of business communities.

Hardly surprisingly, the arrival of tens of thousands of French-speaking people into what had been an English-speaking province was not without controversy. Until well after World War II, the most important institutions for Franco-Ontarians were the Roman Catholic Church and schools, but they did not control either. From its creation in 1904 until 1985, bishops of Sault Ste. Marie (the diocese for Northeastern Ontario south of the Arctic-Atlantic Watershed) were of Irish descent, and the

Franco-Ontarian flag (Credit: Tony Galic)

first two, David Scollard (1904–1934) and Ralph Dignan (1934–1958), developed reputations as inimical to the French language. Bishop Scollard approved Italian-language St. Rita's parish in North Bay before that of French-language St-Vincent-de-Paul because he regarded Italians as more affluent than his French-Canadian parishioners. For economic reasons, Bishop Dignan hesitated to create a separate French-language parish after 1954 in Elliot Lake, because he regarded it as a community with an uncertain future on a secondary branch line of a branch line of the Canadian Pacific Railway. (In reality, it had no rail service).

In 1912 and 1913, the Conservative government led by Ontario Premier James Whitney (1905–1914) forced through the Legislature a law (Regulation 17) that out-lawed French as a language of instruction in Ontario schools. The results were unenforceable and ridiculous. In French-speaking communities, the law obliged French-speaking teachers to speak English to French-speaking students. During World War I, some French Canadians wondered why they should fight the Prussians of Europe when Ontario's English-speaking population provided a more immediate threat. In 1927, another Conservative premier of Ontario, Howard Ferguson (1923– 1930), rescinded Regulation 17. By then, Ferguson, previously an enthusiastic supporter of the Regulation, realized not only its impracticality but the difficulty it created in establishing a friendly relationship with the government of Quebec. Until 1968, the availability of French as a language of instruction would be decided on a case-by-case basis and differ from one part of the province to another. Retention rates of French-speaking students increased, both in terms of numbers and time spent in school.

One of the bastions of Franco-Ontarian culture has been Sudbury's Collège du Sacré-Coeur, a Jesuit-operated secondary school for young men, founded in 1913. During the late 1950s and 1960, its Jesuits played a leading role in the founding of the Université de Sudbury, one of the church colleges that federated to form Laurentian University. However, to some Quebec-based Jesuits, Collège du Sacré-Coeur was academic Siberia. François Hertel, a mentor to a young Pierre Elliott Trudeau, was exiled from Montreal to Sudbury in 1941 as a quasi-punishment for his radical beliefs.

In 1967 and 1968, when fears of Quebec separatism (independence) were strong, William Davis—the Minister of Education in the Progressive Conservative government led by John Robarts (1961–1971)—introduced legislation granting Franco-Ontarians the right to French-language education throughout elementary and secondary school. In 1982, Article 23 of the Canadian Charter of Rights and Freedoms affirmed certain rights of Quebec's English-speaking minority and of the French-speaking minorities of other provinces, and subsequent court battles clarified what that meant. Effective 1 January 1998, the government of Ontario divided school boards along language rather than geographic lines. The result is that Ontario has four categories of school boards: English Public, French Public, English (Roman) Catholic and French (Roman) Catholic.

Since then, French-language instruction has expanded, but use of the French language and of French-Canadian symbols has remained controversial. The Progressive Conservative government of Leslie Frost (1949–1961) established Sudbury's Laurentian University with both English and French as languages of instruction. French-language post-secondary instruction is also available in community colleges across Northeastern Ontario and at the Université de Hearst; yet, even in the more tolerant late twentieth century, many Franco-Ontarians resented the slow step-by-step increase in provincial government support for their linguistic rights. This has been underlined in the decades long struggle for a separate Francophone university, which Northerners wanted in the north but when finally granted went to

Monument to Jacques Cartier

Toronto. When Laurentian University went into insolvency in 2021, it terminated its agreements with its federated universities. The University of Sudbury has since tried to operate independently but the province has not provided support to that stand-alone French university. The local French elite continue to demand a fully funded institution in the north with the Université de Hearst operating as a base.

Given the attitudes of the dominant and intolerant English majority, Franco-Ontarians have often chosen to develop their own separate institutions. In 1926, they created the Order of Jacques Cartier, founded in Ottawa to protect French-Canadian interests. The Order of Jacques Cartier was a reaction to two anglophone organizations perceived as adversaries, the Masonic Order and the Orange Lodge.

In the 1940s and 1950s, Franco-Ontarians developed their own co-operative based banking system, a network of Caisses Populaires. Sudbury even has a co-operative funeral home. In other northern communities, such as Verner, the importance of co-ops and of credit unions is evident in the numerous buildings with co-op signage.

Inspired in part by Quebec's Quiet Revolution, in 1975 Franco-Ontarians based in Sudbury decided to adopt their own flag—green and white, with the fleur-de-lys to celebrate the French connection, and the white trillium (Ontario's official flower) to indicate their commitment to this province. The flag flew for the first time on 25 September 1975 at the University of Sudbury. In 2010, the Ontario legislature approved official status for the flag, with 25 September recognized as Franco-Ontarian Day.

While the flag was important to Francophones across Ontario, 25 September 2010 was particularly special for Sudbury's Francophone community: the 15th anniversary of Collège Boréal, the French-language community college; the 15th anniversary of Le Centre Victoria pour femmes, a shelter for abused women; the 15th anniversary of La Galerie du Nouvel-Ontario, an art gallery; the 25th anniversary of Le Club Richelieu les Patriotes, a service club; the flag's 35th anniversary; and the 60th anniversary of le Carrefour francophone, a cultural centre. The stars performing at the last event were assimilated pianists with non-French names, Philip Chiu and Janelle Fung.

Among the mentioned institutions, Collège Boréal has been especially important in cementing the French language. Formed in 1993, in 2010 it was designated as an official provider of French language under the French Language Services Act. Before that it had spread its language work into many parts of the province, including a campus in Timmins and later one in Toronto.

Even as the twentieth century ended and the twenty-first century began, occasional surges of intolerance occurred. In 1990, the city council of Sault Ste. Marie approved a provocative resolution that English would be the city's sole official language. The following decade, Sudbury's city council voted not to fly the Franco-Ontario flag (even though it had been designed in Sudbury) at Civic Square. Only when English-speaking John Rodriguez defeated incumbent Mayor David Courtemanche in the municipal election of 2006, and used the authority of his office, did the flag appear. Fortunately, the controversy in the birthplace of the green and white flag failed to arouse strong emotions anywhere else.

Despite these concerns for cultural distinctiveness, Franco-Ontarians co-operate across linguistic lines. The Northern Lights Festival Boréal, a musical weekend held at Sudbury's Bell Park every July since 1972, involves people from both sides of the language divide. Laurentian University provides instruction and services in both of Canada's official languages, though French has remained in minority as opposed to parity status, made worse by the insolvency of the university cutting more French than English programs. However, being bilingual can aid social advancement: Louise Charron from Sturgeon Falls became the first Franco-Ontarian justice of the Supreme Court of Canada.

Gaétan Gervais, a noted historian of the Franco-Ontario tradition, has observed a continuing challenge—Quebec's abandonment of French-speaking minorities in other parts of Canada. Since 1969, he maintains, Quebec has turned inward, eager to preserve and promote the French language within its borders but indifferent to its fate elsewhere in North America. Indeed, Quebec authorities often seem more interested in French-speaking countries of Europe and Africa than in the Francophone minorities of other provinces. The federal government has, as is its right and its interest in obtaining votes, offered more support to French-speaking residents of provinces other than Quebec than has the Quebec's government. Simultaneously Ontario's French Languages Service Act of 1986 defined linguistic rights more precisely. Yet, according to Professor Gervais, French-Canadian minorities have been inadvertent beneficiaries of Quebec politics. Whenever Quebec threatens to detach itself from Canada, politicians in other provincial capitals have become aware of problems faced by their French-speaking voters and have sought to improve their situation.

The collective accomplishments of Franco-Ontarians have been considerable. Sudbury-born singer/songwriter Robert Paquette has performed across Canada, in the United States and in Europe. In 1970, Paquette was one of the founders of the Coopérative Artistique du Nouvel Ontario (CANO). Nor has Sudbury been the only Franco-Ontarian cultural centre. Rachel Paiement of Sturgeon Falls was one of CANO's singers. Lise Paiement, also of Sturgeon Falls, was director of *L'écho d'un Peuple*, a famous Franco-Ontarian drama. During his short life, André Paiement (1950–1978) of Sturgeon Falls, was a noted singer, songwriter, playwright and member of CANO. Laurentian University professor Yves Lefier has compiled a reference work of more than a thousand pages about reports written in French about places in Ontario and literary efforts of Ontario's French-language writers. In 1988, the College universitaire de Hearst established a publishing house, Le Nordir. In 2002, Sudbury poet and Laurentian University professor Robert Dickson won the Governor General's Literary Award.

Numerous institutions support the maintenance of French culture. The Assemblée de la francophonie de l'Ontario (AFO) represents Franco-Ontarians from other parts of Ontario—the Ottawa, Welland and Windsor areas—as well as the Northeast. Since the early 1970s many cultural institutions have solidified Francophone culture. Examples include : the annual cultural extravaganza "La Nuit sur l'étang" (Night on the pond), a high quality French-language Théâtre du Nouvel-Ontario, le Centre franco-ontarien de folklore, le Centre de recherche en civilisation canadienne-française, and l'Institut franco-Ontarien de Sudbury. There are significant cultural publications : *Revue du Nouvel-Ontario* (since 1978), *Dictionnaire des écrits de l'Ontario française* (published in 2010, edited by Gaétan Gervais and Jean-Pierre Pichette), and a weekly newspaper, *Le Voyageur*. Radio-Canada's Northeastern Ontario studio is in Sudbury, which is also the site of the French-language community college, College Boréal. Across the northeast are multiple seniors' clubs, Le Club Richelieu (a service club) and Filles d'Isabelle (also a service club). Franco-Ontario culture seems to be thriving more than just surviving in the Northeast.

Resources

Greg Allain, "Les francophones canadiennes minoritaires l'aube du XXIième siècle," *Francophones d'Amérique* no. 14 (2002).

Sheila McLeod Arnopoulos, *Voices from French Canada* (Kingston: McGill-Queen's, 1982).

Jacques Cotnam, et al, eds., *La francophonie ontarienne* (Series: Nordir).

Serge Dupuis, *Sudbury's Francophones : A Brief History* (Sudbury: ACFA, 2021).

W.J. Eccles, *The French in North America, 1500–1765* (Lansing: Michigan State University Press, 1998).

Guy Gaudreau, ed., *Le Drapeau Franco-Ontarien* (Sudbury : Prise de Parole, 2005).

Gaétan Gervais, *Des Gens de Résolution: Le Passage Du Canada Français à l'Ontario français* (Sudbury: Prise de Parole, 2003).

J. Grimard, *L'Ontario français par l'image* (St. Laurent, QC: Éditions Études Vivantes, 1981).

Charles W. Humphries, "Honest Enough to be Bold": The Life and Times of Sir James Pliny Whitney (Toronto: University of Toronto Press, 1985).

Yves Lefier, *L'Ontario en français, 1613–1995: réalités et fiction* (Sudbury: Institut Franco-Ontarien, 1996).

Lucien Michaud, *Cents ans de vie française à Sudbury* (Sudbury: Société historique du Nouvel-Ontario, 1983).

French River

South of Sudbury, the Municipality of French River was amalgamated as an administrative unit in 1999 and includes a large area mostly north of the river. The river had been a natural highway for the First Nations people over some thousand years as they transported trade goods (fish, corn, metals) and changed hunting and fishing grounds. Since Europeans arrived in the 17th century and, until recently, the region's economy has been related to the fur trade and lumbering. The voyageurs' main route from the Mattawa River via Lake Nipissing passed along the French River, which traverses the municipality from Lake Nipissing's many western bays to Georgian Bay, 100 kilometres west. During the nineteenth and well into the twentieth century, lumber production was the main employment, especially as a supplement to small farms.

Access to the region is mainly via Highway 69, which cuts through the western part, and Highway 64, which goes east from Alban and comes southwest from Highway 17 at Verner. Highway 535 is a secondary access from Highway 17 at Hagar south to Noëlville. The terrain is typically Canadian Shield with impressive rock outcroppings, lakes and twisted pines. However, pockets of flat land with good soil exist. Hence, at present cottagers, tourism and agriculture predominate.

The populace is widely scattered on farms and small holdings with a population of 2,800 in 2021. The main centres are Alban (63 people in 2021), French River Station (50), Ouellette, Monetville and Noëlville (about 250). French River Station is no longer a rail stop but has a notable historical station. Ouellette once had a cheese factory and a school but is now reduced to a general store.

Known from 1900 to 1911 as Crosby, Noëlville was renamed for the predominant merchant Noël Desmarais. The village is bilingual and near it are rabbit, buffalo and dairy farms. The village centre is dominated by the Roman Catholic Church, and all significant services are available including service stations, grocery and an 18-hole golf course. It is the supply centre for the very spread-out hamlets and farms that surround it.

Noëlville is known for its annual Family Hockey Tournament, a 40-year tradition. Each February, it brings together much of the community with more than a dozen teams. It has been so successful that family members return home to participate, and it now supports local charities.

A disputed co-generation station that would burn wood chips near Alban might supply needed jobs lost in the closing of lumber and sawmills but might also negatively affect the tourist trade.

Along the river and the lakes of the region are numerous resorts—some fancy, others simple—and campgrounds. The river itself and some of its adjacent public territory is a provincial park (a waterway with some facilities). It is excellent for canoeing with some challenging rapids, and is good for boating, fishing and swimming. The visitor centre, where Highway 69 crosses the river (south side) has two features. The building with displays relating to voyageur days won an architectural prize, and the beautifully arched snowmobile bridge at 1,250 feet long and 12 feet wide is the world's longest and widest. North of the bridge is the well-known trading post, which has a diverse collection of crafts, souvenirs and clothing—and "the hungry bear" is an attraction for children.

Resources

William A Campbell, *The French and Pickerel Rivers, their History and their People* (Sudbury: Journal, 1990).

Ray Love, *The Georgian Bay Ship Canal: Canada's Abandoned National Dream* (Victoria: Friesen, 2021).

Helen Pakkala, *French River: Route to the Past* (Sudbury: French River Heritage, 1979).

Noëlville church

Farmland meets outcrop
(Credit: Laurence Stevens)

Geology or Moving Rocks

⋇

By David Pearson

We often say "solid as a rock" but as we travel through Northern Ontario with an eye on the road cuts and remembering that geological time is measured in billions of years, we can see evidence for the exact opposite, at least on the scale of continents and regions as big as Ontario. It seems amazing and challenges our imagination, but today Ontario is sliding to the southwest by almost two and a half centimetres a year driven by gravity and convection in the hot, partly molten rock tens of kilometres beneath the surface. We call the process plate tectonics and that is what has built generations of mountain ranges, as high as the Himalayas, across Northern Ontario as drifting continents collided, often, but not always to break up again. The 15-kilometre-deep roots of one of those ranges, the Grenville Mountains, are easily seen on the side of the road to Killarney Park. It was one of the longest mountain ranges on Earth, stretching north to Scotland and south to Texas and Mexico. The mountains were built during 100 million years of continental collisions about a billion years ago. The leading edge of those mountains, known as the Grenville Front, is visible in a steep hill on Highway 17, very close to Sudbury.

The rocks on the Sudbury side of the Grenville collision that continue into the La Cloche Hills on the approach to Manitoulin Island, are part of the older Penokean Mountains built by collisions with land masses arriving from the south almost two billion years ago. Although they are older than the rocks of Grenville range, the peaks stand higher today because they are almost pure quartz sandstone, heated and welded during the mountain building, making it very resistant to erosion. It breaks with sharp edges, which made it very suitable for tool making by local Indigenous people, and rings like a bell when struck, which is what gave rise to the name La Cloche for the hills.

North of Sudbury, towards Kapuskasing, are older rocks of the core of Canada, the Canadian Shield, with seven recognized small continents that collided and stayed welded together between three and a half and two and a half billion years ago. They included the deep roots of volcanoes and pools of molten rock that host the mineral deposits, revealed after billions of years of erosion, that are now mined in Timmins and Red Lake. It was in sands, now rock, of the same age as those eroded from the Shield that extremely careful chemical analysis of sulphur atoms showed signs of the first oxygen in the atmosphere. That incredibly important step in the evolution of the atmosphere was created by ancient algae in the oceans, and the oxygen they produced escaped into the atmosphere about two and half billion years ago.

If you drive along the highway to Sault Ste. Marie or to Manitoulin Island, you can catch sight of greyish rocks with visible lines that were layers of sand near a shore. Imagine them being swept by waves and currents at the time the atmosphere was changing. Continuing to Manitoulin Island will take you to limestones that are only about 450 million years old and full of fossils like corals and sponges that are the very tangible evidence of the growing diversity of life on the planet. Unlike almost every other rock in Northern Ontario, they have not been folded into mountains; instead, they are a small part of the evidence for a warm shallow sea across the north. Limestones like those on Manitoulin Island are also found much further north in a down-dropped rift valley between cracks or faults (yes, just like the African Rift Valley but very, very much smaller), now filled by Lake Temiskaming near New Liskeard. A widely felt earthquake on a fracture associated with the faults welcomed in the new century on 1 January 2000. An earlier one occurred in 1935. Near the lakeshore are excellent geological lookout points designed for tourists.

In great contrast to the creeping pace of building and wearing down mountains are the dramatic few minutes it took for a meteorite or comet, 10 to 15 kilometres across, travelling at about 36,000 kilometres an hour from outer space, to collide with the Earth and blast out a huge crater we call the Sudbury Basin. The collision occurred almost 2 billion years ago. The crater would have been about 200 kilometres across and, for an instant, 16 kilometres deep as heat from the impact created a pool of molten rock as much as three kilometres deep that flooded the crater floor, some of it coming from deep below the crater. It has been said that the volume of molten rock was six times the combined volume of the water in lakes Huron and Ontario. The meteorite and a good deal of rock at the point of impact, was vaporized, so Sudbury's ores didn't come from the meteorite. They are not extraterrestrial, instead they separated as nickel and copper minerals as well as others such as platinum, from that vast pool of molten rock, as it very slowly cooled.

The building of the Grenville Mountains almost a billion years after the impact, squeezed the crater into the oval form we see today, especially looking north towards the high northern rim from roads near the town of Chelmsford. Erosion has also worn the crater down to a small remnant of only 60 by 30 kilometres. but that was enough to have attracted Apollo 16 and 17 astronauts to Sudbury in 1971 and 1972. They came to examine the rocks of the crater in preparation for being lunar geologists when they walked on the Moon. You can step into their shoes at one of the most important training sites: the A.Y. Jackson Lookout at Onaping Falls on the road to Timmins. The Apollo 17 crew were especially interested in the rocks of the waterfall that are composed of the so-called "fallback" debris thrown up by the impact. Walk down to those rocks near the river to easily see how it is made of angular fragments that flew up into the air. They were part of a cloud that would have encircled the planet, while about one and a half kilometres fell into the crater. If that doesn't satisfy your yen to visit craters, go to Lake Wanapitei, near Sudbury Airport, which is a youngster, only 37 million years old and only a few kilometres across but interesting enough to have attracted the last two astronauts to walk on the moon.

Much more recently than mountain building, a continental ice sheet, between two and three kilometres thick, like in Antarctica today, shaped the surface of the north. Sliding south from the Arctic, it scoured depressions and polished outcrops like sandpaper with the silt and sand that collected at its base. Some of the scoured depressions became glacial lakes as the ice melted. Eight thousand years ago you could have paddled a canoe from the glacial lake in the Sudbury Basin to the Great Lakes. You could also have explored Lake Ojibway that ran east from Hearst to Timmins and into Quebec. We call that flat potential farmland the Great Clay Belt. Its cousin, the Little Clay belt, is the floor of the lake that spreads from Lake Temiskaming in its rift valley. The weight of the ice pushed down the rocky crust, squeezing partly molten rock aside. Now that the weight has been removed, Northern Ontario is rising from half a metre in the south to three quarter metres in the north per century. Partly molten rock is oozing back under the north from under the floor of the Great Lakes that are sinking.

So, yes, solid as a rock, just slipping and sliding and rebounding from depression.

Resources

John Allan Percival, and Robert Michael Easton, *Geology of the Canadian Shield in Ontario: An Update* (Toronto: Ontario Geological Survey, 2007).
P. C. Thurston, et al., *Geology of Ontario* (Toronto: Ontario Geological Survey, 1991), Special Volume 4.

Icons of the Northeast

Hearst

Despite a slightly declining population (4,794 in 2021, 5,010 in 2011; 5,825 in 2001), Hearst appears prosperous, and may once have been home to Ontario's largest proportion of millionaires. Signs of prosperity include up-market subdivisions and an average family income of nearly $70,000 (similar to Sudbury and more than North Bay). However, the issues of economic diversification and jobs beyond the lumber industry have not been resolved, though a seedling plant, La Maison Verte, produces nine million seedlings annually to assist reforestation. The shift toward research and education offers hope for the future.

Hearst may be the province's most French community at about 90% French-speaking. In the 2016 census of the 3,745 who declared their first official language spoken, 460 stated English, 3265 French. Only 70 declared a non-official language and 10 an Indigenous one. (In more detailed responses of the 5,510 in 2001 who reported their choice of language for the census, 4,855 spoke French at home, 535 English and 35 another language. At that time while 1,525 said that they could speak nothing but French and 245 nothing but English, 3,740 indicated knowledge of both official languages. Only 30 residents indicated that they were not Canadian citizens). Although other Ontario towns and cities are bilingual, elsewhere English usually predominates. In 1977, Hearst's long-serving mayor, René Fontaine (1967–1980) declared his community a "bi-lingual municipality," a first in Ontario. Reflecting a change in attitudes a historic marker erected near Hearst by the Province of Ontario delivers the information in the four languages spoken by residents: French, English, Cree and Ojibwe. The town's multicultural heritage has been commemorated by unveiling a Nations Park in the downtown during its centennial.

Hearst remains a centre of Franco-Ontarian culture. The Université de Hearst (formerly Collège de Hearst) had been affiliated with Laurentian University of Sudbury from 1963 until 2022 when it became independent. It offers social sciences and business and administration programs at three campuses (Hearst, Kapuskasing and Timmins). It is the only university in Ontario to operate on the block plan as opposed to the regular quarter system. In 2011, an archive and research centre (Centre d'archives de la Grande Zone argileuse) opened at the university to preserve historical documents for the region of Hearst and the Great Clay Belt (Longlac to Cochrane) that deal with life, culture and industry, especially logging and mining. Collège Boréal Hearst, a French-language community college whose main campus is in Sudbury, offers courses in business and administration, health sciences, human sciences and some trades. Hearst is the site of the Roman Catholic cathedral of the Diocese of Hearst.

Hearst began with the arrival of the National Transcontinental Railway (later part of Canadian National) in 1911. French-speaking people from Quebec followed the rails west on the advice of the Catholic clergy. Some of the early settlers spoke English, and others came from continental Europe. All came by rail as the highway only reached Hearst in the 1940s. Hearst sits where the northern terminus of the Algoma Central Railway from Sault Ste. Marie meets the Ontario Northland, 208 kilometres west of Cochrane on Highway 11. (In 1994, the ONR bought CN's tracks between Cochrane and Hearst.) The passenger train between the Sault and Hearst ceased in 2015. However, the fall tour passing through the Agawa Canyon is being resumed after a two year pause due to the pandemic. The autumn tours offer spectacular views when the leaves change colour and the Algoma Highlands contours become more visible.

The Province of Ontario named the community for William Howard Hearst of Sault Ste. Marie, then Minister of Forests and Mines, who had become Northern Ontario's representative in the provincial cabinet in 1911 when Frank Cochrane departed for federal politics. Hearst would become Ontario's premier in 1914 and serve through the war until 1919.

After the Japanese attack on Pearl Harbor, on 7 December 1941, Hearst became the site of a camp for unruly prisoners-of-war. Unconfirmed reports claim that once Canada seized the property of British Columbians of ethnic Japanese extraction and forced them to move inland, some spent time in Hearst before proceeding to their new homes. Also, during the war, the U. S. Army built a radar base in Hearst; it was transferred to the Canadian Army in 1943.

Forestry and lumber have always dominated the local economy. Within Hearst, Green First (formerly Tembec among other names) operates a sawmill and Columbia manufactures plywood, particle board and melamine, a timber byproduct used for making resins. West of Hearst at Calstock, Lecours Lumber operates the last privately and family-owned sawmill in Ontario. About one third of the labour force is in forest-related industries. The catchment area for shoppers, students, medical services, sports and entertainment includes an estimated 10,000 people.

Outdoors and indoors, residents of Hearst and nearby communities can appreciate modern amenities. Parks run along the Mattawishkwia River, which flows through the community and stretches roughly parallel to Highway 11. Bicycle and walking paths are common. Hearst's Park Lacours is named for brothers—Alfred, Arthur and Georges—who moved from Quebec during the 1930s and pioneered the local sawmill industry. Snowmobilers can ride 360 kilometres of trails radiating from Hearst, while cross country skiers have 30 kilometres. The Claude Larose Recreation Centre includes twin rinks, an indoor pool, a youth centre and a Hall of Fame Museum. For those unable to make use of those facilities, the Pioneer Nursing Home has 67 beds for the elderly and infirm, and Notre Dame Hospital has 23 acute care beds and 21 chronic care beds.

Recreational attractions include fishing, hunting, canoeing, hiking and snowmobiling. The Information Centre has a theme park that features replicas of some of the area's largest animals because it once touted itself as the Moose Capital of Canada. Other claims to fame include what may well be the world's largest pile of logs, the best sweet and sour chicken balls (per Robert Munsch in *Where is Gah-Ning?*) and, for westbound travellers, the last McDonald's outlet until Thunder Bay.

In its rougher logging days Hearst had many bars. We were told about a group of fellows sitting in one and having a good time when some American hunters entered. One of the drinkers welcomed them. When the Americans asked where to go moose hunting, a drinker told them with winks to his buddies that just east down the road they would find a yellow sign where the moose crossed. They just needed to go there and wait. The Americans left and the drinkers had their laugh. However, in a few hours the Americans returned to thank them because they had indeed shot a moose right after they established themselves near the sign.

Hearst's prominent people have contributed to business, the arts and politics. Hearst is home to Doric Germain (author and French literature professor), Roger Bernard (author and Sociology professor), Louise Tanguay (photographer), Donald Poliquin (author, singer-songwriter, performer), Paulette Gagnon (actor and playwright) and Laurent Vaillancourt (multimedia artist), all of whom had a role in shaping Franco-Ontarian identity and culture from the 1970s through the 1990s. From 1987 until 1990, René Fontaine served as provincial Minister of Northern Development in the Liberal cabinet of Premier David Peterson. City councilor Gaetan Baillargeon made the headlines in 2018 for refusing to swear allegiance to the British Crown citing the colonial past and cultural genocide suffered by his Cree and Ojibwe ancestors. Following the events and in the spirit of reconciliation, Municipal Affairs drew up a new declaration of allegiance allowing Indigenous elected officials to take office without betraying their views about the British Crown.

Producing high calibre hockey players is a Hearst tradition. For example, during his career playing for different teams, Claude Larose was a member of six Stanley Cup winning NHL teams. Other notables include Claude Giroux who played for various teams and the Nigerian-born Rumun Ndur who started his NHL career playing in Hearst minor leagues. Hockey related: Pierre Lebrun is a sportswriter and television sportscaster with Canadian Press, the CBC ("Hockey Night in Canada") and the sports channel, ESPN.

Resources: "Hearstory, the History of Hearst Ontario" is a Facebook site documenting the early history of Hearst.

Killarney east lighthouse and bay

Kapuskasing

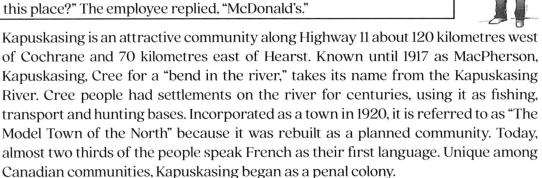

Kapuskasing is an attractive community along Highway 11 about 120 kilometres west of Cochrane and 70 kilometres east of Hearst. Known until 1917 as MacPherson, Kapuskasing, Cree for a "bend in the river," takes its name from the Kapuskasing River. Cree people had settlements on the river for centuries, using it as fishing, transport and hunting bases. Incorporated as a town in 1920, it is referred to as "The Model Town of the North" because it was rebuilt as a planned community. Today, almost two thirds of the people speak French as their first language. Unique among Canadian communities, Kapuskasing began as a penal colony.

The tracks of the National Transcontinental Railway (NTR) reached MacPherson in 1911. (The NTR became part of Canadian National in 1919, and CN sold the tracks to Ontario Northland in 1994.) In 1914, the Canadian government decided to build an experimental farm at MacPherson to see whether agriculture was possible so far north. The soil of the Clay Belt was good, but would the growing season be long enough? The outbreak of World War I that same year determined who would clear the land for the farm, which continues to operate today. The Borden government feared that recently arrived immigrants from the Austro-Hungarian Empire might jeopardize Canadian security from within, and it interned some 1,900 former subjects of the Habsburgs, mainly ethnic Ukrainians, but also unnaturalized Germans. The internees logged the trees, which they then used to erect buildings for the penal colony. Yet, by 1916, Canada had such a severe labour shortage, due to war losses, that the internees were freed (under restrictions), and their camp became "home" to German and Austrian prisoners-of-war. The POWs were in Canada because

Kapuskasing Station and Museum

escape was more difficult from North America than from an Allied country in Europe. The only reminder of the camp today is a site west of Kapuskasing on the south side of Highway 11 opposite the town's cemetery. That site contains a small cemetery for 32 Germans who died before they could be repatriated, as well as separate monuments in Ukrainian and German, that commemorate the sad story.

In 1917, the Conservative government of Ontario led by Sir William Hearst thought that it might establish a colony at Kapuskasing for returning World War I veterans. However, in the election of 1919 the United Farmers of Ontario party defeated the Conservatives, and the government of Premier Ernest Drury abandoned the project. Most veterans lacked agricultural knowledge or experience, in particular, skills that were needed in an area with such a short growing season.

The Spruce Falls Company saved the community. It was incorporated in 1920, and by 1922 its 500 employees were producing 104 metric tons of paper daily. French Canadians from Quebec travelled to Kapuskasing in search of farming opportunities and other employment, and many worked for Spruce Falls. The Drury government hired Harries and Hall, a landscape architectural company, to plan Kapuskasing; they in turn looked to the Garden City Movement, founded in the United Kingdom by Sir Ebenezer Howard in 1898, for ideas. Sir Ebenezer's goals were planned, self-sufficient, architecturally attractive communities with separate residential and industrial areas. The resulting plan allowed considerable green space along the Kapuskasing River, where residents could enjoy outdoor activities. Among the special aspects of the planned town was a circle of commercial institutions from which major thoroughfares radiate. Highway 11 separates the residential area to the north from the industrial area to the south. Other northeastern communities influenced by the movement to plan urban land use include Espanola, Iroquois Falls and Elliot Lake.

In 1926, the Spruce Falls Company reincorporated as the Spruce Falls Power and Paper Company and launched a significant expansion programme. The New York Times and Kimberly-Clark, the maker of Kleenex, owned most of the company's shares, and the company became the sole supplier of newsprint to *The New York Times*, which received its first shipment in 1928. Shipments of Kleenex followed. In a section entitled "Blind Eyes, Blind Pigs and Blind Dates," a local history records that during this phase of industrial development the town had "gamblers, bootleggers and prostitutes," typical of northern boom towns.

One of the bloodiest episodes in Canadian labour history occurred near Kapuskasing in 1963. In January, the Lumber and Sawmill Workers Union went on strike against the Spruce Falls Power and Paper Company. However, independent contractors continued to ship pulpwood, which the mill continued to use. On 11 February, more than 400 strikers converged on Reesor, on the railway line west of

Kapuskasing and east of Hearst. Mennonites, Germans, and perhaps a few people from the Netherlands had settled Reesor in the 1920s, but by the 1960s Reesor's survival was precarious. Its last school closed in 1966, its last store the following year. The strikers' intention was to dump logs stockpiled by a local woodcutters' co-operative. Some of the woodcutters were armed, and they shot the strikers, three of whom died: Fernand Drouin (1935–1963), Irenée Fortier (1938–1963) and Joseph Fortier (1928–1963). Eight others were wounded. At that point, the provincial government led by Progressive Conservative Premier John Robarts decided to impose compulsory arbitration to end the strike. For a time more than 200 workers and 20 woodcutters were jailed. When Stompin Tom Conners wrote a song sympathetic to the strikers in 1969 he reported receiving death threats if he dared to continue to present it.

In 1975, Spruce Falls Power and Paper moved its corporate headquarters from Toronto to Kapuskasing, and in 1980, two years after launching a modernization program, the company earned record profits. The following decade produced a different scenario, with loss of customers and declining revenues, and in 1991 the company said that it could not continue to operate. The Ontario NDP government of Premier Bob Rae came to the rescue. It provided money to sustain operations until Spruce Falls Inc. could buy Spruce Falls Power and Paper. Employees of Spruce Falls Inc. own 54% of the shares, and residents of Kapuskasing and neighbouring communities own another 7%. Tembec Inc., now Green First, owns the rest. Spruce Falls Inc. continues to produce newsprint and other paper products for customers in Canada and the United States.

From 1928 until 2002, one landmark was the Kapuskasing Inn, a place fit for royalty. During their 1951 Canadian tour, then-Princess Elizabeth and her husband Prince Philip stayed there. In 2007, arsonists destroyed any hope of restoration. Near where it stood is the impressive town hall, which overlooks the park surrounding the bend in the river. The new public library, which abuts the town hall, is built with bricks saved from the demolished inn and has a section devoted to Kapuskasing's development. In front of the town hall facing the bend in the river is a large, well-treed park.

General Motors Canada has a site in Kapuskasing for testing engines

94   Internee cemetery, Kapuskasing

under cold weather conditions. The logic is that if cars start on a January day in Kapuskasing, they will start almost anywhere, any time.

Residents of Kapuskasing have numerous amenities. For devotees of winter sports, the Sports Palace has rinks for hockey, figure skating and curling. For those who speak English, the Frank J. Selke Memorial Resource Centre helps with social issues, including employment and welfare. Francophones have two cultural centres: the Centre régional des loisirs (with meeting rooms, small gallery, sports complex, bingo facility, and musical and other entertainment) and La Forge Jos Godin (for hobbies such as woodworking and metalworking). The First Nations people have the Native Friendship Centre and the Kapuskasing Indian Friendship Centre, both of which help with social issues facing Indigenous persons, especially youth. The Golden Age Centre serves seniors.

Tourists and residents can enjoy Kapuskasing's riverside park, golf course and arena. The major tourist site is the Ron Morel Museum outside the former railway station, which is now a bus station. Ron Morel (1922–1976), president of the Kapuskasing and District Historical Society from 1970 to 1975, envisioned the museum, which opened in 1978. Outside the station, and therefore accessible throughout the year, are historical pictures and plaques that review Kapuskasing's history. A steam engine and two passenger coaches sit immediately west of the station; one of the coaches holds information about railway history, the other about Kapuskasing life in general. Winter attractions include a Festival of Lights and snowmobile events. For twenty years the Kapuskasing Lumberjack Heritage Festival was an annual event celebrating the area's logging history but ended with the Covid pandemic.

Resources

The Northern Times, *The First Fifty Years: A Golden Jubilee History of Kapuskasing* (Kapuskasing: The Northern Times, 1970).

The Northern Times, *Kapuskasing, The Model Town* (Kapuskasing: The Northern Times, 1994).

Margaret W. Paterson, *The Yesterdays that Shaped our Today* (Kapuskasing, 1984).

O. Saarinen, "The Influence of Thomas Adam and the British New Town Movement in the Planning of Canadian Resource Communities," in A. Artibise and G. Stelter, eds., *The Usable Urban Past* (Ottawa: Carleton UP, 1979), 82-86.

Kapuskasing Town Hall

Killarney

Located 100 kilometres southwest of Sudbury, the village of Killarney is special. It is close to the diverse wilderness and picturesque rock outcroppings of Killarney Provincial Park. It sits on a channel big enough for large yachts and sailboats to anchor. At each end of the channel are lighthouses. It faces George Island in Georgian Bay, which offers a seven-kilometre hiking trail with at least three distinct terrains: softwood forest, Precambrian outcroppings, and the pink-red rocks of the Huron lakeshore. It has a long legacy as a multicultural (First Nations, French, English) settlement. Its municipality covers a huge area, including parts of Algoma, Sudbury and Parry Sound districts, as well as two provincial parks (Killarney, French River).

Before the first European settlers came in 1820, the Indigenous Ojibwe had fished and hunted from this protected inlet. Smoked fish and dried game meat provided winter sustenance. Steamships arrived in 1836 and were the main form of transport during the nineteenth and most of the twentieth centuries. Killarney served as an important port for the fur trade, for transshipping supplies to North Shore communities, and for fishing. It provided a stopping place from southern Ontario to Manitoulin Island, the North Shore and Sault Ste. Marie. However, the village remained isolated, especially in winter, before highway access in 1962, when Highway 634 linked it to the then-new Highway 69, 40 kilometres south of Sudbury.

In its long history as the oldest European settlement on Georgian Bay, Killarney has welcomed many visitors, including Anna Jameson, who wrote about her stay in 1837: "It was on the shore of a beautiful channel running between the mainland and a large island. On a neighbouring point, Wai-sow-win-de-bay (the Yellowhead) and his people were building their wigwams for the night. The appearance was most picturesque, particularly when the campfires were lit and the night came on. I cannot forget the figure of a squaw as she stood, dark and tall, against the red flames bending over a great black kettle, her blanket trailing behind her, her hair streaming on the night breeze—most like to one of the witches in Macbeth. We supped here on excellent trout and whitefish, but the sandflies and mosquitoes were horribly tormenting; the former, which are so diminutive as to be scarcely visible, were by far the worst."

For many years, Killarney has served as a supply point for yachters and Killarney Park visitors. It is a worthwhile tourist site with a comfortable large lodge, pub and motels, hiking trails—including one near its eastern lighthouse—and fishing possibilities. The lodge has been renovated and large meeting spaces created in wonderfully designed log buildings that fit into the landscape. The world's largest canoe paddle is becoming an icon with which to be photographed. Killarney's fish-and-chips shop, next to the commercial fishery, is renowned; some people even fly from Sudbury to indulge.

Resources

Margaret E. Derry, *Georgian Bay Jewel: The Killarney Story* (Caledon: Poplar Lane, 2007). This is a beautifully illustrated work.

Anna Jameson, *Winter Studies and Summer Rambles in Canada* (Toronto: Saunders, 1972).

Historically informative: http://www. killarneyhistory.com

Killarney east lighthouse and bay

Kirkland Lake and Swastika

The histories of Kirkland Lake and Swastika (located six kilometres to the west) are inseparable. Both are products of the gold rush of 1906 at nearby Larder Lake. Both have strange names. In 1907, a surveyor named a lake in the Township of Teck "Kirkland Lake" in honour of Miss Winnifred Kirkland, a secretary at the Ontario Department of Mines office in Toronto. Miss Kirkland neither visited the area nor saw the lake, which has since disappeared because it has been filled with mine tailings. The community of Kirkland Lake developed beside the lake area. Swastika's name has various possible meanings, including the Cree and Ojibwe symbol for the four winds, which represented universal power. Other possible meanings of the symbol are a good luck charm, peace and good fortune, or sun, sky, deities and light. In 1907, the Temiskaming and Northern Ontario Railway adopted the name for its station. An effort during World War II to change the name of the community to Winston failed, because, as the local people said, their community had that name long before the Nazis adopted the swastika as their symbol. After all, no one suggested that Dresden in southwestern Ontario should change its name! Whenever officials erected signs using Winston, they were torn down. In 1972, Swastika became part of Kirkland Lake.

Kirkland Lake has a declining population, attributed to the volatility of the gold market. The Township of Teck, which included both communities, was home to 25,000 in 1939, but by 1986 Kirkland Lake's population had fallen to 12,000. In 2006, the population stood at 8,248; 6,215 identified their mother tongue as English, 1,200 French, 105 both and 505 as other. Of the total, 2,300 claim to be bilingual indicating diversity beyond English and French. In 2021, the population had declined to 7,750.

Kirkland Lake and Swastika had a host of illustrious founders and lore. In 1911, William Wright and Ed Hargreaves were hunting rabbits near what is now Kirkland Lake. Hargreaves became lost and fired a shot to attract Wright's attention. While Wright was heading in the direction of the noise, he stumbled upon quartz with a significant quantity of gold specks. Next day, the two men staked claims. Others rushed to the area, among them Sandy McIntyre, renowned for his finds in the

Sir Harry Oakes Chateau

Porcupine area near Timmins. What he found would become the Teck-Hughes Mine. The appropriately named Tough brothers ventured out into -50-degree weather and staked a claim in the middle of the night, three hours before competitors arrived. They shared ownership in the Tough-Oakes Mine. J.B. Tyrell, who had previously discovered dinosaur bones in Alberta, established Kirkland Lake Gold Mines, and mining engineer Robert Bruce founded the Macassa Mine.

By 1911, Swastika had a population of 450. A new arrival, appropriately named Walter Mill, launched a sawmill. The Methodist Church, the first hotel and the first school opened. The first baby born in the community, Charles Swastika Culbert, appeared and the first train arrived.

Two of the earliest passengers, Harry Oakes and Roza Brown, became two of the area's best-known personalities. Brown (1854–1947), an emigrant from Hungary, acquired real estate and rented a room to Oakes (1874–1943), who reportedly arrived with only $2.65 in his pocket. Brown became an anglophile par excellence, sending cards and gifts to members of the Royal Family and walking the streets carrying a Union Jack while offering $5 to every young man who would volunteer for military service during World War II. The local museum notes that she "was known as a filthy, shocking, rude, tight-fisted patriotic woman surrounded by barking mutts...."

According to a local laundryman who claimed to be a witness, Oakes left the train in Swastika quite involuntarily, ejected by a conductor because he had no money for ongoing travel. In 1946, Oakes's widow, Lady Eunice Oakes, denied the story and indicated that he had chosen to disembark in Swastika because he was looking for gold. The American-born Oakes had prospected in Alaska, the Philippines, Australia, South Africa and California, and in 1912 with the Tough brothers he staked the claim of Kirkland Lake's first producing gold mine, Tough-Oakes Mine. Subsequently, he became one of the world's wealthiest men.

For more than two decades, Oakes (who became Sir Harry Oakes) lived in

Roza Brown

Swastika and Kirkland Lake, where he built himself a mansion, known as the Sir Harry Oakes Chateau. The Chateau is now the site of Kirkland Lake's Museum of Northern History. Oakes was philanthropic, donating land to the Anglican and Presbyterian churches; books, land and labour to a school; and money to a hospital that opened in 1926. However, he was unwilling to accept a higher level of taxation and, in the mid-1930s when the federal government threatened to tax him at a rate of 80%, he moved to Nassau in the Bahamas. There he lived, in another mansion, until his murder under very mysterious circumstances in 1943. Possible suspects include members of the Mafia, who resented Oakes's opposition to legalized gambling, and even the former King Edward VIII (then Governor of the Bahamas), with whose wife Oakes may have had a dalliance.

In addition to Roza Brown and Oakes, Charlie Chow (1886–1972) supplied local lore. He came from China in 1900 and by 1924 ran a restaurant. Always cautious with his money, but a wise investor, Chow allowed his customers to pay for their meals with mine shares. Over time, the shares appreciated, and he cashed in many. One pay day a snowstorm delayed the train carrying cash to Kirkland Lake and the Royal Bank had insufficient funds. Mr. Chow loaned the bank $250,000 in cash to make the mine payrolls.

In 1919, Kirkland Lake had its first miners' strike for improved wages and working conditions. That same year, the community received its first physician, a Dr. Wilson, who arrived from Swastika. By 1929, the year when Kirkland Lake's library opened, the community had a population of 7,000. Employment in the mines reached an all-time high (4,761) in 1939; by 1944, it had fallen to 2,064. Between those dates one of Canada's most important labour strikes divided the community. From November 1941 to February 1942, the workers at Lake Shore mine were on strike over working conditions and union recognition. The union lost as men who could not survive trickled back to work. However, the towns people and others came to know

The Miners Memorial, Kirkland Lake

actual mining conditions due to arbitration hearings. The strike also galvanized other industrial centres, and eventually the war-time government acknowledged the need for collective bargaining. A monument at the town's entrance bears the names of more than 300 miners who died on the job. The Museum of Northern History, which offers historical displays on mining and many prominent local people, dates from 1967. To house the museum, the interior of the Oakes Chateau received an external and especially noteworthy internal reconstruction (winning architectural awards) in 1981–1982. Unforunatley, the Museum of Northern History will close its doors in August of 2024. Another tourist attraction is the Toburn Gold Mine, the first functional gold mine in the Kirkland Lake area. Launched in 1913, it reverted to the Crown in 1953 when it ceased production. In 2008, the Town of Kirkland Lake took possession. Since July 2009, the Toburn site has offered visitors insight into the former mining operations and working conditions, as well as picnic tables and access to walking trails.

Kirkland Lake is the business and administrative centre for the northern part of the District of Temiskaming. For many years Tembec, now GreenFirst, a giant of the forestry industry throughout Northern Ontario, operated from Kirkland Lake. The town hosts the offices of the regional headquarters of the Department of Veterans Affairs, and it is also home to the Pinegar Youth Correctional Facility and the Kirkland and District Hospital. At least six resident companies focus on the environment: Trans Cycle Industries, Siemen's Canada, Northland Power, A&A Environmental Services and Accurassy Laboratories. The last two of these are based in Kirkland Lake, as are an estimated 300 local businesses, largely retail and service, with no more than 10 employees. The Northern College Institute of Technology, now the Northern College of Applied Arts and Technology, began classes in 1962.

Throughout the 1990s, Kirkland Lake had an unusually high profile. From 1963 until 1990, the Adams Mine—11 kilometres south of Kirkland Lake—had flourished, but when it closed six empty pits with a surface area of some 16 square kilometres remained. To the dismay of environmentalists, authorities in Metropolitan Toronto considered the Adams Mine a place where they could ship their city's garbage. In 1991, Ruth Grier, Minister of the Environment in the NDP government of Bob Rae, rejected the idea, but the Rae government lost the election of 1995. Its Progressive Conservative successor, led by Mike Harris, was considerably more sympathetic to the idea and much less concerned about environmental matters. The issue remained in the news until 1999 when two court decisions rejected the project. Local opposition helped prevent the north becoming a southern dump. Toronto City Council gave its approval on 30 August of that year but in October decided on a closer dumping ground in Michigan.

Though hockey was and is important to Kirkland Lake, one of its attractions related to the sport, housed in a specially created building, Hockey Heritage North, was sold in 2021 after 15 years because of lack of attendance. In it more than 300 hockey players, who came from or made names for themselves in Northeastern Ontario, were honoured.

However, Kirkland Lake is known for much more than hockey players. In 1950, the winning team of curling's Macdonald Brier (Bill Kenny, Tom Ramsay, Lynot

Williams and Bill Weston) came from Kirkland Lake. Toller Cranston, Canadian Figure Skating Champion from 1971 to 1976, who also won world and Olympic medals, hailed from Swastika. Between 1988 and 1993, Lori Laroque, a body builder, became Miss Jr. Canada and won awards in competitions across Northern Ontario, the province and Canada. In 1991, she won first place in Ontario's lightweight division. In 1996, Joanne Lachance Wood won a championship for arm wrestling. The Museum of Northern History honours them both.

Media magnate Roy Thomson moved to Swastika around 1920 and served on several boards, including the Northeastern Ontario Development Council and the Northern Ontario Transportation Commission. He was the first chair of the James Bay Educational Centre in Moosonee and served on its board for many years. Michael Barnes, an immigrant from England who has written numerous books about Northeastern Ontario and is a member of the Order of Canada, lived for 30 years in Kirkland Lake. Vocalist Ken Crowther was born and raised in Kirkland Lake, as was opera tenor Stephen Young. After graduation from the Kirkland Lake Collegiate and Vocational School, Young returned to Kirkland Lake in 1979 as a star in a Canadian Opera Company performance of the Marriage of Figaro, staged at Northern College. Playwright and actor Michael O'Brien was born in Kirkland Lake. David Fox, born in Swastika, taught at the Kirkland Lake Collegiate and Vocational School before performing onstage at Stratford, in film and on television. Michael Mahonen won a Gemini for his role in the CBC series *The Conspiracy of Silence*, about the 1971 murder of Betty Osborne at The Pas, Manitoba. Allan Thicke, born in Kirkland Lake in 1947, had a career as an actor, composer, producer and singer.

Resources

Charlie Angus, *Unlikely Radicals: The Story of the Adams Mine Dump War* (Toronto: Between the Lines, 2013).

Michael Barnes, *The Town That Stands on Gold* (Cobalt: Highway Book Shop, 1978).

Bob Cowan, *Sir Harry Oakes, 1874–1943: An Accumulation of Notes* (Cobalt: Highway Book Shop, 2000). Despite the title, this book includes information on many aspects of life in Kirkland Lake and Swastika beyond the life of Sir Harry Oakes.

John Marquis, *Blood and Fire: The Duke of Windsor and the Strange Murder of Sir Harry Oakes* (Kingston: LMH, 2005).

Laurel Sefton MacDowell, 'Remember Kirkland Lake': The Kirkland Lake Gold Miners' Strike, 1941–1942 (Toronto: University of Toronto Press, 2001).

Cup and Saucer Trail lookout

Manitoulin District and the Islands

Sidebar

Marion Gilmour tells about the origins of Haweaters and the exclusivity of membership:

"When Manitoulin was being settled by people leaving southern Ontario in the 1860s, those who chose to move north were met with much dismay on the part of those who remained. The southerners asked them, 'What will you live on?' but before those departing could reply the southerners offered their own rather facetious answer, 'Haws,' referring to a wild tasteless hawthorn berry that grew in abundance throughout the pastures. From this it is believed the term 'Haweater' originated. It was a description akin to the western Canadian settlers who were called sodbusters, or the eastern herring chokers. At the beginning the word had a very negative connotation.

Fast forward to the last half of the twentieth century. Today Islanders who can trace their ancestry are enjoying a rebirth as a very distinct breed.... Some 40 years ago the local Lions Club established what is known as Haweater Weekend, a homecoming celebration every August Civic Holiday. Thousands cross the bridge or come by ferry. There are festivities of every sort—family reunions, colourful parades, markets selling jams and jellies made from haws, the Hawberry Jamboree and other such events that have elevated the lowly berry to an enviable status (though it grows more profusely where the settlers came from than on the island). Buttons with the logo 'I am a Haweater' vie in number with those that read 'I wish I were a Haweater,' as the once pejorative term has become a term of distinction."

The world's largest freshwater island is big enough to have 108 lakes, some of which have further islands in them. One lake, Manitou, is the world's largest on a freshwater island. Another, Mindemoya, contains Treasure Island, which is the largest island in a lake on an island (Manitoulin) in a lake (Huron) in the world. Also, Manitoulin has the world's longest beach, Providence Bay, on a freshwater island. Over 180 kilometres long and about 80 kilometres north to south, Manitoulin is a large triangle pointing west-northwest with countless indentations on all sides. The coastline is

1,600 kilometres long. The district includes the islands to the north and part of the shore of Lake Huron into Killarney township.

The name Manitoulin can be translated as "God's Island." The English version came via French from the Ojibwe Manidoowaaling, or "cave of the spirit." The reference is to an underwater cave in which lives a powerful spirit. Hence Manitowaning is "den of the Great Spirit" or the home of the Gitchie Manitou. The three First Nation groups, Ojibwe, Odawa and Potawatomi, each have their account of the name and the origins of their peoples on the island per "Manitoulin —The Origins of the Name" by Alan Cobrière.

If water is one defining element of Manitoulin, rocks are another. Fossils embedded in sand and limestone, granite boulders and diverse pebbles plus geodes make it a delight for geologists and rock hunters. The ends of the long sandy beaches such as Carter Bay have an assortment of coloured rocks, making one wonder how they came to be in the same place.

Manitoulin District includes the large islands such as Cockburn, Clapperton, Great La Cloche and Birch Island, which except for the last, are mostly uninhabited aside from cottages dotting the edges. The district goes north to Whitefish River First Nation in the La Cloche Mountains, then east to McGregor Bay and Killarney Park. Killarney village is in Manitoulin District, though Killarney township stretches into Sudbury and Parry Sound districts. The northeast corner of Manitoulin has been amalgamated as the township of Northeastern Manitoulin and the Islands, but locals continue to use designations such as Little Current. It has a sizeable First Nation population and is the most anglophone of northeastern districts.

Manitoulin Island lies in Lake Huron with Georgian Bay to the east and south, and the North Channel to the north. Geologically and geographically, most of the island is a continuation of the Niagara Escarpment and Bruce Peninsula. Limestone cliffs rise to over 300 feet and are the highlight of the Cup and Saucer hiking trail, providing great lookouts. The island is a fossil hunter's delight. Ancient shells, fish vertebrae and other former life forms can be found simply by chipping at the soft stone layers exposed at road cuts or on the shorelines. Someday, the lightened island may rise out of Lake Huron because so many visitors will have carted away so many rocks.

Most visitors and locals acknowledge the First Nations belief about the special spiritual nature of this island. Dream catchers or dream snares (from the Ojibwe word for spider) represent part of that tradition. A willow hoop has a loose pattern of sinews woven over its opening and is decorated with sacred objects such as feathers. Children's nightmares are caught and eliminated, while good dreams slide through. Annual pow wows (at least eight, with Wiikwemkoong, the largest and oldest, dating from 1960) of dancing, native foods, and elaborate regalia reflect the past, but also seek to maintain tribal identity and traditions. Wiikwemkoong has two with the first each 21 June on National Indigenous Day and the second larger one with dancers from across North America on the August civic holiday.

The First Nations ascribed meaning to unusual forms in nature, and explanations were mixed with legends (see entry for Anishinaabek and Mushkegowuk). The island in Lake Mindemoya was thought to resemble a fat old woman. The story developed

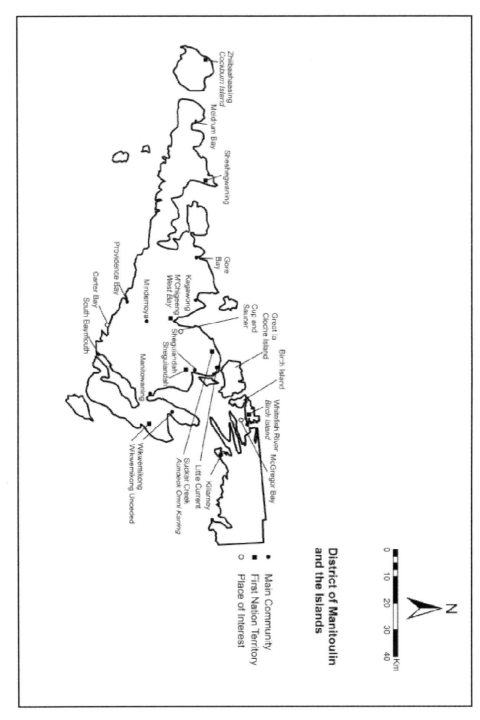

District of Manitoulin and the Islands

> **Did you know?**
> Many settlements, such as Gore Bay, on Manitoulin are older than Sudbury (because the Great Lake waters provided steamer connections before railways and highways). Though all the island had been set aside for Indigenous people in the 1830s, settlers arrived and claimed the land two decades later. During the 1860s among the reasons for interest in Manitoulin was speculation about an oil boom, because its shale rocks were wrongly thought to contain it.

that it was the form of one of the wives of the demi-god Nenaboozhoo, who had hurled her into the lake in a temper tantrum. This legend gave rise to the name of the island as Mindemoya, or old woman. When Europeans came, they appropriated the name of the lake and applied it to their town as well. Another legend relates to what is known as Dreamer's Rock, about 15 kilometres northeast of Little Current at the south part of La Cloche. This rock summit has a hollow where numerous young First Nations males slept and dreamed alone for several days. Whatever they dreamt they were in their dreams, they were destined to become, whether hunter or warrior or fisherman. Near Dreamer's Rock are the so-called Bell Rocks or glacial boulders, which when struck with a hard rock give off a ringing sound audible for a fair distance. That sound was used as a warning or to summon warriors for conference or battle. Europeans learned the meaning and employed it against the Indigenous, preventing them from having secret meetings or perpetuating cultural norms.

With a total resident population of 13,255 (2021), which doubles during summer, three major groups inhabit the island. First Nations, about 40% of the population, hold Ontario's only land to not rest under a treaty, comprising about one third of the eastern end of the island surrounding the village of Wiikwemkoong (pop. 2,728 in 2021). Other substantial Indigenous populations live in the central area at M'Chigeeng (pop. 926 in 2021; formerly West Bay), in the east-central region at Sheguiandah (pop. 150), and on the north shore at Aundek Omni Kaning (pop. 300; formerly Sucker Creek), Sheshegwaning (pop. 100) and Zhiibhaasing near the latter. The last has a small population but boasts the world's largest peace pipe, dream catcher and pow wow drum. All are descended from three tribal groups (or fires): Ojibwe, Odawa, Potawatomi, with Odawa predominating in the Wiikwemkoong area.

The second group of islanders descends from long-time settlers, beginning in the mid-nineteenth century, mostly farmers and later townspeople. Most are spread throughout the central region. These so-called Haweaters, named after a local berry, see themselves as true Manitouliners. Tourists and cottagers are the third major group. They tend to be at the multitude of campgrounds, motels and resorts on the coast and lakes, for the boating, fishing and swimming offered by the pristine cool waters. "Where to Stay Manitoulin" (available at welcome centres) lists more than one hundred places. Most visitors disappear during winter, though snowshoeing, snowmobiling, and cross-country skiing draw some.

The island has a rich and contentious history. Different Indigenous groups had been on the island, but many left it in the early 17th century. Voyageurs used it as a stopping point enroute to Lake Superior. A French Jesuit established a mission near Wiikwemkoong as early as 1648. The traders and missionaries brought diseases that devastated the remaining native population. Then warfare and fires depopulated Manitoulin for nearly 150 years. After the War of 1812, First Nations people began to return. The Crown claimed the land in 1836 as a refuge for Native tribes, though a new mission was established by 1838. At Manitowaning an attempted agricultural, artisanal and missionary settlement for the Indigenous peoples failed to acculturate a native group after 1836 because fishing, hunting and nomadic life continued to disrupt settled existence. An imposed treaty in 1862 reopened the island for settlement, but the Wiikwemkoong chief refused to sign and the eastern area remained unceded. Conflicts, including killings, ensued, partly because the rush for land involved oil speculation, which proved unfounded. By the early twentieth century, much of the central area had been settled by European farmers and merchants.

M'Chigeeng, or "village enclosed by stepped cliffs," has been strongly influenced by Roman Catholic missionaries who arrived by 1854, when a church was dedicated. Since 1974, M'Chigeeng has the offices of the Ojibwe Cultural Foundation, which represents 60 First Nation communities (about 15,000 people) from Sault Ste. Marie east to North Bay, but not Wiikwemkoong. The foundation seeks to advance First Nations' interests and to promote "the heritage, customs, and language of the three fires people [Ojibwe, Odawa, Potawatomi]." Its new offices in a striking building opened in September 1999 at M'Chigeeng. The town has most facilities and services and is especially notable for the abundance of private art galleries. It has a unique half-sunken circular church with Leland Bell paintings of the Stations of the Cross, across from the large cultural centre with museum, gallery and model sweat lodge. Close to the Cup and Saucer formation, M'Chigeeng has its own trail to the top.

The Odawa arrived in Wiikwemkoong during the era of the 1850 treaties and have continuously inhabited the area. In the 1830s, the Pottawatomi of Michigan were forced off their lands and some First Nations from southern Ontario joined them on Manitoulin. In 1862, the island was opened to European settlement, by Upper Canada authorities although Wiikwemkoong territory remained unceded. The community has most services and facilities and seeks to encourage an understanding of its history and to foster the retention of its language. The ruins of the large Roman Catholic Church illustrate the influence of other cultures. Wiikwemkoong has been designated one of Canada's Cultural Capitals. Illustrative of activities blending the old with the new are annual cultural festivals, including the fall fair, ice fishing derby, traditional pow wow, authentic First Nations theatre by De-ba-jeh-mu-jig theatre group, horse pull, Crystal Shawanda Homecoming, whitefish fair, golf tourney and maple syrup fair. The De-ba-jeh-mu-jig theatre was started in 1984 by Debajehmujig Theatre Group and was founded by Shirley Cheechoo, Blake Debassige and colleagues in 1984 at M'Chigeen. In 1989, it moved to Wiikwemkoong and is the only professional theatre on a Reserve. In May 2009, the company added the Debajehmujig Creation Centre in Manitowaning with a large production and training centre. The company's purpose remains to let First Nation youth see their own lives and their own stories reflected on stage.

Sheguiandah, about 10 kilometres south of Little Current on the way to Ten Mile

Point, represents three interrelated places. It is a notable archeological site, proving by tools and markings that it was occupied 9,500 years ago by Paleo-Indians. The site area is protected with restricted land use. A National Historical Site since 1954, the place received little acknowledgement and no development until recently. In the last decade its historical and cultural significance has been given appropriate attention and this site has been developed by an educational trail and signage. Since 2019 tours have been offered through the Centennial Museum at Sheguindah which displays aspects of the Anishinaabek culture through artifacts from the extensive holdings. The geological, archeological and lifestyle of Indigenous inhabitants is delineated. (See https://www.sawatskiconceptreality.com/centennial-museum-of-sheguiandah and https://www.youtube.com/watch?v=bhMn0QMoAf4 the title of the latter may be an exaggeration but the excellent account fully explains the development of the site and what is offered).

Sheguiandah is also two hamlets, one of First Nations established in 1866 and another of Europeans who came in the 1870s. The area has had a sawmill, barrel works, flour mill, cheese factory and wool mill. Now it relies on agriculture and tourism, which includes an annual pow wow. The Howland Centennial Museum presents mostly artifacts illustrating agricultural life in the twentieth century. Its grounds display several relocated log cabins.

The major centres of the European population are in the central region, with the western tip of the island very sparsely inhabited. Little Current (pop. 1,210 in 2021) is beside Canada's last functioning single-lane swing railway bridge, completed in 1913. It ties the island to the northern mainland via a causeway. The town has a lengthy wharf that is occasionally visited by cruise ships but more regularly used by hundreds of yachts and boats. Across the channel from the boardwalk to marinas and galleries and stretching parallel to the main street of restaurants and interesting stores, small piles of coal can still be seen. These piles date from the time Little Current served as a railway depot and supply centre. Well known is Turner's general store, established more than 130 years ago. The family also had a telephone company and other interests, representing the strength of mercantile enterprises in Manitoulin's many ports. The store contains a private museum with photos, maps, and artifacts, and may be the largest supplier of nautical charts in Canada. Little Current, like Mindemoya (pop. 2,235 in 2021), has a hospital, most services, and amenities. Some of the rich and famous people who vacationed on the island generously donated to the hospital's establishment.

For Little Current, the importance of Manitoulin's waters must be underscored. Canoes, sailing vessels, steamers, tugs, ferries, yachts and lake freighters explain much of the history of Manitoulin and the islands. The pattern of development was tied to modes of water transport, for the fur trade, for settler travel, for transporting supplies, for hauling logs, for moving people and cars, for leisure, and for moving aggregates. To illustrate, from among the first missions to Manitoulin, W.Q. Brown reported on 28 June 1866 that he went by the steamer *Waubano* to Manitowaning, then Killarney, and to Little Current where he found "13-14 houses, mostly Indians... one cow, 3 horses and a number of pigs... great many flowers...Indian corn was about 4 foot high, potatoes looked excellent." He noted on 3 July that the *Algoma* arrived with men from Bruce Mines. He used a sailboat or walked to get around the island. During the 1870s, Little Current and Sheguiandah were ports of call for the *Northern Belle* and *Manitoulin*, bringing the mail and surveyors of the island. When the sawmills were developed in the 1880s at Kagawong and Little Current, the logs were moved by tugs, many of which were built locally. Even hardened water was important for travel and contact: in winter the mail moved by dogsled or ice road to Massey.

When the railway arrived in 1913, it made winter movement—four hours to Sudbury—more reliable, but it did not replace Great Lake transport for a long time. Even when the road from Espanola was finally completed in 1930, water remained the primary mode of movement for many tourists and most supplies.

Little Current was incorporated as a town in 1890, three years before Sudbury. By then it already had a newspaper, the *Manitoulin Expositor*, founded in 1879 (the oldest newspaper of the north), the same year Issac Turner established his general store. Little Current had hotels with saloons for travellers, which inspired a temperance movement. Manitoulin would be "dry" from 1913 to 1949, resulting in a great era of bootlegging. It also had or soon developed churches, schools, women's institutes, men's and ladies' hockey teams and a mechanic's institute (as in Bruce Mines, meaning a library). By 1892 a telegraph office operated in Turner's store; later the telephone company owned by the Turners functioned from there as well. Meanwhile, American protectionism, which restricted sawn wood, idled the Manitoulin and North Shore mills until the Ontario government banned the export of uncut logs if coming from provincial lands. Regardless, by the 1930s the sawmill era was over due to declining wood supplies.

The importance of tugs and steamers appeared in other ways. The Sims firm moved mail and passengers through the 1920s by boat. Some steamers created excitement, as when the Manitoulin burned in 1882; others ran aground, while yet others such as the *Manitou* and *Caribou* served travellers and suppliers until the mid-twentieth century. In August 1906, due to a mishap, logs blocked the Little Current channel. As a result, 1,500 people were immobilized because nine steamers and tugs could not operate for days. At that time, Little Current had two large sawmills, Red Mill and Picnic Island. The ruins of the latter remain visible from town. After the decline of lumbering, tourism joined agriculture as the most important economic factor; by 1960 they would be equal in value.

The 1940s began the era of the yacht, later joined by cruisers and recently by kayaks. The yachts contribute to Manitoulin and the North Shore becoming a playground of the rich and famous. The cruiser *North American* arrived in 1948. During all that time, the ferry *Manitoulin* provided service (from 1889 to 1949), being replaced by the *Norgoma*.

Like other towns built mostly of wood, fires were a constant danger due to wood or coal stoves. Little Current had major fires in 1900, 1905, 1906, 1907 and 1910. In the latter two instances, the east and west ends of Water (the main) Street burned completely. Little Current rebuilt and over the next century put in place all the usual amenities of rinks and arenas, hospitals and retirement homes, marinas and docks, but its dependence moved towards tourism.

Among the agricultural developments related to Little Current was the

Farquhar dairy (founded 1935; plants at Mindemoya and Espanola; distribution island-wide), which purchased an ice-cream machine in 1947. The brand has been an island staple since, though no longer made on the island. A member of that well-known island family served as MP for Algoma East from 1935 to 1948. Tom Farquhar began a run of Liberal representatives that lasted until 2008 when Carol Hughes of the NDP won. Farquhar gave up his seat in 1948 so that Lester B. Pearson could run, and Farquhar received that going-to-heaven reward, a Senate seat. A story runs that some further horse trading was involved, including a promised dock for Manitoulin. When Pearson became prime minister, he apparently phoned a prominent Haweater and asked, "Where do you want the dock?"

Manitoulin Island's towns are all walkable communities, mostly with well-maintained gardens, often tended by those retired from rural work. Mindemoya is an agricultural redistribution and supply centre with golf courses and motels. There, a Central Manitoulin Island Museum is combined with the welcome centre. How early settlement in the south-central area occurred can be seen at Spring Bay, west of Mindemoya, which had its own post office in 1890 but now has just a few houses. Between Mindemoya and Providence Bay stand two large cenotaphs, perhaps among the largest in the province, that illustrate the extensive military contributions by small northeastern communities, especially during World War I. Their significance to remembrance and Manitoulin's military contribution to Canada's warfare is described in my co-authored volumes *Untold: Northeastern Ontario's Military Past*. South Baymouth (township of Tehkummah pop. 450 in 2021) on the southeastern tip provides car ferry ties to the Bruce Peninsula via the Big Canoe, as some call the ferry, the *MS Chi-Cheemaun*. It has a marina with charter boats, restaurants, motels, bed and breakfasts, craft shops and galleries to service arriving tourists. Its lighthouse is a noted, lovely landmark.

Gore Bay (pop. 808 in 2021) has been the judicial seat since 1888 and is a transport centre. Its well-maintained old brick buildings along the main street give the appearance of stability. The town is situated at the end of a large bay with cliffs on both sides protecting the bay's waters. The bay has long been known as an excellent sailing destination and offers a large marina. The name may be from the form of the bay or from a steamer by that name. The town was founded in 1890 and soon brick Victorian buildings, including a courthouse and jail, were erected. Gore Bay remains a distribution centre for its agricultural hinterland. Many facilities such as motels, restaurants and bed and breakfasts service tourists, but a range of recreation is offered, including summer festivals and theatre. Amenities include an arena, golf course and community centre.

The Gore Bay Museum is in a charming Victorian building that was once the jailer's residence and jailhouse. Displayed is the lifestyle of early settlers, while an annex serves as an art gallery, with works by artists such as Jack Whyte (deceased). On the western side of the bay is a walkway and large marina with a lookout from the top of the park exhibit building.

Manitowaning (township pop. 1020 in 2016) was originally established in 1837 as a meeting place for First Nations resettling the island. The word has numerous meanings for the Indigenous in their belief system. In one it is the cave of the great spirit. Legend has it that the powerful spirit could move underground between Manitowaning and Little Current.

The town claims to be the first European settlement on Manitoulin Island. Paul's Anglican Church dates from 1845 and claims to be the oldest Anglican Church in Northern Ontario. The Manitowaning Lighthouse, built in 1886, is across from the church.

During the late nineteenth and twentieth centuries, Manitowaning was a major shipping port, and the steamer *Norisle* laid symbolically on display in its harbour until 2023 when it was scrapped. The ship provided cargo and passenger ferry service from 1946 to 1974. As part of the Heritage Bay in the harbour are the Manitoulin Roller Mills building and Burn's Wharf, originally built in 1883. The mill, now a museum, contains some of the original machinery.

Another stately building dating from 1878, which was originally a jail, then the municipal office, is now the Assiginack Museum. Named after a renowned Ojibwe orator of the mid-nineteenth century, it shows artifacts from settlers' pioneer life, and stands near other historic buildings that were relocated to the site.

In terms of economic development, the twentieth century brought tourists. With the railway, artists such as the Group of Seven came to explore La Cloche and the north islands. By the 1920s, the super-rich from the northern U.S. states and Hollywood arrived and by the 1940s became significant to the economy. They found on Manitoulin and the Islands an area with abundant beautiful scenery, sport fish, game, and the lack of people that were overrunning the Muskokas and Thousand Islands. The list of those who came for a weekend or a week or a month, brought their entourages and employed guides, bought supplies and built lodges is long: President Franklin D. Roosevelt, Lana Turner, William Boyd (Hopalong Cassidy), Gene Autry, and Marilyn Monroe among others. The owners of the Evinrude boat motor company had a lodge to which they went by 100-foot yacht; the Eugene MacDonald family from Chicago, who owned Zenith Radio, had an even bigger yacht, with a crew of five.

In 1943, Roosevelt spent the first week of August vacationing on Birch Island, between Little Current and the mainland. A sign on the west side of Highway 6 commemorates the event. Paralyzed from the waist down, Roosevelt loved to spend his vacations on water, and at that point in World War II, the Atlantic and Pacific oceans were too dangerous. Roosevelt's friend Eugene MacDonald advised that McGregor Bay, beside Birch Island, had a delightful mid-summer climate and that fishing in the waters of Lake Huron would be highly rewarding.

The presidential visit was supposed to be a secret, but the high level of security, the comings and goings on water, air and land, and even the presence of the president's well-known dog, Fala, alerted islanders as to what was happening. Roosevelt travelled from Washington to Birch Island on the presidential train, and for decades railway workers on duty as the train passed Sudbury and Espanola could recount anecdotes. Sudbury lawyer E.D. Wilkins happened to be fishing when a launch approached and Roosevelt asked him, "What luck are you having?" Ernie St. Pierre of Little Current was the presidential guide, and the presidential party patronized the Turner store. For a week, the CPR telegraph office in Little Current linked one of the world's most powerful officeholders with those directing the Italian campaign and planning Roosevelt's meeting with Churchill in Quebec City later that month. A persistent local myth is that Churchill secretly met Roosevelt on his fishing trip. That was an impossibility as proven by Churchill's daily log. An exhibit about the visit is available at the Sheguiandah museum.

Encounters with these well-off families holidaying on Manitoulin entered local lore, often in different versions. The Danny Dodge story is well presented at the Kagawong Old Mill Museum. One of the heirs of the Dodge automobile company, Danny vacationed on the island in a lodge overlooking Kagawong Bay. He fell in love with an elegant young telephone operator, Lorraine (sometimes written as Laurine) MacDonald, at Gore Bay. Danny was known for being foolhardy and impulsive, zipping about in a red convertible (presumably a Dodge) or 250-horsepower speed boat. They married despite the reservations of his family on 2 August 1938; she was 19, he was 21. The crucial day was 15 August as Danny and two friends played with some old sticks of dynamite in the garage while Lorraine watched. Apparently, they were lighting and throwing them out the window when one caught on the ledge, fell back, and exploded a pile of blasting caps. All were badly injured, two very seriously. To get medical help at Little Current, they decided to use the boat instead of the car. However, the lake had huge waves and after two hours the boaters were still well out from Little Current. Lorraine, tired of steering due to her injured arm, asked to be relieved. She turned and saw Danny going over the side. At this and other points the story is muddled. Rick Nelson, the curator of the Old Mill Museum who has studied the details, thinks the theories about suicide are wrong. He suspects the waves tossed Danny overboard as he tried to go forward in the boat. After looking for a while, those in the boat continued to Little Current. The news of the disappearance of Danny received international attention. After three weeks of searching, the body was recovered, and the submarine sent to help was not deployed. Was it accidental drowning as the inquest found? Did Danny jump to get into cool water because of

his burns? Or, as one survivor said, did his fear of dying from being the worst injured cause him to jump? Lorraine inherited only 1.2 million of Danny's 9 million dollars.

Today's tourists come for the tranquil, slow-paced life. They come for the deep lake fishing (20-pound salmon, 10-pound rainbow), great hiking and not too strenuous biking, for First Nations gatherings (German tourists flock to the pow wows) and for the flora. In spring and early summer, the roadsides are full of trilliums, anemones, lady slippers and Indian paintbrushes. The tourists come to walk the splendid beaches, with Providence Bay and Carter Bay (restricted) being the most impressive

Providence Bay boardwalk

for their dunes and length. Providence Bay's much-used boardwalk leads to a small museum illustrating the history, flora and fauna of the island.

The School House Museum at South Bay Mouth illustrates nineteenth-century community life. A heritage museum of shipwrecks and lighthouse keepers' lives is in the Mississagi Lighthouse overlooking Mississagi Strait at Meldrum Bay. It is entitled the Net Shed Museum because it is housed in one of the last fishing net repair sheds of the island.

Kagawong means "where the mists rise from the falling waters," referring to Bridal Veil Falls. Today the quiet village belies its industrial past, when a large watermain led down from near the falls to a stone mill on the bay's edge. From 1925 to 1930, the water powered the machinery that processed spruce trees into pulp that was shipped to Michigan to make Sears-Roebuck catalogues. In 1932 the mill was converted into a power plant. The mill building has been restored and houses the Old Mill Museum and village offices.

A novel attraction in the Kagawong area is the Billings Connections Trail: Nature, Art, Heritage. It comprises 35 historical plaques and 9 sculpture sites, bringing together settler and Indigenous history and is intended to serve as an act of reconciliation. Sites include plaques giving short histories and examples of buildings, cemeteries, commercial enterprises, native agriculture, logging, fire and artisanal trades. The sculptures represent aspects of Indigenous and Manitoulin culture.

Among the special attractions of Manitoulin are gatherings of sandhill cranes during the late summer and early autumn (hundreds go to fields near Providence Bay), the Bridal Veil Falls at Kagawong (with smelt runs in spring), the fine sand of the many beaches, misty morning sunrises and colourful sunsets over lakes, and the extensive choice of accommodations for families, fishers, golfers (good short courses at Gore Bay and Mindemoya; full course at Manitowaning). Deer hunters like the fact that nearly everyone succeeds at getting a kill.; an estimate is that Manitoulin has over 12,000 deer. Leisure activities abound, such as watching the swing bridge open to sail and cruise

Bridal Veil Falls in winter

boats, or slowly kayaking through isolated bays, going to livestock or antique auctions, and of course participating in Haweater Days in early August, with dancing, special foods (yes, including hawberries), parades, crafts and fireworks.

Vistas, such as the one from Ten Mile Point over Strawberry Channel and Island, reveal the islands, channels and many-toned blue water. The Cup and Saucer Trail offers spectacular views of cliffs as well as much of the central part of the island's maple tree and cedar forests. One of the best ways to see Manitoulin, including its western, less populated parts, is by driving tours. The island's tourist office offers a brochure "This is Manitoulin." It suggests tours of various lengths, organized by themes such as heritage. Another way to experience the island is by bicycle. Some southern Ontario bikers leave their cars at Tobermory on the Bruce Peninsula, take the ferry to South Baymouth and then cycle the pleasant, mostly flat and hardly trafficked, secondary roads. That can be combined with many hiking opportunities on many marked trails. In addition to the Cup and Saucer, a special one is at Misery Bay Provincial Park with an interpretive centre explaining the terrain, including the many alvars, or worn, flat limestone rocks with intriguing cracks.

Anyone interested in art can explore the numerous private galleries, especially the Woodland School of Native Art. Most towns have galleries, but a few have special offerings. Blake Debassige (deceased) and Shirley Cheechoo show their own and other First Nations artists' work at their Kasheese Studios in M'Chigeeng. The Ojibwe Cultural Foundation there has an extensive gallery, combined with exhibits on the residential school system. At Lillian's Crafts the skills of quill work are demonstrated by the collection in the Quill Box Museum. Ten Mile Point gallery often has works by Leland Bell, whose distinctive work inspired many contemporary artists. Showing native and other well-known artists (Ivan Wheale, Frank Danielson) inspired by the Manitoulin landscape is the delightful (for setting and contents) Perivale Gallery (near Spring Bay) overlooking Lake Kagawong.

First Nation achievers include artists Daphne Odjig, Leland Bell and James Simon, dramatist Shirley Cheechoo, and actors Leroy Peltier and Cheyenne Kitchikeng. The NHL hockey player Chris Simon, world champion hoop dancer Lisa Odjig and country singer Crystal Lynn Shawanda are from Wiikwemkoong.

Resources

Derek J. Coleman, et al, *La Cloche Country—Its History, Art and People* (Espanola: OJ Graphix, 2009).

Mario Coniglio, Paul Karrow and Peter Russell, *Manitoulin Rocks!* (Waterloo: University of Waterloo, 2008).

https://escarpment.ca/ebc-news/manitoulin-the-origins-of-the-name-video-release-alan-corbiere#:~:text=EBC%20News

Geoffrey Corfield, *Northern Ontario and Manitoulin Island: There's More to Northern Ontario Than Just Rocks, Trees and Lakes* (Allanburg: Despub, 2005

http://www.visualheritage.ca/manitoulin/ [exceptional video with historical re-enactments]

Shelly J. Pearson, *Exploring Manitoulin* (Toronto: University of Toronto Press, 2001).

Reflections of Howland, *Little Current and Vicinity* (Manitoulin Genealogical Club, 2010).

Mattawa

Located at the junction of the Ottawa and Mattawa rivers on Highway 17 about 60 kilometres east of North Bay, Mattawa has had the longest continuous contact with Europeans of any place in Northeastern Ontario. Its name is derived from Matawasi'bi ani'cena'bi, which means "Mouth-of-the-River People" in the Algonquin language. The Indigenous had long utilized both rivers for fishing, trade and transport; the confluence point served for meetings for hundreds of years.

From the beginning of the seventeenth century, French-Canadian fur traders, explorers and missionaries travelled from Montreal to Lake Huron via the Ottawa and Mattawa rivers, Lake Nipissing and the French River. They had to use that route because hostile Iroquois controlled what is now southern Ontario. Among the historical notables who passed through Mattawa were coureur de bois Étienne Brûlé (1610); Samuel de Champlain founder and first governor of New France (1615); Jesuit martyrs Jean de Brébeuf (1616) and Gabriel Lalemant (1648); Louis Joliette and Jacques Marquette, who went from Montreal to what is now St. Louis, Missouri (1673); Pierre Esprit Radisson and Médard Chouart des Groseilliers, who went north instead of west from Mattawa and discovered the potential of the fur trade in the area around James and Hudson bays (1685); Louis-Joseph Gaultier de La Vérendrye, who explored the prairie west more extensively than any French predecessor (1731); and, in the post-French period, explorers Alexander Mackenzie (1794) and David Thompson (1812).

Large (six to ten foot), wooden statues of famous figures associated with Mattawa stand along Highway 17 and in Mattawa's downtown core. These include Brûlé, Joliette and Mackenzie, as well as local legends Joe Muffraw, a lumberjack, and Anahareo, who inspired Grey Owl. Joe Muffraw was born in Montreal in 1802 as Joe Montferrand. Anglophones who had trouble pronouncing his surname called him Muffraw. The man had such a reputation for strength that he inspired a song sung by Stompin' Tom Connors and Gilles Vigneault. The song extolled his ability to canoe, supposedly from Ottawa to Mattawa in one day.

A superb boxer, Muffraw/Montferrand became—according to the statue caption— "the most feared and best loved shanty and raft foreman in the Ottawa

Valley." He also was reportedly the source of the Paul Bunyan legend. Muffraw/ Montferrand was enormous (six feet, nine inches in height), and his statue is considerably larger than the others in Mattawa.

Anahareo, neé Gertrude Bernard on 18 June 1906, was born in Mattawa, though she had Mohawk ancestors from their traditional territory in southern Ontario. In 1925 at Lake Temagami she met Grey Owl, an Englishman born as Archie Belaney who gained a reputation as Canada's most famous First Nations person, until exposed as a fraud. He gave her the nickname Anahareo. They married the following year and had three daughters. Anahareo's 1972 book Devil in Deerskins reviews her life with Grey Owl. After a lengthy campaign on behalf of fair treatment for fur-bearing animals, in 1979 she received an invitation to join the Paris-based International League for Animal Rights and later became a member of the Order of Canada.

By the Treaty of Paris in 1763, Great Britain gained ownership of New France, and between 1793 and 1815, Great Britain was at war most of the time against most of continental Europe as well as, from 1812 until 1814, against the newly independent United States. Wood for boat building from the Mattawa area proved indispensable to the British Navy; the lumber could be floated down the Ottawa River to Montreal. Even after the return of peace, Mattawa survived as a logging community, and farmers moved into the area to grow food to feed the woodcutters. The Canadian Pacific Railway reached Mattawa in 1881, and with it came French-Canadian settlers from Quebec.

The fur trade and mining were also important to Mattawa's economy. The Hudson's Bay Company sent trappers to the area during the 1820s and 1830s and erected a log building, Mattawa House, in 1837. That building, on the south shore of the Mattawa River where it flows into the Ottawa River, is now the Mattawa Museum. Displays include artifacts from the First Nations people, exhibits of living conditions in pioneer Mattawa, and biographical information about people associated with Mattawa, including a speaker of the House of Commons, Gilbert Parent. It also houses a huge piece of mica from the Purdy Mica Mine near Mattawa, named for Justin Purdy, who staked it in 1941.

The way Mattawa came to have Canada's first Black mayor relates to S. Firmin Monestine, from Haiti, having a quarrel with his government in 1944. Since he wanted to live in a Francophone environment and Canada was more welcoming than war-torn France or Belgium, he moved to Quebec where he qualified to be a doctor. In 1951, he took a drive to Timmins to explore a job offer, however, he stopped in Mattawa where locals convinced him they desperately needed a doctor despite the predominantly white English community.

Today, Mattawa remains a logging community, largely French Canadian, but it has a declining population. Between 2001 and 2006, the population fell 11.8%, from 2,270 to 2,003, then to 1,993 in 2016 and 1,721 in 2021. In an era when most people have access to cars, increasing numbers of Mattawa residents drive to North Bay for health services, university and post-secondary education, and shopping. Yet, Mattawa has numerous motels and restaurants, some of which offer a spectacular view of the Quebec shore of the Ottawa River. An annual Voyageur Days festival draws well-known entertainers and crowds for music and dance. It serves as the cornerstone of a tourist industry based on fishing, hunting, quad trails and the Canadian Ecology Centre, an environmental education facility.

About 10 kilometres west of Mattawa, a traveller on Highway 17 will see Samuel de Champlain Provincial Park. Apart from the campgrounds, it has two attractions: the Voyageur Heritage Centre and the Canadian Ecology Centre. The former focuses on the lifestyle of those who used the Mattawa River as a highway before the arrival of the rails. An enormous canoe, beside which stand life-sized voyageur statues, dominates the Centre's main room. The ecology centre provides high school courses on the environment and outdoor living, seven to ten days in length, throughout the year. School groups from kindergarten to grade 12 can stay at the Canadian Ecology Centre, which provides meals and accommodation.

Resources
Doug Mackay, *Where Rivers Meet: The Story of Dr. S. F. Monestine: Canada's First Black Mayor* (Toronto: Heritage, 2006).
https://www.canadianecology.ca

Sculpture of Joe Mufferaw

Moose Factory

Moose Factory, on an island near the mouth of the Moose River, has a much longer history than its close neighbour Moosonee. The Indigenous Cree had fished and hunted the area along the river for centuries. The island had long been a meeting and trading place.

In summer 2023 Ontario Heritage unveiled a charming plaque in four languages acknowledging the long-standing Indigenous culture and occupation of the area, incorporating Indigenous perspectives:

"Môsonîwililiw oral tradition describes an ancestral couple, lowered here from a sky world, who were shown how to survive and thrive by animals who also gifted their lives for this purpose. The Creator's laws, including honesty, courage and šawelihcikewin—sharing with gratitude and generosity—were reinforced over generations by lived experience of the benefits or consequences of upholding or ignoring these principles. After receiving hospitality at this Môsonîwililiw summer gathering site, Hudson's Bay Company traders built Moose Fort in 1673, and relations quickly extended beyond commerce to mutual support in hard times. Over the next two centuries, Moose Fort became Moose Factory: a regional transatlantic trade hub marked by cultural exchange and intermarriage. This history influenced Môsonîwililiw expectations for Treaty 9, signed in 1905. Despite treaty violations, many volunteered for Canadian military service in the World Wars. By the mid-20th century, Moose Factory's linkages were shifting towards Canada as it transitioned away from being a fur trade company town. The Moose Cree First Nation's primary reserve was surveyed here in 1948. Veterans helped lead postwar self-governance and treaty renewal efforts, exemplified by the 1973 creation of Nishnawbe-Aski Nation. While Môsonîwi-Ministik is Ontario's oldest English-speaking settlement, its primary history remains with the Môsonîwililiwak." (Quoted with permission from Ontario Heritage).

After the early contexplorers came the fur traders who established a trading post in 1673. It was as the second outpost of the Hudson's Bay Company (HBC), two years after the first one at Rupert House (now in Quebec), Moose Factory's first incarnation was rather brief. In 1686, the Chevalier Pierre de Troyes led an overland military expedition from Montreal, captured Moose Factory, and renamed it St. Louis. The Treaty of Utrecht (1713) returned all lands north of the Arctic-Atlantic Watershed to British control, but the British did not re-establish Moose Factory until the 1730s. A fire destroyed the post in 1735, but by 1737 it was once again functional. A printed version of some of the correspondence written by eighteenth-century residents is available for viewing at the HBC staff house.

The oldest physical sites in Moose Factory date from the nineteenth century. The HBC undertook construction in the 1820s and in 1840 invited a Methodist missionary, the Rev. George Barnley, to the island. The mission of the British Wesleyan Methodist Missionary Society ended in 1847, but in 1851 John Horden of Exeter went to Moose Factory as a catechist. He had a printing press, translated much of the Bible into Cree, and published a hymn book and pamphlets. Ordained in 1852, in 1877 Horden became the first Anglican Bishop of Moosonee. Between 1856 and 1864, the HBC carpenter James King supervised construction of St. Thomas Anglican Church, which closed in 2007, too decrepit to be safe but still available for external viewing. During its lifetime, St. Thomas church was the site of the ordination of 12 decans and 15 priests.

During the 1870s, the HBC erected more buildings, and what was the staff house now houses exhibits of company and local history. In 2022 the staff house became

Cree Village Ecolodge, Moose Factory

St. Thomas Anglican Church, Moose Factory

a National Historic Site. The building represents the types of rooms in which HBC employees lived. While the company's directors were English, most of the employees who lived in Moose Factory came from Scotland, including the Orkney and Shetland Islands in Scotland's far north. Until the nineteenth century, the HBC tried to discourage its Scottish employees, most if not all of them single men, from marrying Cree, but after 1800 it came to terms with the reality of the sexual desires of single or married men far from home and allowed intermingling. By World War I many inhabitants had Scottish names. Near the staff house are other nineteenth-century HBC buildings, including the stone powder house (for gunpowder), which had to remain free of moisture, and a blacksmith shop. Two cemeteries, one exclusively for HBC employees and another beside St. Thomas Church for all others, are nearby.

In 1855, John Horden and his wife Elizabeth established a residential primary school, which continued to operate under the auspices of the Anglican Church until 1969, when the federal government assumed responsibility. Students (mainly Cree) came from the west coast of James Bay and from rivers near that body of water. Teachers at the Bishop Horden Memorial School sought to introduce the young people to Western culture by eradicating their own. The alumni attended secondary school at Shingwauk Hostel in Sault Ste. Marie, now part of Algoma University. It can be a heartbreaking experience to talk to elderly residents of Moose Factory about their experiences in the residential school. In 1964, Moose Factory received its first public school and on 1 April 1969 the federal Department of Indian Affairs assumed responsibility for all First Nations student residences.

In 1951, the Province of Ontario established a tuberculosis hospital at Moose Factory. The hospital staff now deals with a range of health problems, assisted by specialists who fly to Moose Factory at regular intervals, and the facility serves patients from the entire James Bay area.

Numerous men from Moose Factory served in the Canadian military, especially during World War I, often in the railway or forestry corps where they had difficulties with language and discrimination but proved themselves as snipers. More positive was the experience of Johnathan Cheechoo, an NHL player for 17 seasons and winner, in 2005–06, of the Maurice Rocket Richard trophy for the player with the most goals scored in a season.

Resources

Michael Barnes, *Ride the Polar Bear Express: Visiting Moosonee and Moose Factory* (Renfrew: General Store, 1996).

Joseph Boyden, *Three Day Road* (Toronto: Penguin, 2005); an insightful historical novel, despite the scandal about the author's false claims regarding his Indigenous background.

Dieter K. Buse, Marthe Brown and Joe Martin, "The Lindberghs' Arctic Flight," *The Beaver* (April/May, 2002), 38-40.

Edwin Ernest Rich, *Hudson's Bay Company, 1670–1870* (Toronto: McClelland and Stewart, 1960).

Kate Stepheson, *The Community of Moose Factory: A Community Profile* at http://www.wakenagun.ca/Adobe/moosefactory.pdf

Moosonee

Moosonee, Ontario's only saltwater port, is at the northern terminus of the Ontario Northland Railway (ONR), and is readily accessible via the Polar Bear Express, a mixed passenger and freight train from Cochrane. The town is about 15 kilometres south of James Bay, as is Moose Factory, on an adjacent island in the Moose River. Water taxis (15 to 20 minutes) connect the two places.

The name Moosonee derives from the Cree word Moosoneek, which means "at the Moose [River]." In 2006, the combined population of Moosonee and Moose Factory was more than 5,000, mostly Cree. The town of Moosonee, incorporated in 2000, has a population of 1,471 in 2021 of whom about 85% identify as Cree. Unlike their relatives to the north, most of Moosonee's Cree speak English. On Moose Factory Island about 1,500 people live on Indigenous territory and about another 1,000 live in Moose Factory itself. The figures vary because some still live a migratory lifestyle.

Moosonee had been a Cree hunting and fishing area for centuries. As a settled community, it dates from 1903, when the French fur-trading company, Revillon Frères, established a post intended to compete with the Hudson's Bay Company (HBC) post at Moose Factory. Based in France since 1723, Revillon wanted direct access to the Cree trappers who were already selling furs to the HBC. A company-owned sawmill provided the lumber for its buildings, and each year the company vessel travelled between Montreal and Moosonee, laden with supplies on the outbound voyage and with furs destined for upscale New York shops on the return trip. Revillon Frères remained active in Moosonee until World War II and established a museum (now closed) near the waterfront, dedicated to the fur trade and the company's history. In its prime, the company financed mineral exploration expeditions as well as the famous film, *Nanook of the North*, about the life of the walrus hunters who resided farther north.

The first aircraft landed in Moosonee in 1921, and 10 years later Charles Lindbergh, renowned as pilot of the first solo trans-Atlantic flight, stopped at Moose Factory to refuel on his way to Asia. His wife and co-pilot, Anne Morrow, wrote about meeting missionaries and eating local berries with the First Nations people.

The railway arrives in Moosonee, 1932

In 1932, the ONR gave Moosonee greater access to the outside world by extending the railway to near James Bay. Trains continued to operate and transport people and supplies during major forest fires close to the tracks in 1976, 1977 and 1987. Nowadays, Moosonee is the base for aircraft and supply barges headed north to communities along the shores of James Bay.

Moosonee is also headquarters for the Roman Catholic Diocese of Moosonee, large in terms of geography but small in numbers of people. Dedication of Christ the King Cathedral occurred 5 June 1989, though the diocese shares a bishop with the Diocese of Hearst and has only a few priests.

Knowledge of the Cree language appears minimal among most of the youth. Employment and diabetes remain serious challenges. An indication of the changing times was the replacement of sled dogs by snowmobiles since the 1960s. In the 1950s, huskies roamed, even controlled, the streets at night. Now, dogs of any description are rare.

A walk along the waterfront leads to attractive homes and gardens as well as the Ministry of Natural Resources and Forestry's (MNRF) Museum, housed in the provincial government building. The museum displays pelts of fur-bearing animals, stuffed birds, archaeological findings and geological fossils. It usually opens from noon until 3 p.m. Another historic and heritage exhibit is available in an isolated railway car near the railway station, which opens from about 3:10 until 6 p.m., when the train departs on the return journey to Cochrane. It houses exhibits on transportation, local artists and wildlife. Across and down the street is Northern Community College, where Cree students can study trades such as nursing and where tourists can see a few exhibits of special pelts and artistic handicrafts.

Although commercial air service from Timmins is available, most tourists access Moosonee by train. Five days a week throughout summer, the ONR offers the erroneously named but well-maintained Polar Bear Express (PBX). No polar bears roam the territory through which it passes, and it is certainly not an express. The

186-kilometre journey (one way) between Cochrane and Moosonee requires some five to six hours, depending on the number of people who flag it to stop along the way or who decide to be dropped with their canoes or camping supplies beside a river. However, it is far from boring. The PBX has a licensed dining car, a bar car with featured entertainment, and a scenic observation lounge on the top of a double-decker car with a children's play area on the lower level.

The Otter Rapids dam, built in 1958 and a major source of electricity, is one of the sights along the way, as are some rapids and river views. The size of dams, rapids and river are impressive. Train service continues throughout the year, but without the summertime frills.

While it is possible to go from Cochrane to Moosonee and Moose Factory and back to Cochrane on the same day, the best approach is an overnight stay. Both communities offer hotels and guest houses, though the choice of restaurants is minimal, basically fast-food outlets connected with the hotels, but few go to Moosonee or Moose Factory in anticipation of gourmet dining. Those who want to picnic at the waterfront can carry their own supplies or purchase groceries at the Northern store.

Resources
Michael Barnes, *Ride the Polar Bear Express: Visiting Moosonee and Moose Factory* (Renfrew: General Store, 1996).

Eau Claire Gorge

Nipissing, District of

The District of Nipissing (pop. 84,716 in 2021) extends from Lake Nipissing and the French River in the south to the District of Temiskaming in the north, from the Quebec border (the Ottawa River) in the east to the District of Sudbury in the west. The name derives from the Ojibwe meaning "People of the little lake," or "At the little lake." The pronunciation according to First Nations is "Ni-BEES-sing" and the people known as the Nbisiing Anishinaabeg come from Ojibwe and Algonquin people. They lived and traded in the area for centuries, surviving by hunting and fishing but also some agriculture. Indigenous trade routes ran in all directions employing the river systems. In July 2022 over 3,000 people were registered with Nipissing First Nation of whom 800 lived on the reserve.

The district seat (headquarters) is located at North Bay, chosen instead of Mattawa. The main transport corridors are the Canadian Pacific Railway (CPR), Highway 17 (east-west) and Highway 11 (north-south). Created in 1858, by 1884 the district spanned north to James Bay, but later the Temiskaming District was detached.

The economy depends largely on tourism and the forestry industry. In 2007, Mattawa, Calvin Township, Papineau-Cameron and Bonfield formed the Mattawa Voyageur Country tourist region. Being just north of Algonquin Park with many waterfalls, the area shares a similar rolling, forested landscape. The following description generally moves from east to west, then north.

Papineau-Cameron, south of Mattawa, is the oldest settlement in the district. It takes its first name from Louis-Joseph Papineau, leader of the 1837 rebellion in Lower Canada (Quebec). Cameron sits on the northern limits of Algonquin Park and is probably named for Chief Justice Sir Matthew Crooks Cameron. Their combined population was 1,058 in 2016; 982 in 2021, spread along the Highway 17 and the CPR corridor.

Nineteen kilometres west of Mattawa, Highway 630 intersects with Highway 17. Heading south it takes you through the waterfalls of Eau Claire ("clear water") Gorge to the community of Eau Claire, part of Calvin Township, named for lumber merchant Delino Dexter Calvin. Calvin Township advertises access to the Samuel

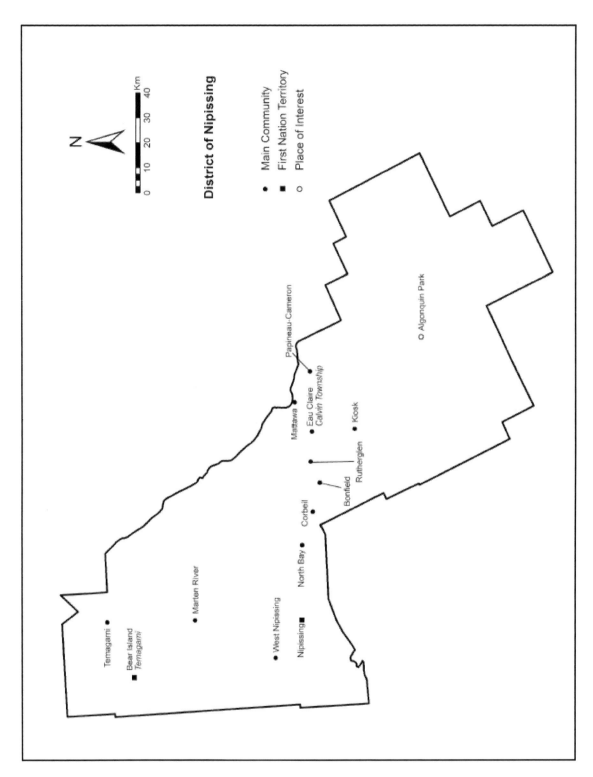

District of Nipissing

de Champlain Provincial Park, the Eau Claire Gorge Conservation Area and the surrounding waterways.

To the south is Kiosk, just inside Algonquin Park. Kiosk, on Lake Kiosk, was once a station on the Canadian National Railway system, and until 1973 was the site of lumber operations. A fire that year destroyed the facilities, and existing laws prevented restoration. The last buildings were demolished in the 1980s, and today Kiosk serves only as an entry point into Algonquin Park. "Kiosk" means "Lake of many gulls" in the Ojibwe language.

Rutherglen, beside Highway 17, has overnight accommodation for travellers who want a motel in the woods, near a waterway. The CPR's James Worthington named the place after Rutherglen, Scotland, which he thought it resembled. Among the earliest settlers were the Shield family, English immigrants who appropriately wanted to settle on the Canadian Shield. One member of the family started the first post office, at a time when the mail was transported by canoe. East of the Highway 630 junction along Highway 17 is the Township of Bonfield (population 1,981 in 2016; 2,146 in 2021). Bonfield, a few kilometres to the south on Highway 531 and the north shore of Lake Nosbonsing, received its first settlers in 1882 when the CPR established a station there. Incorporated as a town in 1905, Bonfield reverted to township status in 1975. The region is a mix of farming, lumbering, and tourism.

West along Highway 17 at the junction with Highway 94 is the Township of East Ferris. Just south on Highway 94 is the village of Corbeil (pronounced "Cor-BEEL"), birthplace of the Dionne Quintuplets. Although the house where the family lived before the birth of the famous girls has been relocated to North Bay's waterfront, the mansion and estate where they spent their formative lives remains in place in this farming community. Another famous resident of Corbeil was Marie-Louise Meilleur, who died at the age of 117 in 1998. For eight months before her death, she was reportedly the world's oldest living person.

Just south of East Ferris is Chisholm Township (pop. 1,318 in 2016; 1,312 in 2021), which takes its name from Kenneth Chisholm, who once served as MPP for Peel. The area is agricultural and most of its people are of German descent.

West of North Bay are magnificent views of Lake Nipissing and then flat agricultural lands. More than 11,000 years ago, before the last Ice Age, gigantic Lake Algonquin included what are now Lakes Huron, Michigan and Nipissing, as well as some of the surrounding land. As the water retreated, it left fertile regions where farmers from Quebec could settle once the CPR provided a link with Montreal. Before they arrived the Indigenous fished and farmed in the area.

Nipissing First Nation is west of North Bay. The population, descended from Algonquin and Ojibwe, has shifted greatly from about 800 in the early seventeenth century down to about 200 in the early twentieth century; in 2020 it had recovered to about 1,000 on reserve and 2,000 off. Before Europeans interrupted the pattern, the Nipissing traded furs and fish for corn and tobacco from southern First Nations and held a central place in trading all the way to James Bay, for some time holding a monopoly over that activity. They even remained prosperous into the nineteenth century, when European trappers and traders took over the fur trade. In 1850, they signed the Robinson-Huron treaties relinquishing parts of their land but since then have insisted that they were signing to save their way of life and to retain control over the northern shore of Lake Nipissing and its crucial water routes.

At present, the Nipissing First Nation is spread over a large area in a series of villages (Garden, Yellek, Duchesnay, Beaucage, Meadowside, Paradise), stretching west from North Bay to West Nipissing. Many small commercial enterprises serve tourists along Highway 17. A health centre is in Garden, water and sewer projects are improving the infrastructure and more power generation is planned. Annual pow wows draw the community together.

The CPR and Highway 17, usually within sight of each other, hug the shore of Lake Nipissing. Amid that farmland, where the Sturgeon River empties into Lake Nipissing, is the town of West Nipissing, until 1999 officially known as Sturgeon Falls, a name locals continue to use.

Beside Highway 11 roughly 50 kilometres north of North Bay is the hamlet of Marten River, which offers tourist amenities and trails for hiking or cross-country skiing. The provincial park at Marten River is the site of a large outdoor museum, which houses displays about the early lumber industry. Visitors can observe the equipment that the loggers used and the difficult conditions under which they lived.

About 90 kilometres north of North Bay on both Highway 11 and the Ontario Northland Railway (ONR) is Temagami (pop. 862 in 2021), a name derived from the Ojibwe Teme-Augama which means "Deep water by the shore." Most of Temagami's permanent residents claim English as their sole or primary language. The community depends on the lumber industry and tourism (camping, hunting, fishing, swimming in Lake Temagami, canoeing). It has numerous resorts, some offering ecotourist experiences because of the extensive, pristine lakes. Lake Temagami is so large and winding that from no shore can one see the other end. The region is highly regarded by environmentalists from southern Ontario, and they help perpetrate urban myths about virgin forests. Most of the terrain was logged in the 1880s as timber registries show. However, a few stands of old-growth forests remain.

Archeological evidence indicates that First Nations may have occupied Bear Island, the second largest island on Lake Temagami, for 3,000 years. In 1943, the Government of Canada purchased Bear Island from the Province of Ontario for $3,000 and offered it to the First Nations. Controversy ensued. Those living on Bear Island disliked and disputed the land boundary terms of the Indian Act of Canada, and in 1968 the federal government announced that it would withhold revenue until and unless those residents agreed that smaller Bear Island designated land would become an official Reserve in accordance with that act. Having little recourse, the islanders obliged, and Bear Island became a reserve in 1971. Access remains by water or air.

Outside infringement and European settlement have a long history. In 1834, the Hudson's Bay Company opened a fur-trading store in the area. That trade remained important but changed with the railways because Europeans competed with First Nations trappers, many of whom had little choice but to become guides for tourists. In 1903, with the building of what is now the ONR to link North Bay with the agricultural Great Clay Belt around what is now Temiskaming Shores, Daniel

O'Connor built a general store and launched a steamship company that offered tours of Lake Temagami. Within three years, he had opened three hotels on the lake. Today Temagami continues to offer motels, restaurants and campsites. Perhaps Temagami's most famous resident was the celebrated conservationist, bigamist, and imposter Grey Owl, one of whose wives, Anahareo, came from Mattawa. Temagami's railway station is now a museum with exhibits on Grey Owl, as well as other features of life in twentieth-century Temagami. The last grocery store closed in the autumn of 2010.

Temagami offers extensive canoe routes and hiking trails. Right on the edge of the village is a trail leading to the fire lookout, which offers a special view of the endless lakes and rugged landscape. An even better experience is a flight over the region, especially in autumn. One waterway extends to the Ishpatina Ridge, whose highest elevation is 693 metres or 2,275 feet. Located 400 feet over the boundary into the District of Sudbury, it is the highest point in Ontario (at 47 degrees 19 minutes latitude, 80 degrees 45 minutes longitude, with access through Lady Evelyn-Smoothwater Wilderness Park). Advertisements proclaim that the White Bear Forest Trails start near Temagami and pass through virgin forest. East of Temagami, the Temiskaming Highland Trail extends 100 kilometres to the Ontario shore of Lake Temiskaming.

Resources

Michael Barnes, *Temagami* (Erin: Boston Mills Press, 1992)

Pierre Berton, *The Impossible Railway* (Toronto: McClelland and Stewart, 1970)

Matt Bray and Ashley Thomson, eds, *Temagami: A Wilderness Debate* (Toronto: Dundurn Press, 1990)

Robert J. Surtees, *Northern Connection: Ontario Northland Since 1902* (North York: Captus Press, 1992).

Bear Island, home of Temagami First Nation

North Bay

North Bay may be one of Northeastern Ontario's success stories. In the last decade, its population (51,500 in 2016; 52,600 in 2021) has been stable or increasing despite a decline of nearly 10% across the northeast. In 1985, the city council decided to beautify and make accessible the waterfront along Lake Nipissing, which had remained an almost forgotten rough zone on the wrong side of the Canadian Pacific Railway. In 1999, the city purchased most of the rail lands, later made the renovated and stately old railway station into a museum and information centre, and in 2010 opened a pedestrian tunnel to provide direct access from downtown. Grants to maintain old downtown buildings—only two blocks from the lake—reinforce the beautification of the waterfront.

At present, protective sea walls and a green space with picnic tables, walking paths, flower gardens, a Heritage Carousel and beach stretch along Lake Nipissing. The former Marathon Beach has been renamed Shabogesic Beach to honour a chief who signed the Robinson Huron Treaty in 1850 and to acknowledge the long time Indigenous presence. Beside King's Landing (formerly Government Wharf), a substantial marina for pleasure craft, is a restaurant symbolically housing the permanently docked *Chief Commanda*. Its successor *Chief Commanda II*, sits ready for afternoon and evening cruises on the lake. The waterfront and downtown beautification programs are examples of North Bay's efforts to provide a high quality of life for its citizens and to attract more enterprises for the diversified economy. Another example is the city's Active Transportation Master Plan initiated in 2019. It provides a framework for encouraging human powered forms of travel: walking, biking, skateboarding, canoeing and mountain biking by creating more bike lanes and walking trails, including asphalted accessible routes. The city is hooked up to the Voyageur Cycle Trail which extends from Ottawa to Sault Ste. Marie (though parts are not very bike friendly) and starting in 2022 has organized two days of special cycle racing, known as Cycle North Bay.

North Bay became a town (instead of a village) in 1891, and a city in 1925. In 1968 it expanded to include the previously separate townships of Widdifield and

Sidebar

Canadian Forces Heritage Officer Doug Newman provides an overview of NORAD's operations in North Bay:

Since 1963, North Bay has been the Canadian headquarters of NORAD (North American Air Defence Command until 1981; subsequently North American Aerospace Defence Command). Like NORAD headquarters inside Cheyenne Mountain at Colorado Springs, until 2006 North Bay's site operated from an underground building. Granite protected the underground facilities to the point that they could withstand a blast of four megatons, estimated to be more than 25 times the size of the blast at Hiroshima. At its height, a staff of more than 2,500 people worked there, but since the Cold War, there has been massive downsizing. By 2009, numbers fell to barely 500, who since 2006 have functioned from a new building located above ground, off limits to tourists.

Until 1983, NORAD's North Bay base monitored aircraft over the State of Maine and those parts of Canada between North Bay and the Atlantic Coast. Since then, it has observed flights over any part of Canada. During the Cold War, it watched for incoming Soviet aircraft, but since then it has acquired new tasks:

(1) In the era before the GPS, North Bay guided pilots lost over the Arctic.

(2) When Swissair Flight 111 caught fire on 2 September 1998, and ploughed into the ocean off Peggy's Cove, Nova Scotia, North Bay contributed to the investigation by monitoring the crash and sending data to the investigators.

(3) Late in the twentieth century, a USAF flight from Greenland, headed for the United States at an altitude of 31,000 feet, disappeared from the screen as it flew near the Labrador coast. A search-and-rescue squad went to the area, as a blip appeared near the ground. A back door had flown off, and almost everything inside flew outside. The plane nosedived, but nobody died.

(4) During the 1970s and 1980s, Colombian drug smugglers contemplated Canada as a route for smuggling drugs into the United States. Seven or eight Colombians flew to New Brunswick. NORAD alerted the RCMP, which arrested all but one. That individual escaped and returned to Colombia, where he was executed. Subsequently, the smugglers decided to use Mexico, where aerial surveillance and police efficiency did not measure up to Canadian standards.

(5) NORAD protects VIPs from aerial security threats.

(6) NORAD investigates UFO sightings, most of which have proven to be ridiculous. On one occasion, someone who had too much to drink reported a bright light in the eastern sky; it was the sun rising for the day.

(7) Technology enabled a general in North Bay to monitor the activities of Canadian military aircraft over Kuwait during the First Gulf War (1991).

Above ground, NORAD has a museum and an archive. They are well worth a visit. Tours can be arranged through the Heritage Office. Phone 705-494-2011, ex. 2261. The museum displays artifacts from the earliest days of aviation through World War I, World War II, and the Cold War. Included are the World War I Zeppelin, the Battle of Britain, Avro Arrow and the Bomarc missiles.

West Ferris. Arguably North Bay has the most diversified economy of any community in Northeastern Ontario. Health and educational services are major employers, as is the Canadian Forces Base. Tourism and transportation are important as are secondary (mining supply) and tertiary (high tech) industries.

The area around North Bay has always been a transportation hub. Indeed, North Bay calls itself the "Gateway to the North" because until the 1960s it was impossible for travellers to reach any destination to the north or west of Canada from the east and south without first passing through it. From a water, rail and road hub, North Bay developed into a regional, commercial, medical and educational centre.

Water travels preceded railways and highways. Indigenous peoples had used the Ottawa and Mattawa rivers for centuries to trade as far north as James Bay and west through the Great Lakes. Later, fur trading voyageurs from Montreal could travel up the Ottawa and Mattawa rivers to Trout Lake, then make a short portage across almost level ground to the LaVase (Mud) Creek, a tributary of Lake Nipissing (That portage now marks the eastern boundary of the Roman Catholic diocese of Sault Ste. Marie). Striking across Lake Nipissing, canoeists could travel down the French River to Georgian Bay on Lake Huron. Early French explorers, fur traders and missionaries had to use that route because the hostile Iroquois (Haudenosaunee) controlled what is now southern Ontario. British explorers, fur traders and soldiers continued to travel via that route after the change of sovereignty in 1763, including fur traders of the North West Company and British soldiers going to and from Fort St. Joseph.

From its terminus in Montreal, the Canadian Pacific Railway arrived in what would become North Bay in 1882. A passenger on the first train was a railway postal worker named John Ferguson. Ferguson often receives credit for the name of what would become his home, where he bought 288 acres of land for $288. He reportedly ordered a package of nails to be sent to the "north bay of Lake Nipissing." The casual geographic reference stuck and became the city's name. Canadian Pacific established a divisional headquarters at North Bay, and a commercial district developed within blocks of the railway station. One of the north-south streets near the station bears his name.

Tracks between North Bay and Toronto (now part of Canadian National) followed within the decade, as did Canadian Northern's main line (also now part of CN) from Montreal to Vancouver. In 1903, construction began on a new line then known as the Temiskaming and Northern Ontario Railway, now Ontario Northland (ONR), linking North Bay with places on the north shore of Lake Temiskaming and, in 1931, Moosonee, almost on James Bay. The head office of the ONR, which links North Bay with the mining/logging/agricultural communities to the north, established its headquarters in North Bay. Since the 1880s, steamboats and other commercial freight and passenger vessels have plied Lake Nipissing.

Until the interwar period, roads around North Bay were few and rudimentary. Even after World War II, they remained rough, muddy and dangerous. The provincial government of Premier G. Howard Ferguson (1923–1930) constructed Highway 11 from Toronto, once known as "the Ferguson Highway." During the Depression of the 1930s, some unemployed men had found work building the east-west Highway 17.

For the first part of the twentieth century, the rail links encouraged North Bay's development as a regional headquarters in religion, commerce and health. David Scollard, first Roman Catholic Bishop of the Diocese of Sault Ste. Marie (1905–1934), chose North Bay as his place of residence because of the convenience of travel to other parts of the diocese. One architectural landmark of the city is the Pro-Cathedral of the Assumption; construction began in 1904. Another is Scollard Hall, originally a boys' boarding school built in 1931. Commercial travellers resided in North Bay and travelled north and west to provide goods and services. In the early 1950s, the Province of Ontario built a psychiatric hospital, with a wide catchment area. In 2010, North Bay's three hospitals (St. Joseph, Civic and psychiatric) moved into one large new facility called the North Bay Regional Health Centre on the north edge of the city.

North Bay's teachers' college, originally called "The Normal School," was established in 1907 at a cost of $100,000. In its first year of operation, the school enrolled 25 students from various parts of the province, each of whom received $1.50 every week for room and board plus one annual return rail trip home. In 1910, the weekly allowance was raised to $4 on condition that the recipient agreed to teach in the district for three years after graduation or reimburse the government. Students came from as far away as Fort William and Port Arthur (now Thunder Bay). The Normal School," renamed North Bay Teachers' College, joined with the fledgling Nipissing University College (then an affiliate of Laurentian University) to build a 720-acre campus overlooking Lake Nipissing. The university was granted its own charter in 1992, and now enrolls around 5,000 undergraduates plus 400 post-graduate students. Nipissing University shares a campus with Canadore College, which has 3,500 full time and 4,500 part time students. The university and college estimate that the two institutions pump approximately $500,000 million annually into North Bay's economy. In fact, educational services are the number one employer in the city. Number two is the Ministry of Community Safety and Correctional Services, which moved to North Bay in the 1990s, taking over the old "Normal School" building.

Moviemaking, TV series and cinema studies have developed quickly in the last decade. The college offers technical courses (editing and composition, digital cinematography, recording engineering). The City of North Bay does not charge a film permit fee. Hallmark Christmas-themed films have repeatedly been filmed in North Bay as have a series of TV shows such as *Cardinal, Carter, the Lake, Essex Country* and *Trickster*. Many of the productions are broadcast by CBC, CTV and educational channels thus attaining a provincial and national audience. Over the past decade the film industry has become one of the key drivers of economic growth in North Bay.

Some background to North Bay's historical development: In 1933, the Department of Transport chose North Bay as a site for emergency landings, refuelling and a passenger depot for Trans Canada Airlines (now Air Canada). By 1938 the landing strip was built, and commercial air travel facilities were in place. During World War II, the Royal Canadian Air Force (RCAF) used the North Bay airport, and after the closure of the base following Hitler's defeat,

private companies and wealthy individuals with their own aircraft flew from there. Air Canada continues to provide commercial flights between Toronto and North Bay, as well as between North Bay and points north.

In 1951, after the outbreak of the Korean War, the RCAF base re-opened. The enlarged base became home to officers of the RCAF and the U.S. Air Force. In 1958, the base became the Canadian headquarters of NORAD, the North American Air Defence Command. Four factors made North Bay attractive to defence planners: the existence of the air base; the cold water of Trout Lake, which could cool the computers of the 1950s; North Bay's role as a transportation crossroad and telecommunications centre; and the Laurentian Shield, which protected NORAD's underground building [the Bunker] from attack. The Underground Complex operated from the equivalent of 68 stories beneath the surface. It closed in 2006 and the base operations moved above ground, but the bunker was used for the sci-fi film *The Colony* in 2012. Locals hope to get a National Historic Site designation for it.

The advent of the diesel engine, competition from Sudbury, and the end of the Cold War became serious challenges to North Bay's continued growth and prosperity. In the era of steam, CPR maintained a substantial staff in the city. Diesels could travel longer distances without refuelling, and in 1953, CPR relocated many of its North Bay-based employees to Sudbury. To the disappointment of residents of North Bay, the Province of Ontario located the regional university, Laurentian, to Sudbury in 1961. As Highway 69 (being renamed Highway 400 as four-laning continues) linked Sudbury with southern Ontario, commercial travellers and medical specialists chose to settle in Sudbury. At the same time, vacationers and commercial travellers often preferred to travel from Toronto to the west via Sudbury rather than North Bay because of the shorter distance. Post-Cold War cutbacks have considerably reduced the size of the air base, and both tourism and travel to vacation destinations have declined.

Secondary industries include firms in the mining and mining supply sector (Abitibi Mining Services, Boart Longyear, JS Redpath, Kaltech Mining Services). Some produce mining equipment, while some serve as consultancy firms, advising mining companies around the world. Expanding tertiary industries include computer and educational research. Perhaps surprisingly, a long-term primary industry is the fur trade, which provides employment for trappers and auctioneers. For two decades,

North Bay has hosted an Annual Fur Traders Convention, where retailers from North America and elsewhere bid on furs. The economic story is not entirely positive. The fur trade has been highly controversial, and many people prefer to buy synthetic products.

North Bay's municipal politicians include colourful mayor Merle Dickerson. After years as a city councillor, he was mayor from 1954 to 1960 and from 1966 to 1971. Ousted mid-term after a criminal conviction for electoral fraud and temporarily banned from public office by court order, he again faced the electorate at the first opportunity and won. Then he held the post for another six years (1974-1980) and from 1982 until his death in 1984. His repeated re-elections probably related to the city's prosperity and expansion during his time in office.

North Bay honours many of its most prominent residents through the naming of streets and parks. Near the downtown core are McIntyre Street, named for Duncan McIntyre, owner of the Canada Central Railway (CCR) and a CPR official after the sale of the CCR to CPR; Worthington Street, named for James Worthington, a contractor who worked with McIntyre; and Ferguson Street, named for McIntyre's nephew, John Ferguson, mentioned above. Bourke Street in western North Bay honours John Bourke, North Bay's first mayor, who developed the western part of the city after buying land from Pembroke's Murray Brothers, after whom Murray Street is named. The Klock family gave its name to the major north-south artery, renamed Algonquin Avenue after World War II in honour of the city's Algonquin Regiment. The local airport is named after Jack Garland, Liberal MP from 1949 until 1964 and Minister of National Revenue in the government of Lester Pearson from 1963 until his death. Parks are named for George Lee, once CEO of the ONR, and Lord Thomson of Fleet, a media entrepreneur who launched his career with the purchase of radio station CFCH in 1931. Bicycle path and multi-use trail Kate Pace Way honours a prominent downhill skier. The Goulet Golden Mile is named for former mayor Bruce Goulet, who worked tirelessly in the early 1970s for waterfront reclamation and redevelopment.

Other prominent celebrities lived or continue to live in North Bay. These include Gerald Bull (1928–1990), who taught at McGill University and was deeply involved in its High-Altitude Research Programme. Bull's assassination in Brussels remains a mystery. One theory is that his killers came from Israel's Mossad, because he was thought to have supplied armaments to countries unfriendly to Israel. Tim Horton, of hockey and coffee fame, lived in North Bay during the 1950s and 1960s with his parents. He and his brother operated Tim Horton Charcoal Broiled Hamburgers (Apparently a friendly rivalry exists between Hamilton and North Bay about which city had the first Tim Horton's, depending on definition). Mike Harris, who grew up in North Bay, became one of Ontario's most controversial premiers (1995–2002). The controversy included the furor when Nipissing University named its new library after him.

Fiction writer Giles Blunt once lived in and now writes crime novels about a North Bay thinly disguised as Algonquin Bay. His novels were adapted into the highly successful TV series *Cardinal*, shot in Sudbury and North Bay between 2016 and 2019. Comic-strip creator Lynn Johnston, author of the syndicated *For Better or For Worse*, for many years made her home near North Bay. One of the storylines in her comic strip revolved around the character Elizabeth attending Nipissing University.

As in so much of Northern Ontario, tourism has enriched the economy. Site of numerous high quality tourist resorts, motels and restaurants, North Bay still offers access to the outdoor life combined with modern comforts and amenities. Foremost among its attractions is Lake Nipissing, the second largest lake located entirely in Ontario. Outdoor enthusiasts can also access the Champlain Trail (Trout Lake and the Mattawa River system). Good swimmers often prefer Trout Lake to Lake Nipissing because of its deeper water, but fishing is purportedly better in Lake Nipissing. Another attraction is the Dionne Quints Museum. The original home of the Dionne Quintuplets, born in nearby Corbeil in 1934, was moved to the southeastern junction of Highways 11 and 17 and turned into a museum. After some controversy, in 2017 it was taken apart and reassembled at the waterfront park close to the North Bay Museum. The Dionne Quintuplets, who were taken from their parents and placed on display as well as having English culture imposed on them, are often credited with putting North Bay onto the tourist map, since between 1936 and 1943 almost three million people came north to view Quintland. A different, more interactive site is at the Sisters of St. Joseph Motherhouse, where a labyrinth offers individuals a reflective healing centre (one of four labyrinths in Northeastern Ontario).

The city is also home to a variety of amateur, student and professional theatre. The Gateway Theatre Guild, for instance, has been entertaining audiences since 1948. TOROS (Theatre Outreach on Stage) and Dreamcoat Fantasy Theatre have offered opportunities for young students to become involved in all aspects of theatre production for the last 25 years. Also, Canadore College has a thriving Acting for Stage and Screen Program that enriches the community with its offerings. The program was created in 2004 by Rod Carley in response to the lack of professional acting training in Northeastern Ontario. The Capitol Centre, the former Capitol Theatre on Main Street, has brought quality arts and entertainment to North Bay since 1987, featuring everything from symphony orchestras to operas to touring dance companies to such musical greats as Tom Jones and Blue Rodeo. The On-The-Edge Fringe Festival offers audiences an alternative theatre experience in mid-August at the Capitol Centre.

From late September to early October, the ONR operates a special tourist train, The Dream Catcher Express, from North Bay to Temagami (return) for visitors to see the changing leaf colours.

The former CPR railway station, on Oak Street in the downtown core, is now a transportation museum. It also records the achievements of people associated with North Bay who had roles in movies, as well as athletes who have won Olympic medals in swimming, basketball, canoeing, boxing and hockey.

The people of North Bay are proud of their hockey and curling traditions. In 1980, goalie Bob Dupuis of the North Bay Trappers played with the Canadian hockey team at the Lake Placid Winter Olympics. In 2007 North Bay won the Hockeyville contest. The North Bay Sports Hall of Fame dates from 1977, supporting sports history, financing scholarships to Nipissing University and Canadore College and displaying pictures and artifacts related to successful athletes.

Resources

Albert Anson, *North Bay: Gateway to Silverland* (Toronto: Emerson Press, 1909)

Michael Barnes, *North Bay: Northern Gateway* (Burnstown, 1997).

Giles Blunt, *By the Time You Read This* (Toronto: Random House, 2006).

Gaetan Gervais, *Les jumelles Dionnes et l'Ontario française* (Sudbury : Prise de Parole, 2000).

W. K. P. Kennedy, *North Bay Past, Present Prospective* (1961)

Franocise Noel, *Family and Community in North Bay: The Interwar Years* (Kingston: McGill-Queens, 2009).

Railway Museum

Aubrey falls

Parks, National and Provincial

The chorus of a popular song by the musical trio The Arrogant Worms repeats the words "rocks and trees and water." These words fully sum up the terrain of Northeastern Ontario. The Precambrian Shield peeks out everywhere to provide ridges and cliffs and impressive rock cuts, the trees of the boreal and temperate forest are varied and profuse, while lakes and rivers abound. To understand the beauty, grandeur, size and diversity of the northeast, Ontario's provincial parks are an appropriate place to start. The system's website www.ontarioparks.com provides detailed information on all the parks, including access points for hikers and canoers.

Though Northeastern Ontario hosts no National Parks, Pukaskwa is close to its edge, where Lake Superior's coastline turns westward, and can be readily accessed via Highway 627 off Highway 17 from Wawa. Among the park's special features is a multitude of ferns and mosses in the valleys of the rivers descending to the lake; similar ones are found only much further north in Canada's Arctic. The Coastal Hiking Trail runs for 60 kilometres parallel to the lake, crossing numerous rivers and creeks, some with suspension bridges.

Among the many provincial parks, Algonquin Provincial Park was the first (1893), and is probably the best known, though it has numerous competitors for diversity, beauty and majestic scenery. Killarney, for example, as a wilderness park featured by the Group of Seven painters, offers colourful quartzite in pink and white, but every park has some special attributes, whether old growth pine, cedars, delicate flowers, eskers, rock walls, wetlands, First Nations rock paintings, or artifacts of settlement and industry.

At present the Ontario park system is administered by zones, of which three are relevant here: Central, Northeast and Algonquin. In those zones, six overlapping types of parks have been designated: recreation (diverse landscape, comprehensive), historical (associated with special event or person), natural environment (no urban development), nature reserve (protected area), waterway and wilderness. The park system is more than 100 years old, so the various designations have come and gone. Further, the province has added to the protected waterways almost annually. Below are the main Northeastern Ontario parks, presented in alphabetical order, with brief

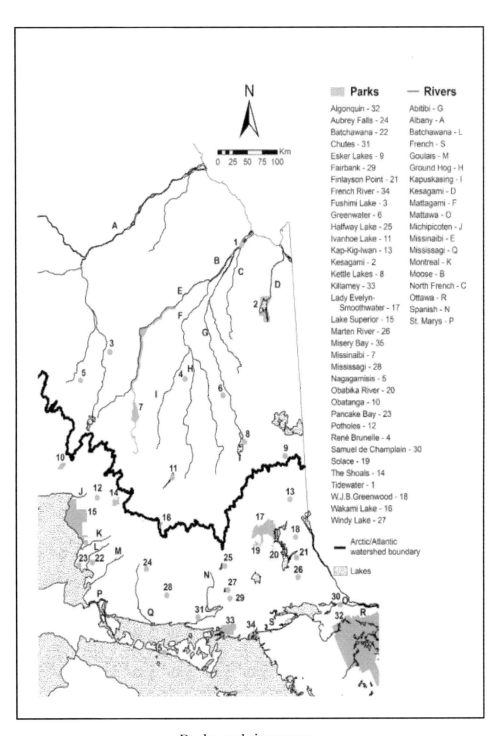

Parks

Algonquin - 32
Aubrey Falls - 24
Batchawana - 22
Chutes - 31
Esker Lakes - 9
Fairbank - 29
Finlayson Point - 21
French River - 34
Fushimi Lake - 3
Greenwater - 6
Halfway Lake - 25
Ivanhoe Lake - 11
Kap-Kig-Iwan - 13
Kesagami - 2
Kettle Lakes - 8
Killarney - 33
Lady Evelyn-
   Smoothwater - 17
Lake Superior - 15
Marten River - 26
Misery Bay - 35
Missinaibi - 7
Mississagi - 28
Nagagamisis - 5
Obabika River - 20
Obatanga - 10
Pancake Bay - 23
Potholes - 12
René Brunelle - 4
Samuel de Champlain - 30
Solace - 19
The Shoals - 14
Tidewater - 1
W.J.B.Greenwood - 18
Wakami Lake - 16
Windy Lake - 27

Rivers

Abitibi - G
Albany - A
Batchawana - L
French - S
Goulais - M
Ground Hog - H
Kapuskasing - I
Kesagami - D
Mattagami - F
Mattawa - O
Michipicoten - J
Missinaibi - E
Mississagi - Q
Montreal - K
Moose - B
North French - C
Ottawa - R
Spanish - N
St. Marys - P

Arctic/Atlantic watershed boundary

Lakes

Parks and rivers map

descriptions of their major features or points of interest. For those with limited access, only a general reference is offered. Many parks, such as Algonquin, Killarney and Misery Bay, have organizations that seek to foster education about their special features and encourage informed use.

- Abitibi-de-Troyes (waterway) on Lake Abitibi is accessible only by air or water and has no visitor facilities. It is 50 kilometres east of Timmins.

- Algonquin (natural environment) has 7,725 square kilometres of lakes, diverse forests, cliffs and ridges. Wildlife, such as loons, foxes, wolves and moose, are frequently seen and heard, as is the case in most of the other parks. Best explored by canoe, many routes with portages are marked (1,500 kilometres). Hiking (6 to 71-kilometre trails), camping and fishing are also popular. Many visitors arrive in fall for the colourful show of changing leaves. The main visitor centre contains extensive exhibits explaining the area's natural and human history. Unique to this park is that active logging occurs in some areas under the purview of a Crown agency and a logging museum is just inside the east entrance. From highways 11 and 17 (west from Mattawa) access is possible, but the main gates are at the south and east edges.

- Aubrey Falls (natural environment) is 80 kilometres north of Blind River where Highways 129 and 556 meet. It has a hiking trail leading to the 53-metre power dam, below which a long bridge and scenic outlooks provide differing perspectives over a spectacular waterfall that cascades in a variety of directions. Jack pine and white birch are scattered among lakes and rock outcrops.

- Batchawana Bay (recreation) is 25 kilometres northwest of Sault Ste. Marie and offers full services, including an information centre. Being on a sheltered bay of Lake Superior means fishing, canoeing, boating and swimming are daily summer activities. Just walking the long beach can be enjoyable.
- Biscotasi Lake Provincial Park (natural) is on the Spanish River and Lake Biscotasi the park has few facilities. It is on a historic water route of the Ojibwe and the fur traders.

- Blue Jay Creek (nature reserve) is on the east side of Michael's Bay on Manitoulin Island; boat or rough trail access only.

- Chapleau-Nemegosenda River (waterway) is on two parallel rivers running into Kapuskasing Lake. Moose, waterfowl and fish are abundant though the park has no facilities; it is about 100 kilometres west of Timmins on Highway 101. From Chapleau it can be accessed via a logging road.

- Chiniguchi (waterway), about 50 kilometres northeast of Sudbury (Wanapetei Lake) and southwest of Temagami, comprises nearly 9, 500 hectares of protected wilderness along the Chiniguchi River, Maskinonge

Lake, Wolf Lake and Matagamasi Lake, including Donald Lake, in Sudbury District though the park office is in Temagami. It has few facilities and is primarily a hiker's and paddler's delight (with some Indigenous pictographs and many waterfalls) as well as a conservationist dream because it includes some old growth forest slowly being protected from mining. Some claim the scenery matches Killarney Park. Canoers can follow this traditional First Nation water highway, including portages used over centuries. Kukagami Lake is not included in the park but is in an abutting protected forest area.

- Chutes (recreation) is one kilometre north on Highway 17 at Massey, west of Espanola. The rapids and small falls of the Aux Sables River are charming with little hint of the earlier extensive logging activities. The interpretive signs at the falls explain the long-lumber chute used to bypass the falls. Campsites (some with electricity), fishing spots and hiking trails along the river and among the big pines make for a pleasant stop.

- Esker Lakes (natural environment) is on top of the Arctic-Atlantic Watershed, 37 kilometres east of Kirkland Lake. Eskers are narrow ridges of gravel or sand deposited by glaciers. More than half the campsites have electricity. Canoeing is relatively easy and portages between the many lakes are marked.

- Fairbanks (recreation) is on the northwest edge of the Sudbury nickel basin with main access from Highway 17 about 35 kilometres west of Sudbury. Swimming, picnicking, hiking, boating and fishing are available. A half-hour hike ends with an outlook on the main lake. The park has recovered from fire damage in 2008.

- Finlayson Point (recreation) is known for superb scenery combining rugged lake-side cliffs, tall pines and 1,300 islands. Canoeing, sailing, boating, fishing and snorkelling are the dominant activities. A five-kilometre trail leads to great views. A summer program and small museum aid understanding of the Temagami Lake region, while a plaque explains Grey Owl, the Englishman who imitated First Nations ways at Bear Island. Apparently, the *North Bay Nugget* knew of Grey Owl's real identity but chose not to reveal the deception until after his death. The park is located about 100 kilometres north of North Bay off Highway 11 near Temagami.

- Five Mile Lake (recreation) is another park showing eskers from glaciations but offers no facilities. It is 140 kilometres northeast of Sault Ste. Marie, just southeast of Chapleau.

- French River (waterway) is easily accessed from Highway 69, about 65 kilometres south of Sudbury. The park stretches for 100 kilometres along the river offering boating, hiking, fishing, swimming and canoeing. As a

Canadian Heritage River, it marks the main waterway of the fur-trading voyageurs. The scenic views are mixed with resorts and campgrounds. The welcome centre at the south side of the river on Highway 69 has won an architectural prize and contains a well-organized museum about the people and places on the river.

- Fushimi Lake (recreation) has full camping facilities, hiking, canoeing, fishing and wildlife viewing. It is 40 kilometres northwest of Hearst off Highway 11.

- Greenwater (natural environment) contains numerous kettle lakes formed by glaciations. It has extensive facilities and offers canoeing, fishing and hiking plus wildlife viewing. It is 32 kilometres northwest of Cochrane north off Highway 11.

- Halfway Lake (natural environment) is the place to see osprey fishing from a high lookout at the end of a four-kilometre hiking trail. Glacial boulder fields can also be viewed. Though full facilities are available for camping and swimming and four hiking trails are identified, the large park offers wilderness and solitude. It is 90 kilometres north of Sudbury on Highway 144, about halfway to Timmins.

- Ivanhoe Lake (natural environment) contains many eskers from glacial deposits, but the special aspect is the "quaking bog," a kettle lake in which the water has been overgrown by floating vegetation. Wild rice and various orchids are among the attractions; there are opportunities for swimming, hiking, fishing and canoeing in a full-facility park. It is halfway between Chapleau and Timmins off Highway 101.

- Kap-Kig-Iwan (natural environment) is on the Englehart River near Highway 11 between New Liskeard and Kirkland Lake. Waterfalls, rapids and rock outcroppings show the two-billion-year-old geology. A suspension bridge spans an impressive waterfall. Full facilities include short hiking trails good for bird watching. Because of the altitude, no blackflies hinder outdoor enjoyment.

- Kesagami (wilderness) is accessible only by air or boat. It is in the James Bay Lowlands about 70 kilometres southeast of Moosonee and follows the Kesagami River.

- Kettle Lakes (recreation) is named for the lakes formed by retreating glaciers about 11,000 years ago. Full facilities for camping, swimming, fishing and hiking are accompanied by cross-country ski trails in winter. It is 40 kilometres east of Timmins off Highway 101 via 67.

- Killarney (wilderness) is considered the crown jewel of Ontario's parks, because of its wild beauty in contrasting colours. Many of the Group of Seven spent much time painting and hiking here, and convinced the government to make it a park. Their iconic paintings emerged as abstractions from this scenery. White quartzite peaks (the highest is Silver Peak, which is on a strenuous, circular 100-kilometre hiking trail) are set against pristine lakes and varied forests to offer endless spectacular views. Twisted jack pines on tiny islands in deep blue water remind of the paintings of Tom Thomson. Campgrounds at the south entrance offer full facilities, but the interior has limited and controlled access. Bog trails, nature education and many activities such as swimming, canoeing (motorboats are not permitted) and hiking are available. The park is near the end of Highway 637 before the village of Killarney, off Highway 69 and about 100 kilometres southwest of Sudbury. Whoever has not been to Killarney has not truly experienced Ontario.

- La Cloche (wilderness) has no facilities but great terrain of ridges and wetlands. It is on the North Shore of Lake Huron, 19 kilometres from Espanola (southwest of Sagamok village off Highway 17, west of Massey). Hikers can reach the few remains of Fort La Cloche, a major supply and stopping point for the North West Company between Montreal and the west.

- La Motte Lake (recreation) has no facilities but offers fishing and canoeing. It is 140 kilometres northwest of Sudbury.

- Lady Evelyn-Smoothwater (wilderness) is west of Temagami. It has great vistas, waterfalls and Ontario's highest point, but is difficult to access.

- Lake Superior (natural environment) has very diverse features and is one of

Agawa pictographs, Lake Superior Park

the province's largest parks. Located on the eastern shore of Lake Superior, it has rugged ranges of big hills through which rivers cascade dramatically to the lake. Many waterfalls and rapids as well as bays and canyons typify the park. Agawa Canyon and Old Woman Bay represent the ever-impressive landscape and parts are easily seen from Highway 17, which traverses part of the park. The forest is a mix   of hardwoods and boreal evergreens so the fall colours are especially noticeable. The park has three campgrounds close to the highway, eleven hiking trails and eight marked canoe routes. Some interior campsites are accessible only by foot or canoe and only the major ones have facilities. A visitor centre nestled among large pines adjacent to a long beach near the northern end of the park offers information about the natural and human history. Fishing can be excellent. The park covers most of the area on both sides of Highway 17 between Montreal River and Wawa. Just north of Agawa Bay a half-kilometre rocky, but spectacular, trail leads from the highway to one of the largest collections of Native pictographs in Ontario.

- Larder River (waterway) is 30 kilometres east of Kirkland Lake and has no facilities, but fishing, boating, swimming and hiking are possible. The river's rapids are challenging.

- Little Abitibi (natural environment) has no facilities. A large waterfall and 300-year-old red pines encourage camping, canoeing and fishing. It is 66 kilometres north of Cochrane via Highway 652.

- Marten River (recreation) contains some huge white pines missed by nineteenth-century loggers. The park has a re-constructed logging camp housed in log huts with good signage. Many animals and an impressive diversity of plants share the transitional forest. Signed hikes and walks illustrate the types of vegetation. The Marten River provides a major canoe route linking numerous lakes. The park has extensive facilities for camping, swimming, and boating. It is 56 kilometres north of North Bay on Highway 11.

- Mattawa River (waterway) between North Bay and Mattawa is a scenic and historic route. This was the main highway of the fur-trading voyageurs. Access is from many points on Highway 17, which runs parallel to the river.

- Misery Bay (nature reserve) is towards the western end of Manitoulin Island south off Highway 640 (after Elizabeth Bay hamlet). Though it has no facilities, it has an interpretive centre explaining the limestone bedrock, alvars and wetlands encountered on the hiking trails.

- Missinaibi River (waterway) has wilderness and the raw beauty of granite and boreal forests. Some facilities are available for backpackers and canoe adventurers, but mostly they are on their own with rapids, waterfalls and wetlands. The south end of the park is 60 kilometres northwest of Chapleau

147

and accessible by gravel road.

- Mississagi (natural environment) is relatively unspoiled by human activity, though evidence of logging exists. Fossils can be seen on the nature trail (protected), glacial boulders are common and some old pines have survived. Full facilities and extensive canoe routes and trails exist. The park is 25 kilometres north of Elliot Lake (Highway 638) with additional access from Highway 17 north on Highway 546.

- Nagagamisis (natural environment) in Cree means "Lake with fine, sandy shores." In addition to the lake, the park has varied vegetation in two distinct regions. Facilities exist and swimming, hiking, boating, canoeing are the main activities. It is on Highway 631 southwest of Hearst.

- Obabika River (waterway), at the north end of the Sturgeon River, west of Temagami, is known for old growth forest and wetlands.

- Obatanga (recreation) is just south of White River. Sandy beaches, short hikes and a bike trail are readily available, but the interior is accessible only by canoe. Pink lady's slippers are common in spring, with eagles and kingfishers year-round.

- Pancake Bay (recreation) has a five-kilometre-long sandy beach with full facilities. Swimming, fishing, boating and hiking are popular. The park is stretched along the Lake Superior shore and many bike the interconnected roads in the campgrounds in spring and fall when campers are fewer, or cross-country ski and snowshoe in winter (though the park is officially closed). In spring, ice is often pushed up the shore by winds to create bizarre forms. A lookout trail offers a spectacular view across the bay from a high point in the hills opposite the beach side of Highway 17. It is 80 kilometres north of Sault Ste. Marie on Highway 17.

- Potholes (nature reserve) show glacial remains and has limited facilities. It is on Highway 101, 35 kilometres east of Wawa.

- Queen Elizabeth The Queen Mother Mnidoo Mnissing (natural environment) park on the west end of Manitoulin Island has no facilities and is non-operational.

- René Brunelle (recreation) is in the clay belt of the boreal forest. It has facilities, self-guided trails, swimming and boating. It is north of Highway 11, 30 kilometres east of Kapuskasing.

- Samuel de Champlain (natural environment) is named for the seventeenth century explorer. The park is on the Mattawa River, which was part of the fur-trade route. Full facilities exist and the Voyageur Heritage Centre explains the life of the traders. The park offers self-guided and themed trails, swimming, fishing and boating. It is 50 kilometres east of North Bay off Highway 17.

- Solace (waterway) is 80 kilometres northeast of Sudbury with difficult access by air and water.

- Spanish River (waterway) is primarily a canoe route along the northern part of that river.

- The Shoals (natural environment) is another esker park in the boreal forest. Basic facilities are combined with canoe routes, hiking trails and excellent fishing. It is 50 kilometres west of Chapleau on Highway 101.

- Strawberry Island (nature reserve) park near Manitoulin Island just east of Little Current has a lighthouse. No activities or facilities exist in this non-operating park.
- Tidewater (natural environment) comprises four islands in the Moose River just 20 kilometres south of James Bay. Small boreal forest trees and lowland hiking trails are the main attractions. Access is by boat or air with limited facilities.

- W.J.B. Greenwood (recreation) offers canoeing, swimming and interesting geological formations. It is on Highway 11 about 110 kilometres north of North Bay, and south of Latchford.

- Wakami Lake (recreation) offers facilities at the main campground, but the interior is worth exploring for wildlife and forests. Short trails and a logging exhibit offer information on the area's fauna and early development. The 76-kilometre Height of Land Trail is long and the main canoe routes challenging. The park is east of Chapleau on a spur road off Highway 129.

- Wanapitei (natural environment) has no visitor facilities and is 35 kilometres northeast of Sudbury on Lake Wanapitei's north shore.

- Windy Lake (recreation) offers some of the best cross country ski trails in Ontario since the park is in the rolling hills on the edge of the meteorite crater known as the Sudbury interruptive. The park has full facilities and is popular with Sudburians for fishing, hiking, boating and swimming. Short trails run through thick pine forests to a high lookout over the lake. It is about 50 kilometres northwest of Sudbury off Highway 144.

Resources
http://www.ontarioparks.com
Gerald Killan, Protected Places: *A History of Ontario's Provincial Park System* (Toronto: Dundurn Press, 1993).
Lori Labatt and Bruce Littlejohn, eds, *Islands of Hope: Ontario's Parks and Wilderness* (Willowdale: Firefly, 1992)

Mattawa River junction with Ottawa River

Retired Ontario Northland caboose

Railways, Budd Cars, Train Troubles, and the Spanish River Train Wreck

Transport in the northeast has gone through a series of modes: canoes, sailing vessels, steamers and railways. Starting in 1880, railways provided access to the landlocked interior, even in winter. First on the scene was the Canadian Pacific Railway (CPR). Built to link Montreal with Vancouver, the CPR reached Mattawa in 1881, North Bay in 1882 and Sudbury in 1883. Its main line then went northwest through Cartier and Chapleau. In 1887, the CPR completed a branch line from Sudbury to the Canadian Sault Ste. Marie, which had connections to the Michigan Sault Ste. Marie and Chicago railways. As highways improved and more people had access to cars and buses, rail passenger service declined.

The railways were built, frequently with immigrant labour discriminated against by the British-born elite, with a series of supply and crew depots every six to ten miles. Many communities in the north grew around the depots. Crews often had to be away from home for long periods, so boarding houses sprang up at some depots, which later became villages and towns. On freight trains, cabooses at the end of the trains provided accommodation for the workers. The main routes of the CPR and CNR ran across Indigenous lands nearly everywhere in Northeastern Ontario without consultation or getting consent, thereby breaking many of the treaties with First Nations. For years the Indigenous protested with little consequence. To illustrate: for decades one of the railway bridges at Garden River has borne the sign "This is Indian land."

In July 1997, CPR leased the 305 kilometres of track between Sudbury and Sault Ste. Marie to the Huron Central Railway for a period of 20 years. Huron Central counted on Sault Ste. Marie's steel industry for viability, and steel constituted 80% of its freight. Because of problems at Algoma Steel, in July 2009 Huron Central threatened to break its lease, and the CPR indicated that it would abandon the line. Negotiations ensued among the federal government, Province of Ontario, railway officials, the City of Sault Ste. Marie, Essar Steel Algoma (by then the owner of Algoma Steel), and Domtar of Espanola. In late 2010, and again in 2020, the parties agreed to loans and subsidies and the Huron Central Railway continues to operate.

After the CPR lines were established, more northerly east-west lines followed, namely the Canadian Northern and the National Transcontinental. The former led to settlement in Hornepayne, Algoma District, the latter to the development of Cochrane, Kapuskasing, Hearst and other communities along what is now the Highway 11 corridor in Cochrane District. The Canadian Northern began as a private corporation on the Canadian prairies late in the nineteenth century, while the National Transcontinental was a publicly owned operation launched by the government of Sir Wilfrid Laurier in 1903. By 1919, the National Transcontinental had proven not to be financially viable, and it became part of Canadian National (CN). Four years later Canadian Northern also became part of CN. In 1993, CN made a successful application to transfer what had been the National Transcontinental to the North Bay-based Ontario Northland Transportation Commission. Ontario Northland provides bus service for passengers and uses the tracks exclusively for freight.

The first north-south railway in Northeastern Ontario was the Algoma Central Railway. Sault Ste. Marie entrepreneur Francis Clergue obtained a charter in 1899. Although his initial intention was to provide a link between his pulp mill and iron mine, the Helen Mine near Wawa, and a projected steel supplier in Sault Ste. Marie, at one time Clergue hoped to extend his railway right to James Bay or Hudson Bay. It never did reach salt water. The Algoma Central crosses the CPR line at Franz and terminates at Hearst, where it meets the CN.

The other north-south railway was built in the east. In 1902, Ontario's Liberal government led by Premier George Ross introduced legislation to build the Temiskaming and Northern Ontario Railway (T&NO) north from North Bay to link Ontario's southern hinterland with the agricultural belt on the shores of Lake Temiskaming. Construction began the following year and led to the discovery of silver in Cobalt in 1903. Profits from silver and the search for gold led to more northerly expansions: the main line to Cochrane (reached in 1909), branch lines to Kirkland Lake and Timmins, and eventually to Rouyn-Noranda in Quebec. Some communities such as Englehart (in Temiskaming District) depended almost exclusively on the railway because they served as supply and crew depots. More than 20 years later, the T&NO extended its tracks to Moosonee. In 1946, the T&NO changed its name to Ontario Northland (ONR), both to avoid confusion with the Texas and New Orleans Railroad and to link the railway with the province. At Englehart, a steam engine recalls a period that ended in 1957 when the ONR converted totally to diesel, the first Canadian railway to do so.

One of the not so secret, but not well enough known, means of transport in Northeastern Ontario is the Budd Car. It is as much a social as a rail service between Sudbury and White River on the old CPR mainline. Some stops are scheduled, such as at Biscotasing and Chapleau, but many are not. Hikers, canoeists, hunters, fishermen and tourists can ask to be dropped at cabins, resorts, lakes or wherever. They can wave down the train to continue their journey on the thrice weekly cars. That option is the same as on the Polar Bear Express from Cochrane to Moosonee and the Agawa Canyon train from Sault Ste. Marie to Hearst.

Many of the local railways, including the multitude of lines near mining centres, have ceased to operate. Dale Wilson, Sudbury rail buff, has traced many of the railways operated by mining companies before they began shipping ores by truck or on main lines from smelters. Some track beds have become hiking and cycling trails, as between Little Current and Espanola.

The Budd Car is not a regular train, but a special two-car self-propelled passenger and freight system. The motor is underneath the car, so no locomotive is necessary. First built by the Budd Car Company during the 1950s, many were in service until the 1980s. Now most are retired to museums, although a few provide backup for light rail systems in some cities. In North America, two lines continue to operate: one in B.C., the other in Northeastern Ontario.

Sudbury and Chapleau old timers who could not afford fly-in fishing or hunting tell of the camaraderie on the Budd Car, which they often termed the "buddy" or "booze" car. Though their drinking may have gained increased stature from the retelling of tales, the exploits and tricks played made good stories. On one occasion, two fellows who had been secretly nipping from a flask but not sharing were told by their buddies that their stop was coming up. They grabbed their packs and when the train stopped, they jumped off, while the others made it as though they were getting ready to do so but stayed on and held the door shut as the train continued. The non-sharers had to walk a kilometre to the actual stopping place, then another to get to the camp on a lake where the others were well established by the time they arrived. Such good-natured pranks were part of northern male worlds during the Budd Car's classic era. Now, one can still escape to the bush, to Biscotasing, to Ramsey, Sultan, Chapleau, or go all the way and see Winnie the Pooh at White River.

Railroad buffs love the Budd cars, and some come from great distances to ride them between White River and Sudbury. Some of those tourists are surprised at the mix of people, baggage, canoes, mountain bikes, fishing and hunting gear plus many 2x4 beer boxes that go onto the cars. In 2010 Via Rail refurbished the diesel cars—it has five of them.

Retired Ontario Northland steam engine

1910 Spanish River Train Wreck

✕

By Andre Laferriere

Railway accidents were frequent, usually injuring or killing train workmen. Monuments at Chapleau and Moosonee honour the "sons of Martha" as they were known in reference to the New Testament activist. In January 1944 the roundhouse at Chapleau collapsed due to a fire from locomotive sparks; in September 1946 a bridge burned near the town because the creosoted ties caught fire.

Most of the attention, however, goes to passengers and one wreck made headlines. On 21 January 1910, one of the worst Canadian train disasters occurred when part of a passenger train on the Sault line plunged into the icy waters at the CPR's Spanish River bridge near Nairn Centre. At 1:00 p.m., a section of passenger train No. 7 broke free of the rail just before the bridge and crashed over the bank into the river. The engine, mail car and baggage car made it over, but the colonist (cheaper immigrant passenger) car and the second-class car broke free, and the rest of the train fell into the river. The second-class car split into two sections and burst into flames, scorching and injuring many on board. Of the seven cars, passengers in the first-class car suffered the greatest loss of life. The car ended up completely submerged in the river. The dining car, still attached to the first-class car, was only partly submerged, while the Pullman car flipped on its side over the bank, allowing the injured passengers to escape. Of 100 people on this fateful trip, more than 40 lost their lives.

On 23 January, *The New York Times*, under the headline "Ice Locks the Dead in Wrecked Cars," described the scene on the following day: "Two of the wrecked cars, the colonist car and the first-class coach, whose ventilators were visible above the water this morning, drifted under the bridge during the day and finally were completely submerged. The dining car remained partly on the bank merged in the river. Little remains of the second-class coach, which was split in two when it struck the bridge girder and took fire. Ice that will bear a man's weight has closed over the first-class coach and the colonist car, and it is impossible to determine their exact locations."

The dead included people from Northern Ontario, Quebec, New Brunswick, Minnesota, Montana, Wisconsin, Michigan and even Norway. Several prominent people perished, including Rev. Childerhouse, the superintendent of the Presbyterian home missions, stationed in Parry Sound; Dr. Allan McLellan, a veterinarian from Sudbury; and W.J. Robertson, a CPR auditor. Four Roman Catholic priests also died in the accident. One of the most tragic deaths was that of Mrs. Stankie, from Ladysmith in Pontiac County, who was on her way to see her ailing husband in Massey, Ontario. Enroute, she received word that her husband passed away. She later died in that fateful crash. A prominent survivor was the Sudbury lumber baron, W.J. Bell.

The tragedy evoked heroism and courage. Mrs. Lindall of Winnipeg, who was injured in the Pullman car, helped other survivors by turning the sleeper car into a makeshift hospital and by binding the wounds of the injured passengers. While the survivors tended to the victims, a passenger and a brakeman from the train braved the cold and rushed to Nairn about five miles away to find help. Robert Burrough, manager of Bell Telephone at Sault Ste. Marie, a survivor of the train crash, recalled his observations of a terribly injured young Norwegian woman who "walked along the river and sat for five hours waiting [for] the arrival of the doctors. While her wounds were being sewed up she did not move a muscle or even wince."

Distinguished by his bravery was Conductor Thomas Reynolds who saved eight lives from the Pullman car by first smashing a submerged window, escaping through it into the ice-covered river, managing to surface, climbing to the roof of the car, breaking into it through the fanlight, and pulling smaller people to safety by their hair. Then he broke a larger hole to allow larger folk to escape. Conductor Reynolds was later awarded The Albert Medal for bravery by the King.

A coroner's jury could not determine the cause of the derailment but recommended that more section-men were needed to keep the rail lines in good condition in the North, that escape openings be installed on the top of passenger cars, and that emergency tools should be carried on passenger trains and placed in convenient locations.

Resources

Pierre Berton, *The Last Spike: The Great Railway, 1881–1885* (Toronto: McClelland and Stewart, 1971).

Darcy Brason-Lediett and Myril Lynn Brason-Lediett, *1910 Spanish River Train Wreck* (Sault Ste. Marie: Whipiwa, 2008).

Robert Surtees, *The Northern Connection: Ontario Northland Since 1902* (Toronto: Captus Press, 1992).

http://www.trainweb.org/oldtimetrains/sudbury/mining.htm (Dale Wilson on Sudbury Area Mining Railways)

Recreation

Northeastern Ontario has better beaches, finer fishing and far fewer people than the south of the province, which has become home to crowded and commercialized "rec" places, often wrecked on the weekends, as locals claim. The golf is half the price for comparable courses. The snowmobiling and cross-country skiing can be done for months; indeed, all winter sports last a season, rather than a day, as is the case further south. The hiking, canoeing, sailing, yachting and kayaking simply cannot be matched—but then neither, in some years, can the blackflies in May or the mosquitos in June.

Boating is possible everywhere because of the endless lakes and rivers, many made accessible by marked launch pads. Going to "camp"—northerners avoid the term cottage—is frequently by boat, or at minimum a boat awaits there. Though often combined with fishing, slowly or swiftly exploring open waters and seeing coastlines from a different perspective reinforces the extent of water in the north. Sea-dooing and water-skiing tend to be close to urban centres, perhaps to flaunt skills and speed. Boat tours are offered on many of the larger waterways, such as Lake Nipissing at North Bay (*Chief Commanda II* dinner and dance cruises), the French River at Wolseley Bay (Rene's Cruises), the St. Mary's River and canal locks (*Miss Marie*) at Sault Ste. Marie, or Sudbury's Lake Ramsey (renamed *William Ramsay*). Sailing opportunities are provided through yacht clubs at North Bay, Sault Ste. Marie and Sudbury. The main sailing and yachting routes are along the North Shore of Lake Huron, around Georgian Bay and along the coast of Lake Superior, though smaller lakes serve as well. The North Channel Yacht Club is mainly made up of members from Elliot Lake and Sudbury. It sails out of Serpent Harbour near Spragge on Highway 17. The Little Current Yacht Club organizes races such as to Mackinac Island (MacMan Race), stopping at Gore Bay with its large marina.

Fishing improves as the roads become tracks and disappear into the bush. From charter boats off Manitoulin, going for big salmon or lake trout and smaller rainbow trout, to fly-in camps organized to get big pickerel, bass, or pike, theoretical and actual fishing is superb. Among aficionados, theoretical fishing is about the one that got away or what lures are best, whereas real fishing is catching bass after a good fight at the secret spot. Northeastern Ontario offers a great variety of species, from bass to pike, from perch to sturgeon, and many types of fishing. A line tied to a belt loop and thrown from shore can sometimes do as well as the fanciest rigging in an overpowered boat.

Hunting, like fishing, is related to technology and size. All-terrain vehicles have made the bush and big game, especially bear and moose, more accessible. However, many small game hunters out for rabbits or grouse are interested mainly in a walk in the colourful fall woods. Ducks and geese are plentiful though the same rule applies as to fishing: the further from main roads the better the possibilities. The exception is Manitoulin Island, which is known for the ease of hunting deer. Using bow and arrow, instead of rifles, to take down moose and deer has become increasingly popular.

Golfing is best along the southern strip near Highway 17 from Mattawa to Sault Ste. Marie. Some championship courses are near this route, but challenging courses also dot Highway 101. Among the championship courses, Sault Ste. Marie's Crimson Ridge lets you shoot over chasms, and Blind River's Huron Pines has many elevation shifts. Elliot Lake's Stone Ridge boasts large inclines, Sudbury's Timberwolf and Lively have tricky greens, and Manitowaning's Rainbow Ridge has ponds and rolling hills. Timmins too has a championship course in Spruce Needles and, like the other northeastern cities, has other worthwhile courses, such as Hollinger. North Bay Golf and Country, like Sudbury's Idlewylde, is semi-private. Some courses are special because they incorporate the rocks of the Precambrian Shield. Indeed, Stonehill in Sudbury may be the true northern course; it has holes that wind between rock cuts, lakes and trees with one hole going through a rock chasm. Sudbury could be called the golf capital of the northeast. Its courses—some featuring no herbicides or pesticides—include three top level (Timberwolf, Lively and Idlewylde), and six medium ones (Cedar Green, Pine Grove, Stonehill, Forest Ridge, Chelmsford, Monte Vista). Nearly every town has at least a nine-hole course, from Alban, Noëlville, and Monetville near the French River, to Wawa in the North, and Mattawa in the southeast, to Chapleau, Hearst, Kapuskasing, Iroquois Falls, and Haileybury in the northeast, or to Espanola in the south-central. All are pleasant. In addition to the 18-hole Rainbow Ridge, Manitoulin has two nine-hole courses: one at Gore Bay (Manitoulin Island) and one at Mindemoya (Brookwood Brae). The one with the longest name, ideal for spelling contests, is Kebsquasheshing Golf Club at Chapleau. Though all the nine-hole courses have not been mentioned, some are little gems when played twice from different tees or finding different ways to avoid trees.

Hiking is well served as the health benefits of walking become more known. The Trans-Canada or Voyageur Trail runs along the southern and western edge of the region. Much of the trail has been completed from the Algoma Highlands north of Sault Ste. Marie going east. Though sometimes misused by all-terrain vehicles, this trail meshes with many local ones, for example, some of Sudbury's Rainbow Routes. All the provincial parks offer trails, with especially diverse ones in Killarney and Lake Superior Provincial Park. Many towns and cities have developed trails and boardwalks to make nature more accessible. An innovative one is at Moonbeam, which runs for 34 kilometres north to a provincial park; they even supply bicycles for the multi-use trail. At Pointe Grondine Park near Wiikwemkoong the First Nations (of Ojibwe, Odawa and Pottawatomi background) offer hiking and paddling trails to experience the land and waters with hiking, fishing and canoeing. Near M'Chigeeng, also on Manitoulin Island, a trail leads up the Cup and Saucer from the First Nation town side. Going all around the island is a marked driving tour, organized by the many First Nations whose land is contacted, entitled Great Spirit Circle Trail. Native Friendships Centres in various towns offer Medicine Walks identifying useful plants and ways to commune with nature. Some explain Indigenous healing via sweat lodges and the purpose of communal drumming.

Rock climbing can be undertaken almost anywhere, though the Cup and Saucer cliffs on Manitoulin Island may be the highest. Guided climbing is available in the Algoma Highlands.

Skiing, both alpine and cross country, is very popular. Searchmont, north of Sault Ste. Marie, and Mattawa offer the best downhill skiing, though Elliot Lake, Espanola, Sudbury and Timmins have runs. The Finns made cross-country skiing and saunas part of Northeastern Ontario culture. Many provincial parks have groomed trails and often the hiking and biking trails around cities and towns become cross-country trails during winter.

Swimming can be bracing, especially if the waters of Lake Huron or Lake Superior are involved. But endless public beaches and isolated coves call for dips, including the possibility of doing it au naturel. The smaller lakes can be warm by the end of May and, depending on the summer, swimmable through September. Many people are surprised to learn that in August the shores of James Bay offer long stretches of warm water.

Of course, the northeast also has hockey, ringette, skating, and curling rinks; soccer fields; pools; courts; plus ball fields and baseball diamonds; but both Canada and Northeastern Ontario have been reticent to reveal where we create all those sports stars, who suddenly are identified as "Canadians" but have been unknowns until they achieve fame in the south or become an export item. About 300 NHL players are identified as Northeasterners and many world medalists, Olympians and dancers hail from Northeastern Ontario.

Rivers

Three systems mark Northeastern Ontario rivers: First those flowing mostly northeast, dominated by the Moose River drainage system going into James Bay. Second, those flowing southeast to drain the eastern highlands south of Lake Temiskaming, dominated by the Ottawa River. Finally, those draining into the Great Lakes or Atlantic watershed, with some going west into Lake Superior or Georgian Bay and others going south into Lake Huron.

The Moose River system drains more than half of Northeastern Ontario north of the Arctic-Atlantic Watershed. The river itself is only 80 kilometres long, but its tributaries (from east to west) such as the North French, Abitibi, Mattagami and Missinaibi provide most of the water that flows into James Bay. Moose Factory is on one of the many islands at its mouth. Some of these rivers, such as the 400-kilometre Abitibi, have been harnessed by dams; others have huge hydro potential. The other large river flowing north along the Quebec border into James Bay is the Kesagami. The Mattagami River, about 450 kilometres long, comes from Mattagami Lake south of Timmins and flows northward into the Moose River.

The Groundhog, like most rivers that eventually contribute to the Moose River, crosses Highway 11 (at Fauquier), while the Kapuskasing crosses at Kapuskasing. The Missinaibi River, about 430 kilometres long, comes from Missinaibi Lake northwest of Chapleau and flows north and northeast to join the Moose River just north of the Mattagami.

The Michipicoten, Old Woman, Gargantua, Agawa, Montreal, Chippewa, Batchawana and Goulais are shorter rivers (50 to 100 kilometres) that descend rapidly west into Lake Superior. Many are used by whitewater kayakers.

Other medium and shorter rivers, such as the Mississagi, Blind, Spanish, Vermillion, Mississauga and Aux Sables, as well as the smaller Onaping and Wahnapitei rivers, drain into Lake Huron. The Spanish is one of few main rivers running south into the Atlantic watershed. From Biscotasing Lake it flows past Pogamasing Lake towards Espanola, then southwest past Webbwood and Massey. It is the second largest drainage system for Lake Huron and a favourite of canoeists.

> **Did you know?**
> A pail of water thrown into the creek south of the road at LaVase east of North Bay has to run westward passing through Lake Nipissing and the French River for a hundred kilometres before going south through Lake Huron and then east to finally end up in the St. Lawrence River. It would have travelled some thousand kilometres going through lakes Ontario and Erie. Meanwhile a pail of water thrown into the lake north of the LaVase portage would quickly run into the Mattawa, then the Ottawa River and be in the St. Lawrence after only a few hundred kilometres. Similarly, a pail of water thrown into the headwaters of the Michipicoten River northwest of Chapleau would descend west to Lake Superior, and then make its way past Sault Ste. Marie to follow the pail of water thrown into the creek south of LaVase. However, another pail thrown just north of Chapleau would go north on the Kebsquasshinghing or Menagosendaa rivers into the Kapuskasing, then the Mattagami and finally into the Moose River to end in James Bay.

The St. Mary's River connects Lake Superior to Lake Huron. It is a fair-sized waterway with canals to bypass the rapids at the Canadian and American cities of Sault Ste. Marie. It flows through George Lake to the North Channel of Lake Huron.

The French River, nearly 100 kilometres in length, exits from Lake Nipissing, divides into two channels at Eighteen Mile Island, then drops dramatically via rapids and waterfalls into Georgian Bay. The fur traders used it as a major route to and from the west. Now it is a major tourist destination, and many cottages dot its shores, especially near highways 17 and 64.

The Ottawa River drains toward the St. Lawrence going southeast from a series of lakes, starting at Lake Temiskaming. It served the fur trade, both the route north towards James Bay—essentially the route traversed by the de Troyes Expedition in 1686—and especially the route west via the Mattawa River, Lake Nipissing and the French River. Now it is known for its whitewater rafting opportunities. The substantial Mattawa River served as the main link westward towards Lake Nipissing and is now a major recreational attraction.

The other main southward running river is the Sturgeon, which flows into Lake Nipissing. Its watershed, like that of most rivers going west, southwest and southeast, supplied the logs for mills, usually located near the river mouths.

Resources
Andy Thomson, *Pogamasing: The Story of a Northern Lake* (Erin: Why Knot Books, 2011).

Abitibi River

French River at Highway 69, looking east (Credit: Laurence Stevens)

Crystal waterfall

Sables-Spanish Rivers Township: Webbwood, Massey, Walford

On 1 July 1998, municipal restructuring created the Sables-Spanish Rivers Township. This included the Township of the Spanish River, the towns of Webbwood and Massey, the Village of Walford and several organized and unorganized townships. This extensive municipality covers 807 square kilometres along the North Shore of Georgian Bay, 75 kilometres west of Sudbury. It parallels Highway 17 and the Spanish River, and includes the Sables River, in and north of Massey.

In 2006, the municipality had a population of 3,237; in 2021 it was 3,214. Most people speak English, and many are bilingual (English and French). Only 175 people have neither English nor French as their primary language. The First Nations population is 435.

The pulp and paper mill at Espanola provided employment for many, while others work for Vale, at the mines and smelters in the Sudbury area. Various enterprises in the municipality, and the municipality itself, provide further employment. Agriculture offers few opportunities for employment. In 2006 the median income was $51,121; in 2021 it was $62,933 or about $30,000 less than Sudbury's.

First Nations surround Espanola, hence the following land acknowledgement has been suggested to commence public meetings: "We begin by acknowledging that we are all on land that has been inhabited by Indigenous people for thousands of years. ...on the traditional territory of the Atikameksheng Anishnawbek, descendants of the Ojibwe, Algonquin and Odawa Nations." The White Fish River First Nation is located just to the south of the town with territory stretching to Birch Island near Manitoulin. Fishing, hunting and creating crafts such as birch bark canoes or quill baskets comprised much of their traditional way of life.

Non-Indigenous settlement in the area began in the late eighteenth century when the North West Company opened a trading and supply post at Fort La Cloche near the mouth of the La Cloche River, south of present-day Massey. By 1865, lumbering had become the base of the economy, with both the Aux Sables and Spanish rivers used to propel logs to market. Agriculture followed, and early settlements such as

Lee Valley, Temperance Valley, Birch Lake, West Lake, Seldom Seen and River Road appeared. Though the hamlets have disappeared, these names continue to be used locally. Nodes of settlement also appeared following the 1885 construction of the Canadian Pacific Railway (CPR) link from Sudbury westward. Many of the workers hired to construct the rail line settled near the rivers and the tracks at what became the villages of Webbwood, Massey and Walford (Station). Webbwood and Walford were both named for early settlers, while Massey commemorated a CPR employee. In all three communities the train station became a congregating point.

Local government began in 1893 with the formation of the townships of Salter, May and Harrow. Massey was the prominent village in that municipality until 1 April 1904, when it secured incorporation and separated itself. On 26 May 1906, Webbwood was incorporated as a town. One of the foremost of the mayors was Barbara Hanley, elected in 1936, Canada's first woman mayor. She was re-elected 11 times.

Highway 17 connects all three of these population nodes, with Webbwood (pop. 600), the most easterly of the three, located nine kilometres from the junction of Highways 17 and 6. Highway 17 is the main street, and the former town has sewer services but depends on wells for drinking water. Webbwood boasts a seniors' residence, a community seniors' centre, an elementary school, a fire hall, a public library, a public boat launch onto the Spanish River, churches, a motel, restaurants, a general store and a post office. South of the highway is a bridge over the Spanish River leading to what residents call "the back road" to Espanola, where many work and shop.

Massey (pop. 1,632 in 2016; 1,606 in 2021) is 16 kilometres west of Webbwood and like Webbwood, Highway 17 is its main street. This town has no septic systems but does have a water treatment plant. The Sable River Golf and Country Club, at the eastern end of Massey, has a nine-hole course. The usual facilities for recreation and education are supplemented by an arena, community centre and pioneer museum, but especially by Chutes Provincial Park just north of town with excellent hiking (trails partly accessible). The Aux Sables River traverses the eastern limits and a beach, commonly called "The Mouth," where the Aux Sables empties into the Spanish River is a much-enjoyed picnic and swimming spot. The bridge over the Spanish River forms a T-intersection with a road, which to the east leads into farming areas and joins the back road to Espanola, while to the west the road leads to the First Nations community of Sagamok Anishnawbek. The former CPR line continues to parallel Highway 17 and the old railway station still exists, but trains rarely stop there. Massey has an annual marathon recognized as a qualifier for the Boston Marathon. For over a decade metal sculptures of horses, moose, motorcycles, mermaids graced the streets but disappeared around 2020, dispersed to other places; for example, the mermaid is in West Nipissing (Sturgeon Falls).

Walford (Station), located along Highway 17, 12 kilometres west of Massey, is now essentially a series of houses. Unlike the two easterly nodes, the main residential area is south of Highway 17, although some development along the highway includes a motel, restaurant, fire hall and community centre.

By 2005, a few Mennonite families had moved to Sables-Spanish River from southern Ontario. They purchased land at the western end of the municipality,

> **Did you know?**
>
> Margaret Clipperton of Walford submitted this story to the CBC by Margie Kring about her meeting with a very special person on the occasion of the Prince of Wales' Canadian tour in 1919. Margie called her piece, "The Visitor."
>
> It was September 3, 1919, and the Prince of Wales was to visit the area. I was at home alone, when two men came to my door. One of them was wearing a blue and white striped suit and he had a red and white dotted handkerchief in his pocket. He said he was thirsty, so I gave him a drink of water. My visitor asked, "Are you going down to the train to shake hands with the Prince of Wales?" "Oh, no," I replied. "He'll greet so many people that his arm will be tired." He asked me where he could find a quiet place to take a walk, so I sent him back to Therriault's on the Sugar Lake Road.
>
> A little while later he came back to me. "Hey English," he said (I had an English accent), "didn't you go to see the Prince of Wales yet?" I told him I hadn't, so he said to me, "Come on. We'll take a walk and go see him." He seemed determined that I should see the Prince, so I agreed. I grabbed my camera, and we went out the front door. I paused just long enough to pick a rose for his lapel. When we got to the station, he put one foot on the track and one on the platform and said, "Would you care to take a picture of the Prince of Wales?" I looked around, "Where is he?" "I am the Prince of Wales," he smiled. "You!" "Hey, English!" Come and shake hands with the Prince of Wales. My arm isn't all that tired. I don't want you to freeze up because you know who I am. Just be your natural self." He presented me with a whole bouquet of roses and I took a picture of him at the station. I still have it to this day.
>
> I was sixteen at the time and guess I expected the Prince of Wales to be wearing a uniform. Maybe that's why I didn't recognize him.

and settled in Birch Lake, and near Walford in Victoria Township, as well as River Road, Seldom Seen Road and across the Spanish River towards Lee Valley. Although the Mennonites have been known to wear traditional clothing, travel by horse and buggy, and eschew many modern conveniences, they do use electricity and motorized farm equipment, and have developed a market in locally produced foods.

This municipality contains more than 30 lakes and rivers. In summer, swimming at the many beaches, camping throughout the wilderness area, fishing and birdwatching are the order of the day, while in winter, cross-country skiing, skating, ice fishing and snowmobiling take over. Among other activities readily available are horseback riding, canoeing, hiking and picking strawberries at a local farm.

The Chutes Provincial Park, located

Prince of Wales
(Credit: Margret Clipperton)

> **Did you know?**
> In addition to having Canada's first woman mayor, Webbwood is the birthplace of Dr. Theodore Drake, the co-inventor of the popular baby food, Pablum. Further, the first provincial police officer in Ontario to die in the line of duty, Constable William Irving, in 1904, was serving in Webbwood.

north up the Tote Road in Massey along the Aux Sables River, has 130 campsites, 56 of which have electricity, and is within walking distance of Massey. In concert with the township, Chutes Park has developed a water trail on the Aux Sables River offering class three and four rapids for kayaking.

The township promotes the Annual Friendly Massey Marathon and the Annual Spanish River Half Marathon the third week of July. The Marathon is an accredited race and is a qualifier for the Boston Marathon. The Massey Agricultural Fair, held each year on the last full weekend of August for over one hundred years, is the longest-running and largest fall fair in Northern Ontario. It attracts people from across the country.

The February Massey Winter Carnival presents both indoor and outdoor family-centred activities. Local gardens are featured at the Massey and Area Museum's Annual Garden Tour in July. The Massey-Walford Horticultural Society Flower Show is held in August at the Royal Canadian Legion in Massey. Also in August, the Massey and Area Museum presents local artists in its Annual Art Show. In September, the Webbwood Historical Society hosts a Fiddling Competition. During fall several craft shows are held, the highlight being the Christmas Tea at the Walford Community Hall.

Although not a part of the municipality, residents of the First Nations community of Sagamok Anishnawbek regularly interact with people and facilities in Sables-Spanish River. Many township residents attend the weekly bingo at Sagamok. This community also hosts the Sagamok Anishnawbek Annual Pow Wow Celebration on the second weekend in July, at the Sagamok Spiritual Grounds.

Resources
Roy Beaudoin, *Webbwood: The First Hundred Years, 1891–1991* (Carp: Gai-Garet Publishing, 1990).

Sault Ste. Marie

Two border communities share the name Sault (pronounced "Soo" though the original French would be "so") Ste. Marie: one in Ontario and one across the St. Mary's River in Michigan. "Sault" is the French word for jump, and the rapids defining the place on the river give the impression of jumping waters. The Ojibwe called it "Bawating" ("place of the rapids") and the confluence of waters served for hundreds of years as an Indigenous meeting place where goods were traded during the whitefish drying season.

Most land acknowledgements for Sault Ste. Marie state that Sault Ste Marie is the traditional territory of the Anishnaabeg, namely the Garden River and Batchewana First Nations, on lands protected by the Robinson-Huron Treaty of 1850.

With a population of about 65,000 (increased 0.5% between 2001 and 2006 but declined to 66,923 in 2016; 64,923 in 2021), the Canadian Sault is significantly larger than its American counterpart. First Nations (Anishnawbek) people account for over 9,500 with many in the nearby Garden River (east) and Batchewana-Rankin (east of Sault; west of Garden River) territories. The Garden River community has its own police, wellness centre and parks, and has a growing population of 3,164 band members and an on-reserve population of 1,292 in 2021 (half under the age of 30). The community centre is symbolically in a round log building, representing the interconnectedness of all beings while the circular shape represents goodness. Batchewana-Rankin has its own police force and an arena with a banquet/bingo hall.

Visible minorities number about 1,000. Almost 55,000 claim English as their mother tongue, compared to 2,000 who cite French and 5,300 other languages. A slight majority are Roman Catholics, with nearly as many Protestants, and a tiny minority are Orthodox, Jewish and Muslim. Ethnically, Italians have been the most notable minority group, well represented in local construction firms and restaurants.

In recent years, Sault Ste. Marie has been coping with serious economic challenges. The biggest single employer, Algoma Steel, has struggled with bankruptcy and undergone numerous changes of ownership and downsizing. St. Mary's Paper Limited, with 400 employees, closed in 2011. A call centre has disappeared. Tighter border controls since 2011 and the pandemic have discouraged American tourist visits. Some French Canadians and conference organizers boycotted the Sault after city council voted early in 1990 that English was the city's only official language. The stance was reversed in 1994 and in 2010 the mayor apologized.

Today, the largest employers are Algoma Steel, with 2,846 employees in 2023; the Sault Area Hospital—centralized to one location north of the city—and the Algoma District School Board, each with over 1,850; and Ontario Lottery and Gaming Commission, with 1,400. Secondary industries include Tenaris Algoma Tubes, with 550 employees. Francis H. Clergue, an entrepreneur from Maine, founded Algoma Steel in 1902, and Dofasco owned it from 1988 to 1991. A strike in 1990 led Dofasco to abandon ownership, and before 2005, when the company again became profitable, it twice needed bankruptcy protection. In 2007, India's Essar Group purchased Algoma for US$1.63 billion. In 2019, it returned to its original name with local owners. Tenaris produces steel pipes. Both federal and provincial governments operate forestry research institutes. The casino and the Lottery and Gaming Commission of the province have helped diversify the economy. In addition, three centres of postsecondary education improve employment possibilities: Sault College of Applied Arts and Technology, Algoma University, and Shingwauk Kinoomaage Gamig, a centre for First Nations studies federated with Algoma University. In remembrance of the residential school at Shingwauk, the site has received a National Historic Site designation.

Apart from the industrial area near the International Bridge, Sault Ste. Marie is most noticeable for its waterways. The renovated waterfront with Roberta Bondar Marina and Roberta Bondar Park and Pavilion, named after Canada's first female astronaut, who came from the Sault, provides regatta and festival spaces. The annual winter carnival, Bon Soo, was held there then moved to Bellevue Park for more space, but post-COVID-19, has been moved to the newly restored Canal District. The fishing derbies, concerts, and summer and fall festivals continue at Bondar Park. The lengthy riverside walkway, the Boardwalk, passes a mix of commercial, public,and residential buildings. It has some commemorative and comical statues and receives favourable comments from most visitors. A 24-kilometre hub trail for biking and hiking traverses much of the central city and connects the waterfront to other neighbourhoods.

Bellevue Park occupies an attractive site beside the St. Mary's River in the city's east end. The park offers a delightful spot for picnics, children's play, and waterfront walking, including on a breakwater for the yacht club.

Near the bridge linking the two countries at the narrowest rapids, Parks Canada manages the Canadian canal, which links lakes Huron and Superior, as a National Historic Site. When it opened in 1895, the Sault Canal enabled commercial vessels to sail on an all-Canadian water route from Montreal into Lake Superior. The canal represented the latest technology, including the world's longest lock and the first electrically powered engine gates. The Sault Canal closed in 1987 when the federal government decided that modernization costs were excessive, but it reopened under the jurisdiction of Parks Canada in 1998. The former administrative and personnel buildings at the canal offer the best examples of Victorian stone

Sault Ste. Marie skyline

architecture in Northeastern Ontario. The mechanical workings of the lock system are well explained by signage and displays. Nowadays, commercial ships use the wider American locks; pleasure craft use the Canadian locks. Lock and waterway tours are major attractions, as is the walkway along the river, especially for birding. The locks too are the site of festivals, especially ones celebrated in common with the American community, such as the Bridgewalk, halted by the pandemic, but returned in 2022.

Sault Ste. Marie has many other attractions for residents and tourists. At the east end of the downtown, within a few blocks of each other, are the Canadian Bushplane Heritage Centre (referred to as the Bushplane Museum; www.bushplane.com) and the Ermatinger Clergue National Historic Site. The latter consists of the Old Stone House and the Clergue Block House. The Bushplane Museum contains replicas of the planes used in fighting forest fires since the 1920s and aircraft crucial to opening the northern part of the province. Videos and simulators engage children as does the ability to enter the cockpits and feel the controls. The Old Stone House is the oldest stone house in Canada west of Toronto. Built between 1808 and 1812 by descendants of Swiss immigrants, the Ermatinger family, its contents offer insights into living conditions in the era of the fur trade. It escaped unscathed during the War of 1812, when battles raged on the streets of both the American and Canadian Saults. The Clergue BlockHouse served as a powder magazine for the North West Company, and in the late nineteenth century, industrialist Francis H. Clergue purchased it and converted it into a home. When he moved to a more luxurious mansion in 1902, he used the Block House as an office. After Clergue left Sault Ste. Marie, others lived there until a fire partially destroyed it in 1974. In 1995, St. Mary's Paper Limited, owners of the land that the Block House occupied, insisted that it needed the site and asked that the building be moved or demolished no later than 30 July 1996. After a study indicated no other options existed, the Block House was relocated to the Ermatinger property. Today, the bottom part of the building contains exhibits from the days of the fur trade. Upstairs, visitors can see furnishings from the late nineteenth and early twentieth centuries, the era of Francis H. Clergue.

An interesting use for an old commercial building is The Loft, housed since 2021 in the completely renovated attic of the former offices of the power company near the Sault canal. Run by the Algoma Conservatory of Music, it contains a high-tech recording studio and a charming venue for performances. The sound quality is simply excellent in a space that can accommodate 180 people.

Residents and tourists can also visit the Sault Ste. Marie Museum at the corner of Queen and East streets, which once served as a post office. It offers displays of the lifestyle in the late nineteenth century, from furniture to dentistry, as well as a fine collection of historic photos, including of notable military contributors from the Sault. Outside is a memorial informing about the internment of "enemy aliens" during World War I. Most were innocent immigrants from the Austro-Hungarian Empire.

In fall, the main tourist attraction is the Agawa Canyon rail tour offered by a private company, Watco using the Algoma Central Railway (ACR) tracks. Tourists can appreciate the scenery, which is particularly spectacular in late September to early October as the leaves change colours. The train traverses almost mountainous terrain on its way through the Agawa Canyon. The train station was recently relocated to the Canal District, a tourist area featuring restaurants and event spaces, near the locks. Also, north about 70 kilometres is the Canadian Carver, a family-owned business known for the animal carvings done on site as well as Indigenous crafts such as moccasins. A local landmark and highway stopping point, it closed after 40 years during the pandemic. It has reopened under the ownership of the Garden River First Nation Economic Development Corporation which intends to continue the high level of crafts sold previously, counselled by the previous owners.

Closer to the International Bridge sits a historic relic, a small canal. The Canadian Sault was the regional headquarters of the North West Company (NWC), a fur-trading company based in Lachine on Montreal Island from 1780 until 1821. The NWC built a canal so that fur-laden canoes could bypass the rapids and move between Lake Superior and Lake Huron. American invaders destroyed the canal during the War of 1812, but a symbolic lock remains as a reminder of that era. The waterfront walkways from the Parks Canada site lead past it.

Recreation possibilities are strong in the area. North on Highway 17, 35 kilometres east of Heyden is Searchmont (www. searchmont.com), a downhill ski resort in winter and a magnet for mountain bikers in warmer weather. The extensive runs are Northeastern Ontario's premier ski hills. Close by, the Trans-Canada Voyageur hiking trail winds its way through the Algoma Hills, which also have many kilometres of well-groomed cross-country ski trails, specifically the trails at Stokely in the Algoma Highlands Conservancy (algomahighlandsconservancy.org). More cross-country skiing and hiking (35 kilometres) are available at the northeast edge of the city at Hiawatha Highlands Park.

The Hiawatha park operated by the regional conservation authority includes a walkway beside Crystal waterfall, a small lake, and marked trails for a circular route. Another conservation area with trails and wetlands is in the western end of the city from which one can continue to many beaches on Lake Superior. Further, Sault Ste. Marie boasts four arenas (the newest is known as the Green for Life [environmental firm] Memorial Gardens), a public art gallery, two boat marinas, convention facilities, two curling rinks, three golf courses (two high level), sixteen fitness clubs, three outdoor sports complexes, one indoor complex with state-of-the-art turf, swimming pools, twenty-two sports fields and seventy-four city parks.

Sault Ste. Marie has a long and complicated history. Ojibwe First Nations held multi-tribe gatherings at the river's rapids for celebrations and trade. Fish was an important staple food which was, in dried form, traded with neighbouring areas. French fur traders and missionaries had outposts on the American shore in the second half of the seventeenth century and the first half of the eighteenth. The Treaty of Paris (1763) transferred New France to British jurisdiction, and Europeans continued to live in what is now Sault Ste. Marie, Michigan. After the U.S. War of Independence, the boundary settlement of 1783 and Jay's Treaty of 1794 forced British subjects who wished to remain British to relocate on the Canadian side, hence, Sault Ste. Marie, Ontario, has been home to Europeans since 1796. A battleground during the War of 1812, its central core has streets whose names reflect the British tradition: Queen and Wellington (the British General known for defeating Napoleon I).

The Ojibwe of the Garden River First Nations Reserve remember their role fighting the French during the War of 1812. Their assistance was acknowledged by the British. According to some reports, their chief, Shingwauk (also written as Shingwaukonce and Shingwaukonse), fought at the Battle of Queenston Heights and personally killed the American who fatally injured the British Commander, General Sir Isaac Brock. British authorities awarded Shingwauk a medal for his contribution to the defence of Upper Canada. Before the Robinson-Huron Treaty of 1850, the Ojibwe controlled land around Sault Ste. Marie as far east as Echo Bay, and Shingwauk envisioned a large Ojibwe homeland there. British authorities rejected it. Ironically, most of the area had earlier been granted to the French and Métis members of the Corp of Voyageurs, who had fought in the War of 1812 to keep the territory British.

International tensions occasionally affected Sault Ste. Marie. In 1838, in the aftermath of a rebellion in Upper Canada, as Ontario south of the Arctic-Atlantic Watershed was known then, shots aimed at the Canadian Sault were fired from Fort Brady, a U.S. Army base in the American Sault. In 1870 and 1885, Louis Riel—a Manitoba Métis—led rebellions against British authority around Winnipeg. A refusal by U.S. authorities to allow the Canadian militia to use the locks on the Michigan side, functional since 1855, prompted the government to build a canal parallel to the American locks. Construction began in 1887, two years after the opening of a branch line of the Canadian Pacific Railway (CPR) from Sudbury.

Soon after the rail line arrived, Francis Clergue envisioned Sault Ste. Marie as a source of hydro power and financial gain. He completed previously failing projects to harness electrical power generated by the rapids. Later Clergue, who supported Ontario's Liberal government, led by Premier Sir George Ross (1899–1905), undermined that government when it became clear that a ship owned by Clergue's Great Lakes Corporation, the Minnie M., had transported more than 20 U.S. citizens to cast ballots in a provincial by-election. Clergue's industrial empire—eventually an integrated monopoly of hydro power, lumbering interests, shipping and mineral refining based on mines near Wawa and Sudbury—lasted a generation and set the pattern of Sault Ste. Marie's development for a century. James Dunn continued Clergue's pattern of obtaining state aid for the enterprises from the 1930s to the 1950s.

Religion proved to be a significant aspect of life in the Canadian Sault. Members of the militia, waiting 13 days in 1866 for attacks by Fenians (who did not attack), dealt with the problem of boredom when someone discovered a cask of communion wine left by a priest. More seriously, both the Anglican and Roman Catholic churches chose Sault Ste. Marie as the site of their cathedrals for their respective dioceses in Northeastern Ontario south of the watershed. During Prohibition in the United States (1919–1933), the Canadian Sault became an entrepôt for Canadian smugglers. Roman Catholic Bishop David Scollard (1905–1934) dismissed one priest who purchased liquor from Montreal in kegs marked "Sublime Olive Oil." The Anglican Church operated a residential school for Ojibwe children, Shingwauk Hall, from 1873 until 1970. It is now a research centre focused on residential schools. In the 1920s, some Protestants supported the Ku Klux Klan as it intimidated the local Italian population, but the racist group had no further support and disappeared.

Sault Ste. Marie became a town in 1887, the year the CPR reached the community. It became a city in 1912. Steelton, the working-class area north of the steel plant, became part of the city in 1918. Until its industrialization, aided by the world wars, the city generally remained a rough lumber, shipping and rail depot. Until well after World War II, Gore Street was an ethnic and cultural divide. Little Italy was to the west, as was French Town and the Finnish and the Ukrainian communities. Not until the 1950s did the first prominent Italian breach the divide and build a substantial house in the east end of the city, where English management clustered near the golf and country club. In 1965, the city was enlarged by the incorporation of Korah and Tarentorous townships.

As a border city, the Sault has a long military tradition. It has hosted militia or regular military units since the late nineteenth century. Like most places in Northeastern Ontario, it contributed a high proportion of men and women to both world wars. Like Manitoulin, the city intensively honours those contributions with monuments, cenotaphs and special places of remembrance scattered around the city. During World War II, the city's industrial plants were considered important to war production, especially the steel plants. Barrage balloons, meaning large helium-filled balloons, were tethered with steel cables around the plant. Ironically, in 1942 a windstorm tore loose the cables and some balloons escaped. The cables hit power lines and shorted out the electricity to the steel plants, shutting down production for more than two weeks.

In the last half century, major changes have occurred in education. In 1967, Algoma University College (AUC) opened as an affiliate of Laurentian University in Sudbury. Affiliate status meant that AUC's curriculum and standards fell under the jurisdiction of the Senate of Laurentian. Located since 1971 on the grounds of Shingwauk Hall, with a superb view across the St. Mary's River, AUC became Algoma University in 2008. What is now Sault College started as the Ontario Vocational College in 1965. With around 5,000 students it contributes to the local economy by supplying trained craftspeople.

Politicians from Sault Ste. Marie have played a prominent role in Ontario politics. Sir William Hearst, Conservative premier of Ontario from 1914 to 1919, was a resident, as was James Lyons, Ontario's Minister of Lands and Forests in the

Conservative government of George Howard Ferguson (1923–1930). In 1964, Arthur Allison Wishart became Ontario's attorney general in the Progressive Conservative cabinet of Premier John Robarts. In 1975, John Reginald Rhodes became Minister of Housing in the government of Progressive Conservative Premier William Davis. Russell Ramsay, his successor, served Davis as Provincial Secretary for Resource Development (1981–1982) and as Minister of Labour (1982–1985). When the New Democrats formed Ontario's government, Sault Ste. Marie MPP Bud Wildman served as Minister of Natural Resources and Minister responsible for Native Affairs (1990-1993), then as Minister of the Environment and Minister of Energy (1990-1995).

At the federal level as well, MPs from Sault Ste. Marie have held responsible positions. James Kelleher served as Minister of International Trade (1984-1986) and Solicitor General of Canada (1986–1988). As Minister of Trade, Kelleher had responsibility for negotiating the Canada-US Free Trade Agreement, which took effect in 1989 and later became the North American Free Trade Agreement. As Solicitor General, he directed the reorganization of the RCMP and the early years of the Canadian Security and Intelligence Service (CSIS), after surveillance in Canada was transferred from the former to the latter. Ron Irwin was Canada's Minister of Indian Affairs in Jean Chrétien's Liberal government from 1993 until 1997.

Nor have politicians been Sault Ste. Marie's only notables. Angelina Napolitano, an Italian immigrant born in 1883, won worldwide notoriety in 1911 when convicted of murder. Pregnant at the time of her trial, Napolitano's defence—that her husband had battered her—did not convince the jury, and the judge sentenced her to be hanged one month after the baby's birth. Following protests in Canada and abroad, the Canadian government commuted the sentence. The Esposito Brothers, Phil and Tony, were stars with the National Hockey League, and both played in the famous Canadian-Soviet hockey showdown in 1972. When Phil retired in 1981 after playing on three NHL teams, he was second only to Gordie Howe in terms of career goals and points.

Resources

Joseph E. Bayliss, *River of Destiny* (Detroit: Wayne State, 1965).

Ian Brown and Francis Heath, *The Ermatinger Family of Sault Ste. Marie* (Sault Ste. Marie: Creative Printing, 1985).

Aileen Collins, *Stories of the Past: 300 Years of Soo History* (Sault Ste. Marie, 1967).

Francis M. Heath, *Sault Ste. Marie: City by the River* (Burlington: Windsor Publishing, 1988).

Duncan McDowall, *Steel at the Sault: Francis H. Clerge, Sir James Dunn and the Algoma Steel Corporation, 1901–1956* (Toronto: University of Toronto Press, 1984).

William Newbigging, *Northern Soldiers: The History of the 49th Field Artillery Regiment, RCA* (Sault Ste. Marie: Regimental Senate of the 49th, 2021)

Steamers

Until the Industrial Revolution, travellers relied on sails for crossing oceans and large lakes, and on canals for navigating inland waterways. Technological progress during the nineteenth century offered faster, easier transportation options and some lakes and rivers of Northeastern Ontario were big enough for steamboats. Lake Nipissing, Lake Temiskaming, and the Ottawa River and even logging settlements around Lake Temagami profited from their use. All the Great Lakes were ideal, even if dangerous due to shoals, rocky islands and storms. Lighthouses along the North Shore of Lake Huron and around Manitoulin and parts of Lake Superior remind of those perils. Many northeastern communities, such as Killarney, Gore Bay, Algoma Mills and Wawa developed due to steamers.

Steamers arrived before railways. Factories elsewhere could build sections of the boats, which horses would drag through winter snow to the point of embarkation, where they would be assembled. The arrival of trains created a new role for steamers. Trains operated along predictable routes at predictable times. Steamers on adjacent waterways could haul goods or deliver passengers to depots along the tracks. In other words, the steamer services complemented the rail service and offered new opportunities for a less strenuous lifestyle.

Life aboard a steamer was difficult and until the 1920s passengers were more likely to be immigrants or workers than tourists. Most of the time, the weather was sufficiently cold that people had to remain inside, with the smell of coal dust, or even the coal dust itself. Fires were frequent, and if sea sickness and turbulent weather did not provide enough unpleasantness, the constant danger of the ship sinking and people on board drowning certainly did. The paddle steamer, *Waubuno*, linked Collingwood with Parry Sound and the French River from 1874 until 1878, and then sank, resulting in the loss of all aboard. The *Manitoulin* burned in Manitowaning Bay in June 1882, and her successor, the *Asia*, sank with substantial loss of life three months later near the mouth of the French River. The *City of Owen Sound* sank in the North Channel. Collisions were also a hazard, especially in the relatively narrow, fast-moving, often shallow St. Mary's River. Long absences from home, a requirement during the limited shipping season on the Great Lakes, were hardly conducive to a wholesome family life; yet the sailors and the entrepreneurs who financed steamers provided a lifeline so that residents of what is now Northeastern Ontario could receive food, mail and other essentials.

Until 1855, steamship service to what is now Northeastern Ontario was intermittent. *The Penetanguishene*, a sidewheeler owned by Charles Thompson of York (Toronto) and launched in 1833, made a couple of trips from Sturgeon Bay in Simcoe County to Sault Ste. Marie and St. Joseph Island, but by 1836 her owner decided that northern trips were not economical and reverted to sail. Even the initial exports of copper from Bruce Mines depended on sail for transport. However, in 1846 the *Gore*, also owned by Thompson, inaugurated a run from Sturgeon Bay to Manitoulin Island and then onward through the North Channel to Bruce Mines and Sault Ste. Marie. In 1847, the government extended mail service to those points, and the resulting subsidy allowed the *Gore* to visit twice each month, and weekly during the warm months from 1850, by which point the *Gore* was also making three trips into Lake Superior each summer. Advertisements claimed that the *Gore* could provide transportation from Toronto via Sault Ste. Marie to Lake Superior within 60 hours. In 1852, Thompson's larger *Belle of Buffalo* replaced the *Gore* but quickly came to grief. From May until the end of the 1852 shipping season, the *Detroit* travelled the northern route, but by 1853 the *Kaloolah* (known as the *Collingwood* from 1856) provided ongoing service.

Manitoulin Island, the North Channel, and Sault Ste. Marie became considerably more accessible in 1855. That year, the Ontario, Simcoe and Huron Railway (now part of Canadian National) began to transport passengers to Collingwood. There they could board a steamer for points north and west. Thomas relocated his southern terminus from Sturgeon Bay to Collingwood, and in 1857 leased the *Collingwood* to the railway. Also in 1857, the Toronto-based North West Transportation Company sent the *Rescue* from Collingwood to Fort William (now Thunder Bay) at least five times, and by 1856 and 1857 the Rescue and the paddle steamer, *Ploughboy*, managed by rival E. M. Carruthers of Toronto, were competing for traffic to Sault Ste. Marie. While the Gore was only 125 feet long, the Collingwood and the Ploughboy exceeded 170 feet. In 1873, after train service reached Owen Sound, Great Northern Transit sent the *Silver Spray* and the *William Seymour* to Sault Ste. Marie.

Financial and legal problems forced the Rescue to remain in Collingwood during 1861, by which point the *Ploughboy* was too decrepit to go beyond Sault Ste. Marie. However, the ill-fated *Waubuno* competed with the *Silver Spray* on the route to Sault Ste. Marie in the early 1870s. The *Waubuno*'s successor, the Northern Belle, briefly had the route to herself, but as of 1880 had to compete with the *F.B. Maxwell*. In the 1880s and 1890s, the *Wiarton Belle* linked Owen Sound and Manitoulin Island.

Throughout the 1880s, steamers provided service to Lake Superior, service that continued even with the opening of trans-continental rail service in 1885. The Great Northern Transit Company, co-owned by William Beatty Jr. of Parry Sound, owned the doomed *Manitoulin* and *Asia*, as well as the *Atlantic* (700 tons) and the *Pacific* (1,000 tons), which served this same route. The *Spartan* and the *Magnet*, sidewheelers owned in Owen Sound, connected Owen Sound with Algoma Mills.

Chief Commanda, on North Bay's waterfront

Between 1888 and 1890, the Owen Sound Steam Transit Company provided almost daily service to Algoma Mills and Sault Ste. Marie. Rail transit offered year-round service, but during the shipping season, steamer costs were lower, especially as Sault Ste. Marie and communities along the North Channel were not situated on the CPR's main line. In competition with the CPR, the Owen Sound Steam Transit Company had three ships: the *Cambria, the Champion*, and the *Carmona*. By 1888, one steamer was usually in the North Channel every day. In 1891, the North Shore Navigation Company launched the *Kathleen* (renamed the *City of London* the following year), which sailed to Algoma Mills. A sister ship, the *City of Midland*, joined her in 1892; and five years later, the North Shore Navigation Company added the *City of Collingwood* (1,400 tons) and the *City of Midland* (1,000 tons) to the Sault route. Great Northern Transit of the White Line dispatched its *Majestic* (1,000 tons), which briefly sailed from the Bruce Peninsula to the North Channel, until 1898 when the *Collingwood* and the *Majestic* were transferred to Lake Superior. That same year, fire ended the *Pacific's* career. As the century ended, Collingwood's Northern Navigation Company continued to send numerous ships to the area.

The first steamboat on Lake Nipissing, the *Inter Ocean*, was hauled in sections from Chapman's Landing along Nipissing Road to the water's edge. On 8 November 1893, another steamer, the *John Fraser* (built by the Fraser Lumber Company), burned and sank with the loss of most on board. Nobody could survive in the frigid waters, but the alternative was to remain aboard the *John Fraser* and burn. That event was the most devastating shipping disaster in the history of Lake Nipissing. During the 1920s and 1930s, lumber companies downsized, and steamers like the *Aletis*, the *Chief Commanda*, and the *Chief Commanda II* found other roles. They transported groceries and other essentials from North Bay across Lake Nipissing to water access resorts and cottages on the French River. They also transported passengers who simply enjoyed the ride and threw bread to the gulls as they escaped the city's heat, or who wanted to dance on the moonlight cruises.

The first steamboat to reach Temagami, the *Marie*, arrived in 1902. The *Marie* served on Lake Temagami, which is much smaller than Lake Nipissing; she was a mere 33.5 feet in length, double the size of a normal canoe, and weighed 3.74 tons. The *Marie* arrived intact, pulled through the snow by 16 horses.

In 1903, the year of the building of the Temiskaming and Northern Ontario Railway from North Bay to the Little Clay Belt, entrepreneur Dan O'Connor launched the O'Connor Steamboat Company Limited, subsequently relabelled the Temagami Steamboat and Hotel Company. In 1905, two more steamboats arrived, the *Spry*, with capacity for 10 passengers, and the *Wanda*, with space for 30. O'Connor erected Temagami's first resort, the Ronnoco Hotel, to house steamboat passengers during their stay.

Steamer service continued well into the twentieth century, but its importance diminished. As train service improved, roads and highways became available and increasing numbers of people owned cars, steamers became less practical. Weather limited the number of months when they could operate, and trucks could carry goods relatively short distances from source to destination without any unloading and reloading along the way. Passenger service from Simcoe County via Sault Ste. Marie to Fort William remained viable until completion of the missing stretch of Highway 17 northeast of Lake Superior in the early 1960s. Diesel gradually replaced steam on the upper Great Lakes, as the large diesel ships could travel longer routes, usually with wheat from the prairie west to overseas markets. Today, steamer use is reserved for tourism.

Resources
Andrea Gutsche, et al, *The North Channel and St. Mary's River. A Guide to the History* (Toronto: Lynx, 1997).
W. R. Wightman, "The Canadian Steam Packet Service of the Upper Lakes," *Inland Seas XLLVI* (Winter 1990), 248-264.

St. Joseph Island

St. Joseph Island is at the mouth of the St. Mary's River and a short drive south of Highway 17 along Highway 548 between Desbarats and Echo Bay. Human habitation has been traced to the 17th century though when First Nations spread into the island from the north shore is unclear. They were Ojibwe, Odawa and Potawatomi of Algonquin ancestry. From the mid-17th century, the island became a stopping point for French explorers, fur traders and missionaries. The British gained control after the Seven Years War in 1763.

In the 1870s the island contained one-third of all of Algoma District's 54 miles of roads. Today Highway 548 encircles the island, which at its south end has a national historic park at the site of Fort St. Joseph (1796-1812). Beside the fort is a bird sanctuary. Connecting these destinations with the island's two communities, Richards Landing and Hilton Beach, are well-paved but lightly trafficked roads over gentle hills, perfect for bicycling. Campgrounds and motels are available, and the towns have restaurants that provide fresh fish from Lake Huron.

One of the island's exports is maple syrup, and producers include First Nations. Another is pudding stone, whose bright colours of small rocks embedded in larger differently coloured rock make it attractive to jewelers. In the mid-nineteenth century, English settlers gave the stone that name because it resembled boiled suet pudding.

Throughout the calendar year, St. Joseph Island hosts a range of activities. February has a ski loppet and an ice fishing derby. April is the month for a maple syrup festival and a maple syrup soirée. May features the Mountain Maple Run/Walk, in which participants run or walk on cross-country trails. In June, the St. Joseph Island Soap Box Derby, a barn dance and a coureur-de-bois rendezvous occur. On the last Saturday of June, a Canadian Arts Festival at an open-air gallery is held at Richards Landing, and each Saturday from mid-June to mid-September an open-air market operates at Hilton Beach.

Summer is particularly active Canada Day (July 1) brings the Canada Day Tractor Parade and a host of picnics and fireworks. July is the month for the Annual

Northern Riders Horse Show, the annual Arts at the Dock (multimedia art show) at Hilton Beach Marina, the Hilton Beach Summer Festival, and community nights at both Richards Landing and Hilton Beach. In July and August, a Wednesday evening concert series takes place at Hilton Beach. The first week of August, Algoma's artists display their paintings at the Doug Hook Art Show at Richards Landing. On the third weekend of August, also at Richards Landing, a corn fest includes runs and walks of both five and ten kilometres. Other August events include a Museum Village Collectors Day, a Horticultural Society Flower and Vegetable Show, and the St. Joseph Island Plowing Match at Richards Landing, plus a sailing regatta off Hilton Beach. A triathlon, which involves swimming, cycling and running, attracts participants from small children to adults. In summer, the permanent population of roughly 2,300 (in 2021) swells to between 4,000 and 5,000. Autumn events include agricultural fairs, a self-guided tour of local artisan studios, and a Giant Christmas Craft Show.

Permanent attractions of St. Joseph Island include Adcock's Woodland Gardens (acres of flower gardens and ponds at U line and 5th Sideroad), the House of History (a historical museum at Hilton Beach), the "Over the Rainbow" Doll Museum (two kilometres from Richards Landing), and the St. Joseph Island Museum (five kilometres south of the bridge going onto the island).

First Nations people had been living on St. Joseph Island for thousands of years before the first European settlers located there in 1796, starting the process of encroachment and displacement. By then, French, British, and American fur traders, missionaries, and soldiers had lived at Michilimackinac, at that point on the Upper Michigan Peninsula where Lakes Huron and Michigan meet, or on Mackinac Island in Lake Huron. By the boundary settlement of 1783, both the peninsula and Mackinac Island became US territory, although the British soldiers and those civilians wanting to remain British subjects stayed until Jay's Treaty of 1794 forced them to relocate to St. Joseph Island. Accompanying the soldiers were civilians, who established a small community of their own, right beside the fort. Thomas Duggan, the storekeeper, managed his business on St. Joseph the way he had on Mackinac Island. Louis Dufesne, a French-Canadian blacksmith renowned for his competence, was among other early pioneers. Dr. David Brown, who arrived from Scotland around the turn of the century, is better remembered for his problems with the bottle than for his medical skills. The Askin family, Métis fur traders who lived on St. Joseph Island for two generations between 1796 and 1812, served as interpreters, as did other Métis.

Resources

Joseph and Estelle Bayliss, *Historic St. Joseph Island* (Cedar Rapids, Iowa: The Torch Press, 1938).

Mildred Hadden, et al, *The St. Joseph Island United Church Pastoral Charge History, 1878–2008* (Rains Homestead Century Farm: Sheep Skin Press, 2008).

Sudbury, City of Greater

From:
"The Girls are out to Bingo and the boys are getting' stinko
And we think no more of Inco on a Sudbury Saturday Night"
Stompin' Tom Connors, 1967
To:
"Science North and Dynamic Earth: Northern Ontario's most popular tourist destination"
—My Sudbury 2010

Though known as a mining and smelting centre, Sudbury started as a lumber camp and railway depot. At present it is a much more middle-class, than working-class, city. It has become the prime location for government, commerce, health and social services, higher and technical education, research and media in Northeastern Ontario. Located 380 kilometres north of Toronto, it is at the junction of major rail lines and highways (CPR and CNR, Trans-Canada Highway from Ottawa to Sault Ste. Marie, Highway 69/400 from Toronto, and Highway 144 to Timmins).

Proof of Indigenous occupation has been found southwest and northeast of the city. Two Ojibwe First Nations territories are present, Whitefish Lake to the southwest and Wanapitei to the east. On the south end of Long Lake, archeological excavations have shown habitation going back more than 8,000 years, though it seems none for the era 500 B.C. to 1000 A.D. The Whitefish Lake First Nations claim compensation is owed them for utilization of resources on their lands as well as for treaty monies. Though some Indigenous continue hunting and fishing traditions, most work and live in the urban area.

The rich mineral deposits discovered during the 1850s and confirmed during railway construction in the 1880s eventually turned out to be one of the world's largest deposits of nickel, iron, copper, gold, silver and platinum. Thus, mining and smelting mostly supported the city during the twentieth century, and the associated roast beds used to smelt the ore created a desolate environment for which Sudbury became

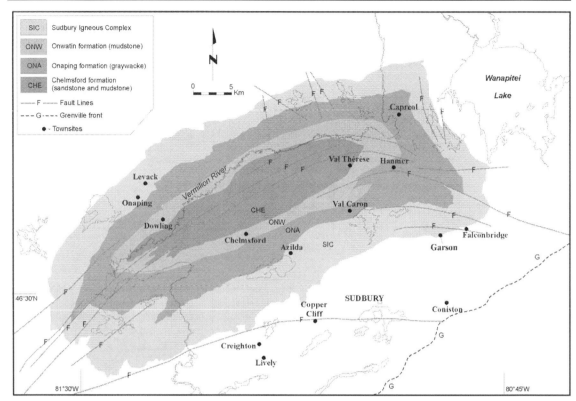

The Sudbury Basin: a 50 km long by 20 km wide meteor impact crater
(Credit: Léo L. Lariviére)

well known. Though many companies have changed and merged, two dominated until recently: International Nickel Company (Inco), now Vale, and Falconbridge, now Glencore. However, late development of refining and hardly any manufacturing meant that until very recently mining boom and bust cycles determined the city's history.

The most populated city in Northeastern Ontario, with 166,004 (in 2021) inhabitants, Sudbury is spread over a large area. It covers 3,627 square kilometres, which includes 330 lakes, and hence is the largest municipality in Ontario. The present City of Greater Sudbury was formed in 2001 by an amalgamation of surrounding towns and townships, some unincorporated. Many persons in the outlying areas still identify with the previous small lumbering, mining or rail centres, such as Lively, Naughton, Whitefish and Copper Cliff to the west, Onaping, Chelmsford, Dowling and Azilda to the northwest, Capreol, Skead and Falconbridge to the northeast, or Garson and Coniston to the east. Other organizational combinations have also existed due to outlying town amalgamations during the 1970s, so that some locals refer to Walden, Rayside-Balfour, Nickel Centre and Valley East, since those identifiers continue as town names on arenas and community centres. Sudbury also partly contains the world's largest lake in a city, Lake Wanapitei to the northeast.

Like most of the towns and cities of Northeastern Ontario, Sudbury emerged due to its geographic location, in this case because the CPR arrived at Lake Ramsey in 1883. Indeed, the village was renamed from the lumber camp Ste. Anne-des-Pins by a railway commissioner in honour of his wife's English hometown. What changed the lumber camp and railway depot into a mining centre was the geological composition of rocks exposed when blasting railway cuts. A CPR blacksmith, Tom Flanagan, noted many metals in 1883; soon many prospectors, such as the Murray brothers, Charles Crean and Thomas Frood—after whom mines would be named—were in the area staking claims of what most thought was copper or gold. By 1886, the first mine was operative under the direction of Samuel J. Ritchie. At the time, limited uses, mostly coinage, existed for nickel, but the discovery of how to separate it from other metals, use it as an alloy, and then apply it to armaments increased its value and markets. The Spanish-American War in 1898 demonstrated the superiority of nickel-plated armour on ships, and soon all navies demanded nickel-plating. However, in 1900 most employment in the Sudbury district remained in lumbering and railways. The pre-World War I naval race and then the war sky-rocketed the demand for nickel, which resulted in mining becoming the predominant industry in Sudbury.

The main theory for the existence of so many minerals is that about 1.8 billion years ago a meteorite hit the earth to create the Sudbury basin, an egg-shaped indentation, or irruptive, running southwest-northeast (about 50 kilometres long and 20 wide). The average annual value of ores mined and smelted is about five billion dollars.

The present city covers more than the basin, with the original town near its southern periphery at Lake Ramsey. Along the edges are most of the nickel mines, identified by their protruding six-to-eight-storey high headframes. Also marking the horizon are old industrial chimneys from the smelters. The main remaining smelters are at Copper Cliff and Falconbridge; Coniston closed in 1972. At 1,250 feet, the world's second tallest industrial smokestack stands beside the smelter in Copper Cliff. Known as the Inco Superstack, it has become one of the symbols identifying Sudbury to outsiders but has been decommissioned and may be taken down. Another symbol is the Big Nickel (a 30-foot replica of the 1951 Canadian nickel coin), built in 1963 near the Copper Cliff slag heap. Though some refining is done near Copper Cliff, most smelted ores are processed in southern Ontario and Wales.

Sudbury's mining history went through phases, starting with prospectors searching for outcroppings of minerals and staking claims. Men such as Rinaldo McConnell, James Stobie, and Aeneas McCharles—after whom more mines would be named—told of the many hardships involved in exploring the bush. These were very determined characters. For example, when he heard of the Sudbury finds, Stobie paddled a birchbark canoe from Bruce Mines to Algoma Mills (in Algoma District), and then walked more than a hundred kilometres to Sudbury. That was easy, given that previously, as an electoral returning officer, he had walked to Thunder Bay from Sault Ste. Marie in winter, some 700 kilometres.

Most of these men sold their claims to individuals or firms with the capital needed to develop mines and smelters, another phase of development, so in the late 1880s about 20 mining companies existed. The latter included Ritchie's Canadian Copper Company and the associated Orford Copper Company. They dominated mining in Sudbury, especially when Francis Clergue's mining and smelting enterprise ran into financial difficulties. In 1902, combining many of the mines, the International Nickel Company (Inco) was incorporated, though Ritchie would be shunted aside by the New York bankers. Inco became the dominant nickel company in the western world until the 1960s. In 1929 it acquired Mond, another major Sudbury producer selling mainly to European markets. For much of the period of Inco's dominance the only other major Sudbury company developed in the late 1920s, Falconbridge, agreed to divide markets with Inco.

To illustrate: between 1887 and 1902 Canadian Copper took out 71% of all ores mined in the area. In 1902 Inco smelted 60% of the world's nickel. During World War I, its position was consolidated though Mond grew as well. An important side issue was the demand for refining in Canada, especially once it became public knowledge that Inco continued to sell and ship nickel via submarines to Germany during wartime. The early 1920s brought a major mining downturn or bust with reduced armaments, but the 1930s brought renewed growth, especially as the fascist powers initiated a new arms race. Sudbury thus weathered the Great Depression better than many industrial cities, and many men, especially from the drought-stricken prairies, rode the rails to seek work in the nickel mines or the huge smelter built in 1929 in Copper Cliff.

Though nickel and copper became the dominant metals, for a short while Sudbury had Canada's most productive gold mine. From 1909 to 1917, at the southwest end of Long Lake, a rich vein provided the basis for a large mining operation which employed a double shaft, blasted a large glory hole and resulted in an arsenic contaminated area. When the main lode ended and no continuation could be found, operations ceased though many attempts have been made to find it since.

During World War II and the Cold War, economic growth continued at a rapid pace while two novel developments occurred. Since the United States wanted to limit its dependence on Inco, it also made agreements for purchases from Falconbridge, which by 1958 was producing over 50 million pounds of nickel annually. Second, both companies began to diversify and to look for other uses for nickel, as well as other sources of ores when Australian and American companies began to develop mines. Though mini recessions, such as that of 1957, and the ending of American stockpiling of nickel, cut into the companies' and the city's prosperity, generally growth and Inco dominance were the pattern until the 1960s. A few nickel statistics

Sudbury's Superstack, with rainbow
(Credit: Laurence Stevens)

illustrate Inco's and Sudbury's decline thereafter. In 1950, Inco produced 247 million pounds of the 260 total Canadian output with about 60 million in the Communist bloc. By 1970, Inco stood at 531 million pounds out of the 1,220 Canadian total, with about 370 from the Communist bloc. New Caledonia, Australia, and others had moved from 10 to 230 million pounds, from nil to 180 and from 3 to 299 respectively. By the recession of the early 1970s, both Inco and Sudbury would feel the downturn. Though Inco would recover to make its highest profits ever during the mid-1980s, the city suffered because of the workforce reduction and the lack of other industries or major services.

The people of Sudbury reflect Canada's diversity in terms of self-identified groups promoting their heritage and culture. At present almost 5,000 First Nations people live in Sudbury with another 5,000 identifying themselves as Métis, together forming about 6.4% of the population; the fastest growing segment. The Native Friendship Centre seeks to help urban integration and Laurentian University offers Native Studies and proclaims itself tri-cultural. Technical colleges too have special programs involving First Nations. Whitefish Lake First Nation is an enclave in the amalgamated city. The population is about 1,000, some of them living near Lake Panache and some of their lands leased to cottagers. Its territory was ceded by the Robinson-Huron Treaty, but borders and resource utilization remain in dispute.

The diverse ethnic make-up, though mostly European until the last three decades, and those groups' contributions to Sudbury's development district are symbolically represented by the" bridge of nations" on the main rail overpass into the city's core. Flags from more than 70 countries offer a colourful welcome and heritage identifier. Each of the countries identified by the flags pays for its own representation and the replacement of worn-out flags. The flags include the Franco Ontarian flag.

Though one quarter the population was francophone in 2016 and 2021, some 12,000 claim Italian, about 12,000 German, and about 7,000 Ukrainian or 5,000 Polish as their ethnic background (per 2021 census). Smaller numbers identify with Serbian, Croatian, or Scandinavian heritages (among others). They came in waves during the twentieth century for railway, lumbering and mining jobs. They provided skilled labour and, during the 1940s, were heavily engaged in the fight for union recognition, slowly leading to improved wages and working conditions. While a tiny minority of Chinese people were present from the town's beginnings, more Far Eastern, Caribbean and African people have settled in the last two decades. The 2021 census identified 1, 135 Chinese, 465 Filipino, 265 Pakistani, 210 Vietnamese, 910 African, 310 Hindu, 225 Punjabi, among others. The attempt, especially from the 1930s through the 1970s, to maintain the cultural heritage of Europeans is illustrated by the many ethnic festivals with traditional foods and costumes, which melded during the 1970s into a Canada Day multicultural food fair. Most of the European groups had social and sports organizations and built themselves a community hall, while the newer immigrants tend to have social and cultural clubs. Add the many halls built by the unions, plus the social clubs such as the legions, among others, and the result is that Sudbury is blessed with a multitude of meeting, and especially dancing, places. During the 1950s, some 30 dances with strict rules might be held on

Sidebar

Agnes Salo remembers the trip to downtown Sudbury from the Kelly Lake area in the west end of town (during 1940s):

"We then passed the brewery and next we turned right to Elm Street. Now, it seemed a far way to get to the Livery Stable. I'm not sure what street that was on, but I think it was around Drinkwater St. (maybe that is where the name came from?). We left the horse and buggy there for hay and water, and then we started walking.

Our first stop was the market on Borgia Street to see father. It was probably for money. I didn't like that walk because we had to pass the Queen's Hotel on the corner of Borgia and Elm Streets. There were always half-corked men loitering there, spitting, smoking and talking loud, sometimes calling to us. On the other end of Borgia Street was a dry goods store called Toronto Bargain Store. There was a fish market in the back of the market and the CNR station was on the left side. There was another way to the market which meant crossing the railway trestle and that was scary. I was afraid of falling down to the ground from the space between the ties!"

Saturday nights, in contrast to the wilder drinking in the 30 or so miners' pubs about which Stompin' Tom Connors sang.

Sudburians often claim that the city has been an especially tolerant place, accepting newcomers and integrating them. Those of Chinese or German descent would probably have a different perspective about certain eras, as would First Nations generally. After a minor incident involving young females soliciting in 1922, Chinese restaurateurs were forbidden to hire female waitresses. Attempts were even made to limit the Chinese to two restaurants. After World War II, German speakers experienced subtle discrimination and crude remarks about them as Nazis, and other groups were shunned during the Cold War, especially during labour struggles. Sociologists and First Nations researchers have found racial undertones in Sudbury similar to other parts of the country. Some so-called Red and White Finns and Red and White Ukrainians began to cross old social and ideological divides only in the late twentieth century.

Among the meeting places for Francophones, who have a larger presence in terms of population—during the 1950s they outnumbered those who spoke English in the metropolitan area—and institutions than the use of the French language would imply, was the Carrefour francophone with art gallery and meeting rooms. These groups now have a new striking home in the downtown at La Place des Arts, which includes the French theatre. The Théâtre du Nouvel-Ontario (TNO) is a small semi-professional group with a tradition of staging provocative and thoughtful productions. In social groups too, Francophones have a strong presence; the assertive generation of the 1970s challenged those who looked only to the Clubs Allouette and Richelieu. The students who had emerged out of the radical movements of the 1960s, or even those fundamentally conservative ones trained in Jesuit institutions such as the Université du Sudbury (since 1913 as Sacré Coeur College), sought symbols of identity such as a Francophone flag (now flown at city hall) and public use of their language and representation in the established institutions. Though divided in terms of tactics, all agreed on the need to reconfigure the French elite (from assimilationist to parity) and to reinforce minority rights and identity. The French tradition in Northeastern Ontario received a strong boost with the federal push for bilingualism and local French institutions such as Collège Boréal and the TNO, and especially the officially bilingual Université Laurentienne.

If the people of Sudbury are becoming more diverse, as immigration from Europe has almost ceased, so is its appearance. Greater Sudbury's core has little aesthetic unity, though perhaps its beginnings as a railway depot and mining camp help to provide perspective. However, attractive clusters of buildings date from the 1970s, such as the triangular city hall, theatre centre, St. Andrew's Place, the Bell Building, and St. Mary's Ukrainian onion-steeple church—all along the thoroughfare created by post-1967 urban renewal, formerly in or abutting the Borgia area. The YMCA complex with pool and Older Adult Centre seem to not have done any more for the regeneration of the downtown that urban renewal in the late 1960s and early 1970s did not accomplish. During the last decade, city council has repeatedly sought ways to reverse the decline and made financial investments with limited improvements.

A hallmark of the city is that major roadways from the downtown to the suburbs wind between rock outcroppings and lakes to give a different configuration than the mostly rectangular pattern so dominant in North America. New Sudbury, developed in the 1950s towards the northeast, and the urban sprawl in the flat agricultural lands of "the Valley" to the north, look much like the gridded suburbs elsewhere. Generally, the city can be visualized as a ball of twine with loose strings running in all directions. The economic undercutting of the city core started with the building of

Science North from Lake Ramsey

the New Sudbury malls during the 1960s, then the development of shopping centres at the south end (near the higher income area) and finally the stores and cinema complex on rocky land towards the east since the 1990s. However, the latter have also expanded Sudbury's market area to around 250,000, or half the population of Northeastern Ontario.

Outside the core, the spectacular lakeside Science North complex (from 1984) and Laurentian University's campus illustrate what can be achieved in a setting of rock and small trees. The largest lake, Ramsey, southeast of the core, has a three-kilometre walkway, passing beaches and pagoda overlooks. The walkway, partly a boardwalk cantilevered over the water's edge, leads to Science North. That two-part, mostly glass, building was constructed to represent snowflakes on rocks. An underground passageway connects the IMAX® Theatre and restaurant-entry building with a large cavern, above which the main structure is situated. A spiral walkway in the latter building leads past a major geologic fault and the suspended skeleton of a Fin whale. Physics, biology, human kinetics, astronomy, and a butterfly gallery are among the learning and exploring possibilities. Dynamic Earth, a Science North attraction, is located three kilometres west overlooking regreened slag heaps that now appear like rolling hillsides. It offers explanations of the city's geology and mining history. A special glassed-in elevator takes visitors seven storeys underground to experience the evolution of mining during different historical periods. Dynamic Earth is the home of the Big Nickel, Sudbury's iconic landmark, which was initially perched above a desolate spot overlooking slag heaps and within easy sight of the refinery chimneys pouring out pollution. Science North is partly funded by the provincial government, and it has drawn over seven million visitors in 25 years. It is the only science centre in the world with an in-house IMAX-film production unit and has produced four IMAX films and become known as a premiere hands-on science education centre.

Laurentian University (established in 1960) sits amid three lakes and may have one of Canada's most attractive campuses. How many universities have their own beach next to a private golf course and conservation area? With a strong sports tradition (basketball, volleyball, soccer) and excellent facilities (the only Olympic pool in the northeast, though in need of repairs), Laurentian offers many recreation-related programs. Its biological science programs have supported the regreening of the Sudbury area, while other science and engineering departments co-operate with the mining and refining industries in research activities. Its physics faculty attained international acknowledgement through the Sudbury Neutrino Observatory, a huge underground experiment: the equivalent of a 12-storey egg-shaped hole was created 7,000 feet below ground in the still-active Creighton Mine. Monitors installed on a sphere filled with heavy water trace neutrinos and better forecast the time the sun will continue to supply energy. The Centre for Rural and Northern Health Research—an enterprise undertaken with Lakehead University—has developed the university's health research capability and demonstrated the need for improved health resources in the north. In 2011, the Living with Lakes Research Centre, moved into a special ecologically designed building. The university's historians, film analysts, political scientists and commerce faculty (among others in both languages) research regional issues (pollution in context, homelessness, health resources), and provide advice and information to local institutions such as the media and business. Hence the university is one of the economic and cultural engines of the city, contributing at least $200 million annually. After teething difficulties in its first two decades, Laurentian University improved its reputation and grew to serve 9,000 full-and part-time students. Together with Lakehead University in Thunder Bay, Laurentian has been able to create a medical school, operative by 2003—the first in Canada in 30 years and adding about $100 million per annum to the regional economy. In 2011 a new school of architecture opened in the city's downtown as opposed to on campus. Like the medical school, the school of architecture is a common enterprise of the university and the city. However, despite predictions, it has not had much impact on the appearance of the downtown. Arguably Sudbury would not have been able to undertake the environmental renewal of the area, the international film festival since 1989, or the creation of schools of medicine and architecture without Laurentian's presence.

Similarly, the move of the Ontario Geological Survey to Sudbury in a large building on campus brought many well-paying jobs and relates directly to the potential of Earth Sciences at the university. However, until recently Laurentian University relied very heavily on government grants and received many special ones for its bilingual programs, illustrating the continued reliance on the public purse when the mining industry has downturns. Cambrian College and Collège Boréal too are significant factors in providing a skilled labour force and contribution to the diversification of the economy. Norcat, located at Cambrian, is known for its mining technology program and has become an Ontario Centre of Excellence. Both colleges have augmented Sudbury's cultural life, often in conjunction with faculty from the university.

An explanatory aside regarding Laurentian University is necessary. On 1 February 2021, the university filed for creditor protection. This shock came after the faculty association repeatedly had asked for precise information on the financial state of the university. Within three months nearly 200 persons (including over 100 faculty) were laid off without severance and the actual debt owed by the university, rumored to be $50 million, mounted to nearly $320 million. Soon the public discovered that the funds to create and run the numerous new programs and buildings added during the 2010s did not exist. Under the leadership of Dominic Giroux, president from 2009 to 2017, and a board of governors headed by Floyd Laughren, Michael Atkins and Jennifer Witty, the university had run up deficits, but proclaimed publicly that for seven years they had had balanced budgets. The Auditor General of Ontario's report examining the cause of the problem, underlined the long-standing financial mismanagement and underscored that the (ir)responsible presidents and boards of governors need not have gone to creditor protection. A much-reduced university, perhaps only a technical college, is emerging from the mess. So far not one administrator or leader has been held accountable, indeed, most, like Giroux, have moved to high positions in other public institutions. Confidence in the university has not been restored even with a new board of governors. With reduced programs and fewer choices, will students return to the level of previous numbers? So far, the answer is no, or at least ambivalent.

A major Sudbury attraction is Bell Park on the northwest edge of Lake Ramsey.

It has beaches, picnicking, play areas and floral displays. The three-kilometre walkway from Science North runs along its northwest shore. Just off the walkway is an aesthetic Mining Heritage Sculpture. Originally proposed in 1967 by Mine Mill's Ladies' Auxiliary in a very different form, it symbolizes building community but avoids acknowledging miners' deaths (probably influenced by the mining companies) as many northeastern communities' monuments do. Close by in the park is the Grace Hartman amphitheater (named for the first woman mayor appointed in 1966), which was reconstructed in 2011, losing its earlier charm. It is known for hosting Canada's longest continuous folk music festival, Northern Lights Festival Boréal. Since 1971 this festival has showcased established national performers from Valdy to Ian Tamblyn, Buffy Ste. Marie, Rita MacNeil, Ashley MacIssac, Murray McLaughlin, Bruce Cockburn, Jane Siberry (among many, many others), and locals who later gained national reputations such as Robert Paquette, Patti Cano, and Pandora Topp.

Festivals are weekly events during summer. Starting with Blues for Food in mid-June and culminating in Cinefest Sudbury—Canada's fourth largest international film festival, held during mid-September—they attract summer tourists. Some of the larger festivals include Canada Day, Italian Festival, Northern Lights/Festival Boréal, Dragon Boat Festival, Blueberry Festival, Greek Festival, Whitefish Lake Pow Wow, Garlic Festival, Summerfest, Ribfest, Jazz Festival and Mini Pow Wow held on National Indigenous Day, as well as weekly Bell Park Gazebo concerts. Similar to the above events, the East Indian community has an annual event celebrating the sub-continent's foods, dress and dancing.

The outlying towns continue their own festivals, including special ones such as the anniversaries of Copper Cliff 's Italian Club or Capreol Days. Even some areas in the city, such as Gatchell or Minnow Lake, have their own annual events with ball games and barbecues.

Mining Heritage Sculpture
(Credit: Michelin Tremblay)

The Sudbury winter festival offerings are sparser, though snowmobile races at Whitewater Lake, winter carnivals in surrounding communities, and skating lanes on Lake Ramsey draw many. The Pond Hockey Festival on the Rock is a very successful recent addition, with upwards of 80 teams competing in February on Lake Ramsey at the bay between Science North and the Sudbury Yacht Club. The major cross-country ski trails are in the Conservation Area, and at the University, west in Walden, northeast in Capreol and at Windy Lake.

The above-mentioned events have been in place for a long time. Recently added are Fierte Sudbury Pride week with parades and dances. The Indie Cinema presents many films on LGBTQI issues, including themed film festivals. Adding to the diversity is an annual Afro community celebration of both African and Caribbean culture at Bell Park.

An event that deserves mention is the Little Native Hockey League (LNHL). 2021 marked the 50th anniversary of this competition, which attracted teams from across the entire province, but mainly from the north. It moves to different communities yearly but has been hosted by Sudbury eight times since inception. In 2011 more than 110 teams competed at the Sudbury arena. Since 2018 the event was held in larger cities due to lack of sufficient accommodation for the size (4200 players in 2020) of the event but in 2023 it was hosted by Nipissing First Nation, near North Bay.

The major museums are mostly on the city's edge. Capreol has a well-structured railway museum partly in a heritage house, Copper Cliff has a log cabin museum focusing on life in the early twentieth century, Lively in Walden has the Anderson Farm showcasing immigrant agricultural life in the north, and Rayside-Balfour has one in the public library (a renovated firehall in Azilda). Using a former dairy farm owned by a Finnish family who came in 1901, the Anderson house and barn have been renovated to illustrate self-reliance well into the 1930s with looms and blacksmith forge. The Flour Mill Museum and Log Cabin are just north of the city centre in a predominately Francophone area. Hence the cabin shows Franco-Ontario lifestyles; the Heritage House had been the home of the foreman for the Ontario Flour Mill Company, which operated the huge silos next to a branch line of the railways that cut through "French Town."

Among the many attractions are the cultural institutions. The Art Gallery of Sudbury has one of Canada's most extensive collections (2,000 items), including numerous pieces from the Group of Seven and related local artists (such as Nelly Lowe and Bruno Cavallo). Situated in the Bell Mansion on a site overlooking Ramsey Lake, the stone heritage building is named after the lumber baron who donated for public use the property surrounding much of the west end of the lake that is now Bell Park. Plans are underway to build a new gallery and library but have not materialized. The city opened its new archives to the public in 2012 in the Edison Building in Falconbridge. The building was donated to the city by Falconbridge/Xstrata for a community archive. The city has two semi-professional theatres plus seasonal offerings from university, college and other amateur groups. The Sudbury Theatre Centre has a 289-seat building. The fine statues on the east side of the building are often thought to be dramatic figures but were the hundredth anniversary gift to the city by the Chamber of Commerce and represent early community figures. The theatre was part of the series of new buildings such as the city hall and provincial building, which improved the appearance of part of the downtown in the 1970s. The theatre group has been active since 1967 and its building opened in 1982.

The music scene in Sudbury is varied. The symphony is a mix of professional and amateur players among whom some independent sub-groups such as the Northern Brass stand out. Choral groups are mostly church-related, though the Bel Canto Chorus is a non-denominational singing group which has held twice-annual concerts for 40 years. The Jubilee Folk Ensemble seeks to support cultural development by combining a world-wide musical heritage with social issues. Northern Lights Festival Boréal hosts irregular coffee houses at private homes, where touring performers mostly present folk music. The Townhouse and Laughing Buddha offer diverse fare in eclectic surroundings and the Sudbury arena hosts the big shows, while Laurentian University's auditorium accommodates mid-sized events.

Sudbury has strength in media and communications because it is the only Northeastern city with a sizeable market and was one of the first to install a highspeed cable system. Fourteen local radio stations offer a variety of news, classical, easy listening, rock and inspirational messages (three are in French). CBC radio broadcasts in both languages with repeater stations throughout Northeastern Ontario. Only one television station, MCTV, aside from the public service station, presents broadcasts locally with rebroadcasts in other northeastern centres such as Sault Ste. Marie, North Bay, Timmins and Espanola. As CKSO-TV it was, in 1953, Canada's first private television broadcaster, though for many years it was affiliated with the CBC. The daily paper, the *Sudbury Star*, has a long history of conservativism continuing the traditions started by William Mason and James Meakes. Popular locally was the bi-weekly *Northern Life*, which also published numerous specialty magazines such as *Northern Business*, *Sudbury Living* and even a regional medical journal. The turn to electronic publishing has undercut printed newspaper like elsewhere. The firm has been sold to a Sault Ste. Marie owner and the newspaper converted into an electronic media outlet, Sudbury.com. *Le Voyageur* is a weekly as are the two university newspapers (French and English).

Though some 4,000 persons still work for the two major mining companies, education and health employment have passed mining and smelting as the main employers. The near-total dependency on mining-related work changed during the late 1970s and 1980s to a heavy dependence on public sector jobs, many of which meant a new dependency—on largesse from Ottawa or Toronto. However, some diversification has occurred and by the twenty-first century Sudbury has been surviving economic problems in similar fashion to other mid-sized cities. Lack of youth employment and cultural venues for the 18 to 30 age group remains a problem shared by most northern communities, though Sudbury had previously obtained significant public sector jobs, such as the transfer of the Ministry of Northern Development and Mines and the Ontario Geological Survey. The taxation data centre processes income tax for much of Ontario and provides stable employment as well as seasonal part-time work for about 2,000. The supply side of the mining industry—some 400 firms employing about 8,000—has expanded to include markets around the globe, as well as serving the local mining and smelting companies. The latter have expanded to include two new players, FNX Mining and

First Nickel (though operations and production depend on nickel prices).

The regional hospital opened in 2010 after 10 years of scandals about the level of increasing construction costs and many difficulties in amalgamating three separate institutions under Vicki Kaminski's leadership. Yet, it has become the main teaching, research, and health centre of the north, though both Sault Ste. Marie and North Bay also have created one-site hospitals. The northern medical school has succeeded in placing more doctors in the north though a shortage remains. Whether the mega-hospital, combined in Sudbury with the Cancer Care and Research Centre and the Children's Care Centre, will provide adequate services remains an open question; northerners often suffer long wait times to see specialists in the larger southern cities. The new structures have brought more modern technology and high-risk patients extol the level of care.

Opportunities for women have expanded in recent decades. The first female city councillors only took office in the 1950s and remained a tiny minority. By the twenty-first century, women had achieved the top posts at Laurentian University (Judith Woodsworth), at Cambrian College (Sylvia Barnard), at Boréal (Gisèle Chrétien), at the head of the hospital board (Carol Hartman), at the agency dispensing regional development funds, with Fed Nor (Louise Paquette) and the first elected mayor has been added (Marianne Matichuk). However, always underrepresented in Sudbury's elite positions have been those with a labour background.

Sudbury's colonial history reflects the uneven growth of a mining centre. A few aspects can be highlighted here. The village became a town in 1893 with Stephen Fournier as mayor. The total population in 1911 was 4,150 plus 3,000 in Copper Cliff, with about 20,000 in the much larger census district. By 1921, the population of Sudbury had nearly doubled to 8,000 while Copper Cliff 's declined slightly and the total in the district doubled. The demand for metals during World War I directly affected economic and demographic growth. However, conscription caused dissent between the pro-British elites who supported it and French Canadians who thought voluntary efforts sufficed; some churches divided as a result of the disagreements and streets were renamed. This conflict would be restaged during World War II. Already before the first war intolerance towards non-British and non-French persons had seen the major company, Canadian Copper, seek "white men" as employees. Despite that, the ethnic element, meaning mostly Finns, Ukrainians and Italians, doubled from 15% to 30% of the population in the region by 1921. The early 1920s brought a great economic downturn as nearly all the mining companies stopped production and unemployment led to demands for relief and numerous protests. By the mid-1920s, a sharp recovery resulted from finding other than military uses for nickel. In 1930, the town became a city and by 1931, its population had again doubled to over 20,000 as the increase in ethnic Europeans continued but nickel demand or prices and corporations with their own interests determined the fate of the city.

World War II consolidated the growth, with the city's population at 42,000 by 1951 and the metropolitan area at 80,000. That growth would shift into higher gear during the next decades, doubling the city's population to 80,000 in 1961 and increasing the region's to 110,000. By 1973, when the Regional Municipality of Sudbury was formed, the total was 163,000. The 1970s layoffs halted growth and the enlarged city has remained near 160,000 since.

During the era of great growth, one important development was the unionization of the workforce. In the 1940s Sudbury may have had Canada's highest paid male workers (its employed women were among the lowest paid), but working conditions were horrendous. Deaths and injuries in the mines were frequent—at least 318 fatalities between 1886 and 1930, and authoritarian bosses were the norm. Attempts to alleviate conditions in the mines and smelters led nowhere, so unionization became the goal. The companies and the Sudbury Star were strongly anti-union and represented the old patrician attitudes aided by the usual accusations of foreign radicals and communists misleading the hard-working people. During the depression, communists and socialists (especially from among Finns and Ukrainians) fought for social justice. Only during World War II would the International Union of Mine, Mill and Smelter Workers (Mine Mill), with government help—during a time of such labour shortages that women were encouraged to work at Inco plants—achieve bargaining rights. From 1944 to 1965, Mine Mill represented workers at Inco and Falconbridge and built a large union movement that organized many trades beyond mining and smelting, especially in retail. However, in the Cold War era the United Steelworkers of America took over many Mine Mill organizations. During the 1960s, Sudbury had one of the most bitter, and sometimes even violent, union struggles. The Steelworkers won with the help of the local elite from politicians to religious and educational leaders. Ironically, within a decade the mining unions began their slow decline as the number of labourers were undercut by recession, mechanization, and rationalization (replacing workers with more and bigger machines and blasting larger mine cavities).

After the 1958 strike by Mine Mill against Inco, Mine Mill lost Inco workers to the Steelworkers, though it was able to retain those at Falconbridge. A union with a large cultural program and with newspapers in various ethnic languages was replaced by one that focused mostly on bread-and-butter issues, though no unionists could avoid dealing with working conditions. Hence, the Steelworkers too had to address the cancer-causing sintering plant, the increasing fatalities during the 1960s boom, and associated compensation issues. They too have had long strikes against Inco—four months in 1969, six months in 1978, and most recently a year against the Brazilian giant, Vale, which purchased Inco in 2006. With the twenty-first century the unions' 50 years of social gains—pensions, improved working conditions, high salaries for skilled labour—have all been challenged, or even reversed.

Inco and Falconbridge generally enjoyed a period of prosperity from the 1940s until the downturns of the early 1970s shifted the nature of mining in Sudbury. By then the companies encountered a public concern about pollution. The Superstack was built in 1970 to help solve the acidification of the lakes and sulphur fumes descending as regularly as tidal flows, but in fact it was also necessary to handle the increased volume of production. Like other pollution controls, it came after much public pressure and increased governmental regulation; later it would be exploited as a symbol of the company's pollution efforts. Emissions have declined to about 10% of 1970s levels though more improvement is possible.

The 1970s were economically transformative for Sudbury in several ways. The dependency on mining became a dual dependency on mining and public funding. The image of the city as the most polluted place in Canada did not shift much, but the Superstack provided the potential for change. In the late 1960s, urban renewal started to modernize travel arteries and the downtown. In the 1970s, numerous new off-white buildings including a new city hall appeared, almost symbolizing a new beginning. Simultaneously the first moves to diversify the economy, as called for by the New Democratic Party representatives for years, began. In 1968, more than 20,000 people worked for the two major mining and smelting companies. At present that figure is about 4,000 and declining though production continues to increase. In 1971, mining accounted for about half of all the jobs in the Sudbury district with a labour force of 75,000. Today the service sector employs 80%. In 1971, men outnumbered women in the age group 18 to 30 (107 to 100); the demographics of a typical mining centre. By 2000 women outnumbered men, especially in the over age 65 category.

Since the 1970s, Sudbury has struggled to find alternative industries and only has partially succeeded. In 1976, Sudbury 2001, a committee comprising union, municipal, media and educational leaders noted the massive decline of mining employment and sought a unitary front to obtain institutional transfers (government ministries, research centres, taxation data centre) and start-up funds from provincial and federal sources. It sought to make Sudbury the education, health, and research hub of the north, to promote trades, to focus the university on some centres of excellence, and to beautify the city, among many other goals. Some of the efforts led in interesting directions. In 1979, the Regional Municipality of Sudbury leased the closed minimum security prison at Burwash (Camp Bison 20 kilometres south) to develop a goat farm producing mohair under the leadership of a man named Schaffernicht. By 1981 it closed, and the leader had fulfilled the literal translation of his German name: create nothing. However, in general, initiatives such as the science centre for tourism, support for regreening the landscape and most importantly, a common effort to face an uncertain future emerged. Some would argue that the creation of the school of medicine resulted from a similar unified effort, an approach that seems to have been lost since then. Others, outside Sudbury, suggest the city has been the recipient of much governmental largesse, referring to it as "Hogtown North."

Though many attempts had been made to plant trees and improve the appearance of the landscape, only the 1970s witnessed the beginnings of a large-scale regreening program and attempts to reverse the impact of pollution. The great impetus came from the need to provide work for unemployed miners, so Laurentian University, the city and the companies cooperated with the federal government and started a program of liming hillsides and lakes, grass seeding and tree planting. Keith Winterhalder (who has been written out of accounts by some of his successors) from Laurentian's biology department had experimented with ways to grow vegetation on barren hillsides. Inco earlier had experimented with a program called "Rye on the Rocks," mostly in response to complaints about dust from its mine tailings. After 1977 a large and systematic make-work project was underway to re-green the major, most visible, corridors. By 2022 more than 10 million trees had been planted. The success was apparent within two decades, and by the 1990s was winning international environmental awards. However, many areas away from the main roads remain untouched, since only about 10% of the barren lands have been reclaimed. Further, Vale has sought to extend deadlines mandated by the provincial government for reduced emissions and heavy metal controls at its plants in Copper Cliff. How bad was pollution earlier? People remember sulphur fumes burning leaves off plants, gardens turning brown, and fallout damaging vehicle paint. The hamlet of "Happy Valley" east of Falconbridge had to be relocated because it was directly in the way of sulphur emissions. Those conditions are gone, but the controversy about the results of soil testing for heavy metals, and the high local incidence of industrial, especially respiratory, diseases, demonstrate that much remains to be done.

Reflective of the more diversified new economy in Sudbury are the more than 300 firms supplying mining companies throughout the world with technology and services. A study in 2014 revealed that about 14,000 persons are employed in aspects of mining and smelting enterprises, even if Vale and Glencore employ only 4,000. Further, industries such as computer networks, film production, music (local bands such as The Birthday Cakes; coordinators such as Music and Film in Motion), design, and publishing (Éditions Prise de parole in French and Latitude 46 Publishing in English) are part of the expansion of the tertiary sector, which may, in the future, match education and health services.

Many notable events are remembered by locals, but some also received attention far beyond the city. In July 1930, Junction Creek, which runs through the centre of the city (subsequently channeled underground in the downtown), flooded drastically but its banks have since been controlled. In 1958, 1978, 2001 and 2009 strikes at Inco and Falconbridge lasted for three to twelve months, setting Canadian records for time lost. In August 1970, a tornado swept through the city from west to east leaving much destruction and killing four persons. One event that confirmed many outsiders' views of "barren" Sudbury was the 1971 visit of American astronauts, when they wanted to practice on what were assumed to be rock formations like those found on the moon.

An anecdotal historical note: yes, Sudbury had the first parking meters in Canada, starting in 1940.

Sudbury has had many sports moments and notable personalities—and sometimes claims persons who lived in adjacent towns. Without listing all of Sudbury's recreational facilities, in addition to a large arena built in the 1950s, plus hockey and skating arenas scattered throughout the amalgamated city, Greater Sudbury has six curling rinks, seven public pools, tennis courts, soccer fields (local clubs include ethnic groups such as the Croatians and Italians), cycling, a multitude of playgrounds and eight major golf venues. Sudbury Downs offered harness racing and a casino but was terminated due to the pandemic. In the area fishing and hunting are highly popular, often combined with snowmobiling or ATVing. Swimming is possible for three to four months in more than 300 lakes with their good beaches. Lake Ramsey has a yacht club for sailing. Recreation is buttressed by an extensive system of hiking trails such as the extension of the Voyageur Trail near Fielding Park with its bird sanctuary, or the extensive, mostly accessible trails at Kivi Park. Rainbow Routes provides maps of 26 trails, including the Jane Goodall trail near Coniston on

Highway 17, plus those in the conservation area in the southeast of the city next to Laurentian University; skiing and hiking trails abound.

Alex Bauman won Olympic Gold in 1980, undoubtedly because Laurentian University had a proper sized pool and an excellent trainer, Jeno Tihanyi. In sports, especially hockey, the infrastructure and support provided by the public now seems essential. Hence, the achievements of earlier generations who had no indoor rinks, special pools and diving platforms, high-tech skis and golf clubs should be especially acknowledged for overcoming difficulties. Despite not having a full, covered professional arena until 1954, Sudbury had numerous hockey teams that won the Memorial Cup during the 1930s. Sam Rothschild was the first Jewish player in the NHL. At least 15 NHL players hailed from Sudbury, including Todd Bertuzzi, the Foligno brothers, Brian Savage, Ed Giacomin and Eddie Shack. In all the focus on hockey, it is mostly forgotten that Sudbury had a soccer team, made up mostly of Europeans, which in 1932 won the provincial championship. From 2016 to 2022, a developer pushed for a new arena outside downtown, causing much controversy about its environmental impact and its finances, and was eventually abandoned.

Sudbury women have performed well on Canadian women's and world hockey teams, including Tessa Bonhomme and Rebecca Johnston. In track, Robert Esmie shared Olympic Gold on the 100-metre team. Sudbury's long-serving mayor during the 1940s, William Beaton represented the best of amateur athletes, and the annual Beaton classic challenge bears his name. The Finns especially had a tradition of creating their own fields, diving boards and meets, including some who skied to Timmins and Sault Ste. Marie to compete in cross-country ski events (and then skied back after the meet!).

In politics many gathered local experience before moving to the provincial or federal level. Frank Cochrane, for example, had been Sudbury's mayor before becoming a provincial and federal cabinet minister. Numerous other Conservative cabinet ministers such as Charles McCrea, Welland Gemmell and Jim Gordon represented Sudbury, and most were on friendly terms with the mining companies. Gordon may have been more successful in obtaining quid pro quos for the city from the mining companies, despite causing a stir when he accused Inco of holding the city to ransom during the 1978 strike. Floyd Laughren served in the NDP government of the 1990s as finance minister and deputy premier during a tough recession. Though accused of high deficits, that government helped save many jobs in the northeast, especially at Iroquois Falls and Sault Ste. Marie. Ironically, Sudbury's working population received little and later Laughren was among the Laurentian University and hospital boards which facilitated Dominic Giroux's rise and destruction of the university's finances. By contrast, the federal Liberal representatives Jim Jerome, Doug Frith and Judy Erola asserted that they obtained funding for the Taxation Data Centre in the late 1970s and for Science North in the early 1980s—though many politicians make such claims when team efforts were often involved. In this instance such teams were encouraged and forged behind the scenes by Tom Davies, the chair of regional government. During the 1990s Liberal Diane Marleau represented Sudbury in the federal cabinet and had as many difficulties regarding cigarette taxation as Minister of Health Erola had when she was Minister Responsible for the Status of Women. Erola suggested that childless women who stayed at home might not be contributors to the economy. She eventually lost her cabinet position. Many NDP MPPs, such as Bud Germa, Sharon Murdock and Eli Martel did not serve in a cabinet, but Martel was well known for his unorthodox approach to exposing Inco's pollution and other social problems. His daughter, Shelley Martel, would become the youngest Ontario cabinet member, but unfortunately also the only cabinet minister to take a lie detector test to confirm that she had not been truthful. Perhaps the prominence of Sudbury's politicians has been as much due to their controversy as their achievements representing their constituents' interests in hard times.

In business, the Desmarais family became the owners of one of Canada's largest financial empires, Power Corp. It owned bus lines in Sudbury starting in 1951. The shift to a public bus system came in 1972 after one of the Desmarais buses stalled and the exhaust leaked into the rusty bus, causing serious illness to the passengers. Another financier from Sudbury, Robert Campeau, built and bankrupted a huge real-estate and department store empire.

Nationally known because of successful union organizing of Mine Mill in the 1940s was leader Bob Carlin. Yet, by the 1950s he was known for causing union infighting through his political stances. Later, due to its size and progressive policies, Mine Mill union leaders such as Nels Thibault and Mike Solski were attacked as communists. So was Weir Reid, the controversial recreation director of Mine Mill who built a youth culture that included summer camps, ballet and theatre. He was noted at his death in 1971 by *Time Magazine* as "the last angry socialist."

Francophones have represented Sudbury well in the arts. Two have won Governor General's awards: the historian Michel Bock who trained at Laurentian University won for non-fiction, and Robert Dickson who taught at Laurentian for poetry. Francophone Senators include Jean Noël Desmarais appointed in 1993 and Marie-Paule Poulin in 1995 (resigned in 2015 due to ill health).

Among the musicians and singers from Sudbury are the jazz guitarist Reg Schwager (member Order of Canada) and the tenor Joey Niceforo, who sings with the world touring Destino group. Niceforo told a Sudbury audience in 2009 that he decided to become a singer after scoring a goal against his own team while playing hockey. Among those who acknowledge their Sudbury roots are the CTV weather woman, Susan Hay, and the creator of the outdoor clothing line, Alex Tilley.

While Alex Trebek and Karen Fowler have become noted TV hosts and producers, a prominent artistic post has been achieved by Marc Mayer as director of the National Gallery of Canada and Antoni Cimolino as director of the Stratford Festival. Richard Rose has been a theatre director since the 1980s, including at the Tarragon in Toronto. Bruce Mau is noted as a designer, and some Sudburians had hoped he would help transform their city's appearance but has not had any impact aside from appearances at the school of architecture. Sean Costello is a horror/thriller novelist using mostly northern places in his stories. Roger Nash was the inaugural Poet Laureate of Greater Sudbury, and past president of the League of Canadian Poets. Dr. Ray Wiss of the Sudbury hospital emergency ward turned his medical tours of duty in Afghanistan into two well-known books recalling his experiences as a medic. Paul Field undertook the first Canadian open-heart surgery (coronary by-pass) at the Memorial Hospital in 1968.

Communities Surrounding the Sudbury Core

The outlying towns and villages have as much history as the core city but are sometimes not given recognition. Some small communities such as Long Lake and company towns such as Copper Cliff had trajectories parallel to but often different from the large centre, like boom-and-bust communities.

The Town of Nickel Centre included Coniston, Falconbridge, Wahnapitae, Garson and Skead, which had amalgamated in 1973. On 1 January 2001, Nickel Centre became part of the City of Greater Sudbury. The 1996 census, Canada's last before the incorporation of Nickel Centre into Sudbury, indicated a population of 13,017.

Wahnapitae, at the easternmost end of Greater Sudbury, sits astride the CPR and Highway 17. The tracks from Montreal reached Wahnapitae before they reached Sudbury proper in 1883. In Ojibwe, the name Wahnapitae may mean "A place to cross the river," "Wrinkled by the wind," or "A place where people gather beside the water." Entrepreneurs from Michigan bought timber tracts beside the Wanapitei River, as the arrival of the rails coincided with the depletion of forests in Michigan. Lumberjacks cut trees along the banks of the Wanapitei River, and the current carried the logs into Lake Huron, whence they proceeded to markets. As early as 1886, a barge named *Wahnapitae* hauled the logs across Lake Huron to destinations in the United States. Employees and farmers in Wahnapitae, Ontario, developed a community with its own schools, churches and businesses, but as Highway 17 improved and almost every family owned a car after World War II, most commercial operations moved some kilometres to the west. Wahnapitae today has a few stores and a service station primarily for motorists on Highway 17, but it survives as a residential area.

Between Wahnapitae and Sudbury on Highway 17, Coniston takes its name from a place in Northwestern England. A superintendent with the CPR, T.R. Johnson, read a novel about events that happened in the English Coniston. He suggested the name, and the villagers liked it. John and Peter Butler, along with their parents, were the first farming settlers in 1902. Two years later, five other families followed them. Their farms produced hay, rye and oats.

Coniston did not remain an agricultural area for long. In 1905, the Canadian Northern Railway (now part of CN) reached Coniston, as did a CPR line from

Toronto three years later. The St. Clair Construction Company built the Coniston Woodworks Lumber Mill at Coniston. Mond Nickel (subsequently part of Inco) then established a smelter. It was a divided community with workers in peripheral Polish, Italian, French and Ukrainian "towns," while company managers lived along the main streets in larger residences. Typical of company towns, recreation services such as the arena (1970) and curling rink (1957) contrasted with the barren landscape. Air pollution from the mining and smelting operations killed most of the vegetation, and, as in Wahnapitae, better shopping opportunities in Sudbury and the closing of the smelter hollowed Coniston's commercial core. Regreening efforts of the last 40 years have made it a more attractive residential community.

Two of Coniston's most famous residents were Hector "Toe" Blake and Mike Solski. Blake began his hockey career in 1927 as a goalie for the Coniston Boy Scouts team, but he soon became a forward with the Sudbury Cub Wolves. Blake was part of the team when it won the Memorial Cup in 1932. By the 1940s, Blake was a left winger for the Montreal Canadiens, playing alongside Maurice "Rocket" Richard. Blake has a place of honour in the Hockey Hall of Fame, including coaching teams to 8 Stanley Cups. Solski, a smelter worker from the age of 17, became a union organizer and leader of Mine Mill. Slandered as a Communist, he retained credibility in Coniston, where he served as mayor from 1962 until 1972, then the amalgamated Nickel Centre from 1973 to 1978. On 15 November of that year, he was presiding as mayor over what would have been one of his last meetings. A deranged man, Romeo Kerim, burst into the room and shot him three times. Solski survived what was one of the few assassinations attempts against a Canadian mayor, although his arms were permanently damaged. Between his departure from political life and his death in 1999, Solski was an active Liberal and author of books about Sudbury and his union.

North of Coniston lies Garson, and Falconbridge is northeast of Garson. In 1856, the Province of Upper Canada (what is now Ontario south of the Arctic-Atlantic Watershed) created the Township of Garson, named for William Garson, MPP for Lincoln County. The Hudson's Bay Company dealt in furs in the area, and logging followed. The Emery Lumber Company started to cut trees in 1882, one year before the arrival of the CPR a few kilometres to the south. Horses pulled sleds to the tracks, and the CPR carried them to Wahnapitae from where the Wanapitei River carried them to Lake Huron. The lumber boom ended in 1910 as pollution from the smelters destroyed the trees.

Falconbridge takes its name from William Glenholm Falconbridge, justice of the High Court of Ontario, and chief justice from 1900. Falconbridge too began as a supplier of lumber, especially to Chicago, still rebuilding after the Great Fire of 1871. In 1901, 1902 and 1903, the famous inventor Thomas Edison visited Falconbridge in search of nickel, but he failed to find any and abandoned the attempt. His claim reverted to the Crown, but in 1911 the Longyear Company purchased the claim, then joined other mining companies who together created Falconbridge Mines Limited. Operations only began in 1928.

That year, Thayer Lindsley went to Falconbridge. Lindsley and his brother had become interested in Canadian mining operations while they were students at Harvard. Lindsley, as president of the mining company Ventures, purchased

Falconbridge Mines Limited, and he renamed it Falconbridge Nickel Mines Limited. Lindsley served as its president until 1944. The price Linsley paid after his arrival in Falconbridge for the company's assets, $2,500,000, was reportedly the highest to date for any mining property near Sudbury. In 1929, Falconbridge Nickel Mines Limited found nickel only 30 metres from the place where Edison had searched in vain. The company built bunkhouses, then a school, post office and general store. Again, a typical company town emerged with some amenities (parks, arena) and large houses for managers.

Skead, to the northeast of Falconbridge, dates from 1924 as a lumber centre. Wahnapitae First Nations had utilized the area for hunting and fishing for a long time. Using nearby Lake Wanapitei, the Skead logs would proceed down the river to Lake Huron. That year, Sudbury's lumber baron, William J. Bell, purchased the Sable and Spanish River Lumber Company, which, despite its name, operated on Lake Wanapitei's north shore. Bell gave the company a new name, the Spanish River Lumber Company, and arranged construction of a mill at Massey Bay. Then he renamed Massey Bay "Skead," the middle name of his wife, Katherine Skead Bell. The Spanish River Lumber Company erected bunkhouses, a cookhouse and stores in Skead. The Depression forced the mill to close for more than a decade; however, a 1941 forest fire destroyed the Poupore Lumber Company's mill in Gogama, and Poupore Lumber moved to Skead. The new sawmill became operational 6 August 1943, and Skead was revived.

Valley East, a town until 1997 and briefly a city until its incorporation into Greater Sudbury in 2001, consisted of several previously separate communities: Lumsden, Hanmer, Capreol, Bowell, Wisner and Blezard. The census of 1996 indicated a population of 23,537. While the rest of the Sudbury Region has had a population decline since 1971 until recently, Valley East's has expanded by 25%.

Valley East's previous history is one of successive mergers and status changes. Hanmer Township was incorporated in 1904, Blezard Township in 1906, and Capreol Township in 1956. Hanmer and Capreol amalgamated in 1967 to become, briefly, the Township of Capreol-Hanmer. In 1968, the new township expanded to include the unorganized townships of Boswell and Wisner, plus the northern part of Lumsden. Later in 1968, the Township of Capreol-Hanmer amalgamated with Blezard Township to become the Township of Valley East. With the arrival of regional government in 1973, the township became the Town of Valley East.

Valley East's economy has depended on logging, agriculture and mining. The first Europeans to do more than pass through what is now Valley East were loggers. However, mines did exist: by 1890 the Canadian Copper Company was operating one at Blezard, reportedly the first mine in Ontario with underground electrical lighting. Early in the twentieth century, the valley's soil provided an outlet for the surplus population of Quebec's farms. They could grow food for the area's mines and loggers. Since the 1920s and especially since World War II, however, agriculture has declined in importance. Pollution from Inco's roast beds and smelters made farming almost impossible. Across the Sudbury District, the number of active farms declined from 1,634 in 1951, to 416 in 1971. Blezard was part of that trend. There, the number fell from 54 to 14 between 1951 and 1961. Clearly, farmers found it more profitable to sell their land for subdivisions than to farm. Even so, potatoes from Valley East remain available in Sudbury's grocery stores.

Capreol's history is intertwined with that of the CN rail system. It sits astride CN's main transcontinental line; Sudbury Junction at the east end of LaSalle Boulevard in Sudbury was never more than a whistle stop. Capreol takes its name from Frederick Chase Capreol, a founder of the short-lived Northern Railway of Canada. Soon, the Grand Trunk Railway, later acquired by CN, purchased the Northern Railway. While Capreol has a lengthy park along the river, of greatest interest to tourists will be the railway museum, which has locomotives and cars as well as a house full of well-organized photos.

Until 1920, no road linked the agricultural and rail settlements with Sudbury, and the towns remained self-contained. When the road did materialize, many thought that it had far more curves than necessary, and they suspected that the contractor received payment according to the length of the road.

Valley East has a variety of public and secondary schools, divided by four categories: English and French language, public and Roman Catholic. Its industrial park has expanded in recent years, and the Elizabeth Centre provides long-term care for 128 people, who live in a modern, attractive building. The centre takes its name not from the Queen but from the first name of three residents, including the original landowner, Elizabeth Mrochek. The Trans Canada Trail passes through Valley East, and shorter local hikes offer recreational opportunities.

Rayside and Balfour, which at the end of 1972 merged into the Town of Rayside Balfour, owe their origins to the Canadian Pacific Railway. Farmers from Quebec, who followed the tracks from Montreal, at once began to clear land. In 1921 Rayside comprised 97% French, while places like Garson were at 29%. In 1996 the population stood at 16,050, most of whom spoke French as their primary language. This made Rayside-Balfour unique among the component parts of Greater Sudbury.

The Township of Rayside had become a municipality in 1890, the Township of Balfour the following year. The village of Azilda was part of the Township of Rayside. Chelmsford, named by a CPR engineer from England, separated from Balfour and became a town in 1909. Its two mines, Errington and Nickel Offset, closed during the Depression and never re-opened. In 1968, the Township of Balfour absorbed Chelmsford, as well as the townships of Creighton and Morgan. It became part of the City of Greater Sudbury in the amalgamation of 2001. The town, with around 6,000 people in 2021, served and serves the northwest area of the city and has good recreational facilities, including golf course and arena.

The first woman who settled in what became Azilda was Azilda Bélanger. She had 12 children and as a Métis was known for healing powers with medicinal herbs. Her husband who worked for the CPR became mayor of the village. Another Azilda pioneer, Zotique Régimbal, by then in his early twenties, squared timbers as the CPR moved westward. When the second Riel rebellion erupted in Manitoba in 1885, the CPR had not yet become operational. Régimbal was responsible for leading the troops through that part of the forest still without rail tracks, about 50 kilometres. Régimbal later became clerk-treasurer of Rayside and secretary of Rayside's first school board. In 1904, he moved from Azilda to Sudbury, where he was an employee of Laberge Lumber, founded by an entrepreneur from Rayside.

West of Sudbury, from 1886 until its closure in 1905, Copper Cliff was the site of the richest copper mine owned by the Canadian Copper Company. That mine's disadvantage was its depth, the deepest of its 13 levels operating at 1,052 feet (384 metres). Depth meant expense. Nickel closer to the surface was more economical to mine and became the basis of the economy. The opening of a smelter in 1888 created employment but caused extensive environmental damage over a wide area.

One of the world's largest smelters and industrial plants would develop east of Copper Cliff after 1929, with huge tailings and slag dumps. Canadian poet Earle Birney (one of many visiting poets and painters responsible for making Sudbury's landscape part of the Canadian mindscape) compared the then-three smokestacks to an industrial Calvary sacrificing lives. His imagery would be ruined when the world's largest industrial smokestack (at that time) replaced the smaller ones and became operational in 1971.

By 1900, Copper Cliff was a self-contained community. The village became a town on 15 April 1901, and during the interwar period its population was temporarily larger than Sudbury's. Finnish and Italian enclaves predated World War I and maintained clubs separate from the mostly English managers, who lived in large houses away from the smelter. Little Italy, a small cluster of houses next to the refinery on streets named after Italian cities, had an Italian bakery and stores that have disappeared. The Italians had small gardens but most important were roses which won many prizes at horticultural shows since the plants loved the acidic conditions of the soil impacted by ore extraction. In the company town era, Copper Cliff 's high school, which operated from 1937 until 1980, had a well-deserved reputation for excellence in sports, especially hockey. The town had its own police force and shopping area, even its own newspaper, the *Copper Cliff Courier, from 1902 until 1918.* As of 11 November 1915, the Copper Cliff Suburban Electric Railway linked Copper Cliff with downtown Sudbury, and thereby enabled workers to live in one place and work or shop in the other. Bus service replaced streetcars between 1947 and 1950, and thereafter increasing numbers of people owned their own cars. In 1972, under regional government, Copper Cliff amalgamated with the city. As Inco had its regional headquarters in Copper Cliff, it supplied the town with amenities such as an arena, park and curling club, but paid no taxes to Sudbury, home of most of its labour force.

Like Copper Cliff, Lively was a child of Inco, albeit a more recent one. Established as a company town in the 1950s, it served as a residential site for Inco employees, primarily those who worked at the Creighton Mine. Lively's name—taken from Charles Lively, an early settler—became the butt of jokes. "Where do you live?" "Lively, Ontario." "Yes, but I live in swinging Saskatchewan. Where in lively Ontario do you live?" In the 1970s, Inco left the housing business but gave its employees the first option to buy the homes in which they lived. Lively, an attractive spread-out community with many amenities (such as a fine golf club), survives as part of Walden, complete with a secondary school.

North of Lively is the ghost town of Creighton, near a mine of the same name. Mining began in 1900, and some 900 miners lived in the area. The usual urban amenities—post office, school, doctor's office, stores, banks, theatres (movies) and churches—followed. Creighton exemplified a company town, where the Canadian Copper Company, later Inco, owned the land and the buildings, including homes, maintained the streets and provided water and sewage services. The population began to decline in the 1960s, and Inco decided that Creighton's costs were too high. Although the mine remains active, the last workers abandoned their homes in 1986, and Inco demolished the town.

Other places in Walden include Naughton, originally McNaughtonville, Whitefish, Beaver Lake and Worthington, all still lightly populated, as well as the ghost towns of High Falls and Victoria Mines. Naughton, once site of a Hudson's Bay Company post, was home to hockey player Art Ross of the Boston Bruins, a member of the Hockey Hall of Fame since 1945. The original hamlet of Worthington (1892-1927) occupied a different site until the mine and some of the town collapsed into a sinkhole. Nobody died, because a foreman had noticed unusual geological activity and ordered everyone to evacuate the area. Water subsequently covered what had been Worthington. The legendary hockey figure Hector "Toe" Blake was born in Victoria Mines.

Finally, about 30 kilometres northwest of Sudbury on Highway 144 is Onaping, which in turn consisted of separate communities: Dowling, Levack and Onaping. The most famous attraction is the High Falls, beside which is the A.Y. Jackson Lookout, named for the Group of Seven painters who made it famous by a series of paintings— one of which was stolen from a high school and never recovered. High Falls drops 46 metres.

Beside the falls are hiking trails, picnic tables, public restrooms and a display of rocks extracted from Inco mines as part of a Geological Tour. Signs identify the rocks and explain their probable origin. Amid the display is some mining machinery. A drive from Sudbury to High Falls resembles a drive across the Canadian prairies to the foothills of the Rockies: first the flat farmland of Valley East, then the appearance of the northern rim of the Sudbury Basin, and finally the rock and hill country of the northern rim. The major industry of Onaping is mining, and its famous people have included cyclist Eric Wahlberg and NHL players Dave Taylor (Los Angeles Kings), Dave Hannan (Pittsburgh Penguins) and Troy Mallette (Ottawa Senators). It has Sudbury's main downhill ski slope and is close to Windy Lake Provincial Park's excellent hiking and cross-country ski trails.

The Myths of Sudbury

Did you know?

Canada's most productive gold mine, operative from 1909 to 1917 when the mother lode was lost, was at the southern tip of Long Lake, just southwest outside of Sudbury.

Together the 1.7 trillion tons of ores—reduced to 40 billion pounds of nickel, 36 billion pounds of copper, 70 million ounces of platinum, palladium and gold and 283 million ounces of silver—dug out of the Sudbury Basin plus known reserves represent over a trillion dollars in today's terms. The basin is the richest mining district in North America and one of the top ten in the world, with about $5 billion extracted by four companies annually—Vale, Xstrata, FNX Mining and First Nickel Inc. The cost of extracting ores is high: at least 318 workers died between 1886 and 1930 in Sudbury operations; during the 1960s, the bonus system resulted in about 2 deaths per month.

Leo May invented a sturdy tin lunch pail for miners after others fell apart and were not capable of being sat on or treated roughly. It is still being fabricated by his daughter.

Sudbury is enveloped in contrasting myths. One surrounds pollution. Once considered the prime example of the western world's worst industrial pollution, now the myth is being propagated that it has a restored landscape. Neither version quite fits reality. The destroyed area resembled many industrially blighted places, such as the steel and rustbelt cities in the United States. Certainly, the open-pit mining and clear-cut lumbering made a barren landscape by the twentieth century. Then sulphur fumes from huge open pits, in which logs were burned under metal-bearing rock, devastated a long strip of land, at least four kilometres wide and thirty in length northeasterly from Copper Cliff. The reach of the fumes from the smelters acidified lakes in many directions but mostly towards the northeast. After 1971, the Superstack pushed those fumes and pollutants into the atmosphere. They landed as far away as

Sweden. The dilution of the fumes, the reduction to a tenth of the sulphate released in the smelting process, and the restoration of the scarred landscape starting systematically in 1977 has reversed the devastation. Some forty-foot (twelve-metre) evergreens and much bush growth have begun to improve the landscape, while fish are surviving and multiplying in the lakes. However, much work remains to restore the area's original beauty and to clean up the metals in the soil, as well as to reinstate the fact that Sudbury itself has always been surrounded by a sea of green.

At different times in the past 50 years, the city has been described as dying and among the ugliest of North America. That mythical version is supported by the repeated effects of a boom-and-bust economy dependent on distant markets. True, the downtown is marred by parking lots and many decrepit buildings. No cityscape, in the sense of any coherent style, exists, even if a few attractive buildings are scattered about the city. The entrances to the city could stand a clean-up. In this regard another myth argues that Sudbury is a "hidden" secret, with its numerous lakes, lengthy boardwalk, and special architecture in its science centre. City boosters make much about an environmental award and about a magazine once listing it as one of the best places to live in Canada. Between those extreme claims is the reality of charming suburbs, of walking trails and being close to nature plus some attractive buildings. Yet, the reality includes a struggling infrastructure (like many Ontario cities) and few modern venues for sport and culture. In the 2020s attempts to systematically rebuild the crumbling road system began but the infrastructure deficit remains.

Another myth is Sudbury as a union town. During the late 1950s and early 1960s it had Canada's largest union with more than 25,000 members. However, despite the numbers and attempts to develop cultural and political institutions, the two main mining companies Inco and Falconbridge, aided by the churches and Cold War attitudes and augmented by internal union strife, restrained union influence. Lawyers, publishers, merchants and teachers always ran the city in alliance with the companies. In 2009–10, a year-long strike by 3,000 Steelworkers at the main mining-smelting complex recently taken over by the Brazilian conglomerate, Vale, found limited support from the community. Even one group of Steelworker unionists refused to support another. Likewise, a 2010 strike by support staff at the new medical school was mostly seen as a nuisance and not a reflection of the low-wage, nor the questionable working conditions of the technologists.

A related myth is that since the 1970s the city has attained a diversified economy. Though publicly funded institutions such as the university, new medical school, colleges and taxation data centre have undercut the total dependence on mining and smelting, Sudbury remains highly dependent on resource-based production (with high metal prices) and government support, as shown by the provincial bailout of the university.

What then is Sudbury? It is Northeastern Ontario's main city with nearly one third of its population. It is the prime centre for business, social and health services, education and media as well as mining and mining services. For tourism and smaller conventions, it has most major hotel chains, some bed and breakfasts and numerous campgrounds. It is a widely dispersed entity. Three icons and symbols represent Sudbury's reality very well: the Big Nickel, with small training mine and numismatic park surrounded by barren grounds representing production of nickel regardless of environmental results; Inco's Superstack representing both the relentless drive to extract and simultaneous awareness of pollution; Science North, a beautiful complex on the city's main lake next to preserved wetlands and tied to the Bell Park walkway, representing the new partly-diversified and service-dominated economy in which education and research are the hope for a future very different than the nickel-reliant past.

Resources

Dieter K. Buse and Graeme S. Mount, *Untold: Northeastern Ontario's Military Past 2 vols* (Sudbury: Latitude 46 Publishing, 2018, 2019). Broader than Sudbury but many local examples.

Wallace Clement, *Hardrock Mining: Industrial Relations and Technological Change at Inco* (Toronto: McClelland and Stewart, 1981).

Copper Cliff Museum, *A Bit of the Cliff: A Brief History of Copper Cliff, 1901–1972* (Copper Cliff: Museum, 1982).

Donald Dennie, *A l'Ombre de l'Inco* (Ottawa: UOP, 2001)

Guy Gaudreau, ed., *L'Histoire des Mineurs du Nord Ontarien et Québécois, 1886-1945* (Sillery: Septentrion, 2003).

Greater Sudbury 1883–2008 (Sudbury: Laurentian, 2008).

Wayne F. Labelle, *Valley East, 1850-2002* (Field, 2002).

David Leadbeater, ed., *Mining Town Crisis: Globalization, Labour and Resistance in Sudbury* (Halifax: Fernwood, 2009).

Scott Miller, *Leading the Pack: 50 Years of Sudbury Wolves History* (Sudbury: Latitude 46 Publishing, 2022).

Graeme S. Mount, *The Sudbury Region: An Illustrated History* (Windsor: Windsor Publications, 1986).

Nicola Ross, *Healing the Landscape—Celebrating Sudbury's Reclamation Story* (Sudbury: City of Sudbury, 2001).

Oiva Saarinen, *Between a Rock and a Hard Place: A Historical Geography of the Finns in the Sudbury Area* (Waterloo: Wilfrid Laurier, 1999).

Oiva Saarinen, *From Meteorite Impact to Constellation City: A Historical Geography of Greater Sudbury* (Waterloo: Wilfred Laurier, 2013).

Mike Solski, *The Coniston Story, 2 vols* (Coniston, 1982 and 1990).

Carl M. Wallace and Ashley Thomson, eds., *Sudbury: Railtown to Regional Capital* (Toronto: Dundurn Press, 1993). Most comprehensive and informed overview but only to the 1970s.

Stacey Zembrzycki, *According to Baba: A Collaborative Oral History of Sudbury's Ukrainian Community* (Vancouver: UBC Press, 2014.)

Sudbury, District of

The District of Sudbury emerged from the districts of Algoma and Nipissing in 1894 and is situated between them, going south to Georgian Bay and the La Cloche Mountains, and north to just above the Arctic-Atlantic watershed. For hundreds of years various Ojibwe bands hunted and fished in nearly all its southern area whereas Cree lived in the northern part. The City of Greater Sudbury is almost at its centre. The district expanded northwest to include the area around Chapleau in 1910. The following describes the smaller communities of the district in a clockwise direction. The townships of French River and Killarney, the towns of Chapleau, Espanola and Sables-Spanish River have individual entries elsewhere in the text.

Biscotasing, population claimed as 22 in 2016 (or ghost town), swells to 300 during summer. It dates from the arrival of the CPR in 1884. The fur trade provided some employment, but the primary reason for the town was a temporary sawmill that opened in 1884, largely because of the needs of CPR construction crews. A permanent sawmill opened the following decade. Lumbering ended around 1927 because of a shortage of trees. Nowadays canoeists, fishermen and campers can

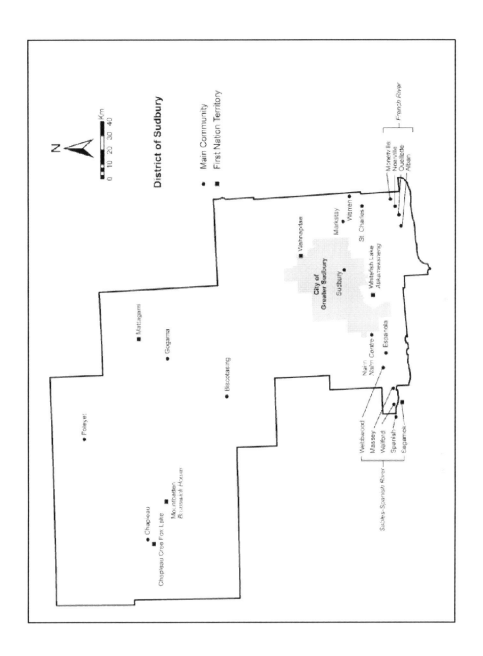

District of Sudbury

travel there by car, train (Budd car), or float plane. Perhaps Biscotasing's most famous resident has been Grey Owl, a British immigrant who falsely adopted a First Nations identity. He also resided in Mattawa and Temagami.

Foleyet (population 216 in 2006; 177 in 2016; 165 in 2021), on Highway 101 between Chapleau and Timmins, was a base for construction of the Canadian Northern Railway (now part of CN) in the early twentieth century. Once the Canadian Northern was operational, Foleyet became a divisional point, where crew changes occurred. Today it is largely a centre for hunting and fishing.

An unconfirmed story about Foleyet's name involves the Foley brothers, whose construction company erected some of the community's first buildings. The brothers wanted to name the place for themselves and became angry when they learned that a Foley Post Office existed near Parry Sound. They reportedly stormed, "We'll name this place Foley yet!"

Mattagami First Nations is just east of Highway 144 on the lake of the same name, meaning "meeting of waters." The Anishnaabe, here comprising Ojibwe and Cree bands, lived off fishing and hunting for centuries. In 1906 they signed a treaty with the crown to share the land, but in the 1920s parts of their territory were flooded because of a hydro dam. In 1952 they were compensated with additional land. In 1962, the band elected the first Indigenous all women council with a female chief. In 2023 the band claimed 695 members with about 200 residents in the area. Some provide support services to tourists in an area known for pickerel fishing. An annual "Walleye Catch and Release Derby" takes place in June.

Gogama, population 310 in 2021, takes its name from the Ojibwe word for "jumping fish," which points to the possibility of successful fishing. Located off Highway 144, 196 kilometres north of Sudbury, not far past the Arctic-Atlantic Watershed sign, the town had no highway connection to the outside world until the opening of Highway 144 between Timmins and Sudbury in autumn 1970. Perhaps Gogama's most famous resident is Joe LaFlamme, an émigré from Quebec, who reportedly could tame moose and wolves by speaking to them in Ojibwe. He mushed his team of half-wild wolves down Elm Street in Sudbury, Bay Street in Toronto and Broadway in New York. An anecdote about an aspiring local politician relates that he once promised that, if elected, he would work for a road "into Gogama." One of the listeners protested, "We don't want a road to Gogama, what we want is a road out of Gogama." Gogama began as a Hudson's Bay Company post, and its store still operated in the 1950s. Recently the economy has received a boost from nearby gold mining from which Timmins and Sudbury have also benefited.

Canadian Northern Railway (now Canadian National; CNR) reached Gogama between 1911 and 1914, and the first settler arrived in 1919. Mattagami First Nations had hunted and fished the area for a long time, but their forest-based economy was displaced by white settlement, so they moved further east. Until the Depression, the town was dependent on forestry. The company Cochrane and Laforest operated a mill from 1919 to 1932; members of the Poupore family operated another mill from 1919 until a fire destroyed it in 1936. At first, the Poupore mill's main customer was the CNR, which needed railway ties. Later, as the CNR's requirements diminished, Poupore survived by selling lumber to the mining company Falconbridge. Today the

La Cloche mountains near Willisville

economy depends on tourists who want to hunt, fish, or snowmobile.

About 40 kilometres east of Sudbury, Markstay-Warren stretches along Highway 17 at the easternmost limits of the district. Between those villages is Hagar, 10 kilometres from Markstay and six from Warren. Markstay-Warren, which amalgamated in 1999, had a population of 2,475 in 2006, a drop of 5.8% since 2001, but increased to 2,656 by 2016 and 2,708 in 2021. Residents reported the language spoken most often at home as follows in 2016: English, 1,750; French 890; both, 15; other 10. Markstay is heavily Francophone, Warren more pluralistic. Only 50 individuals said that they could manage to function only in French. Ten claimed no knowledge of either language. Almost 20% have a College Diploma or a trade certificate, and more than 5% have university degrees.

The CPR reached what is now Markstay-Warren in 1883, and French-Canadian Roman Catholics from Quebec followed. The Veuve River parallels Highway 17 and the CPR tracks, and by 1885 a community with a station called Rivière-Veuve existed. The local economy depended on lumber. Toronto's Warren family opened a sawmill in 1890 and called the investment the Imperial Lumber Company. Agriculture followed, and after World War II when Highway 17 was paved, residents of Warren were willing to drive the 60 kilometres to jobs in Sudbury. Ontario Hydro (now Hydro One) and the Ontario Provincial Police provided further employment, although by the end of the twentieth century the Hydro One office closed and the Ontario Provincial Police detachment downsized. One of the attractions of Markstay-Warren was the low cost of real estate, but as gasoline prices have risen, some residents have moved closer to jobs in Sudbury or North Bay.

Ten kilometres south of Hagar, St. Charles sits amid an agricultural area, for which it is a supply centre. Although heavily Franco-Ontarian, most of its signs

> ### *Did you know?*
> - Biscotasing may have been the first place in Northeastern Ontario to use aircraft to monitor forest fires.
> - Gogama's Joe LaFlamme mushed a team of half-wild wolves down Elm Street in Sudbury, Bay Street in Toronto, and Broadway in New York.

appear either in both English and French or in English alone. Ironically, the main street is King Street. Unlike many rural communities the population is relatively stable at around 1,300 (1,357 in 2021).

Nairn Centre (township population 477 in 2011; 342 in 2016; 373 in 2021) is 40 kilometres west of Sudbury on Highway 17 and the branch line of the CPR. Some lumbering continues, but it is primarily a highway travel stop. During the 1901 smallpox outbreak, Dr. Max Mackenzie King, brother of the future prime minister, volunteered to gain medical experience. One day Dr. Mackenzie King travelled 60 kilometres by dogsled despite temperatures of minus 30 degrees so that he could vaccinate 25 lumberjacks. Haunting Dr. King and the government of Ontario was the memory of an 1885 epidemic in Montreal, where some 20,000 people had taken ill and 3,000 had died.

South of Espanola, the La Cloche Mountains and lakes towards Killarney were a favourite area of the Group of Seven artists. Many resorts dot the area in which hiking, canoeing and fishing is popular. The village of Willisville, a small company-owned hamlet, served a quartz mine that is now nearly automated. The road to the village provides marvelous lookouts towards Manitoulin.

Resources
Suzanne R. Charron, *Wolf Man Joe Laflamme: Tamer Untamed* (Sudbury: Scribner Press, 2013; Latitude 46 Publishing, 2017).
Derek J. Coleman, et al, *La Cloche Country: Its History, Art and People* (Espanola: OJGraphix, 2009).

Gogama Hudson's Bay Company store

Bison, near Englehart

Temiskaming, District of

The District of Temiskaming (population 32,200 in 2016; 31,4224 in 2021) has its judicial seat at Haileybury, now part of Temiskaming Shores. The name "Temiskaming" means "Deep Waters" in the Algonquin language, appropriate given the depth and size of Lake Temiskaming, which straddles the Ontario-Quebec boundary. The Algonquin had no written language of their own. Missionaries later created one, and the word has been written in English as both "Timiskaming" and "Temiskaming," but today the latter is more common. The district's only city is Temiskaming Shores. Its towns are Cobalt, Englehart, Kirkland Lake and other communities and include Latchford, Earlton, Larder Lake, Virginiatown and Matachewan First Nation. Here the communities are described from south to north and west.

Latchford, population 370 in 2011, 313 in 2016, and 327 in 2021 is located on the Montreal River (not to be confused with the Montreal River which runs into Lake Superior), 16 kilometres south of Temiskaming Shores on Highway 11. Temagami First Nation lived a traditional life of hunting and fishing in the region based on the rivers and lakes. Latchford dates from the arrival of the Temiskaming and Northern Ontario Railway in 1903. First named "Montreal River Station" and situated at the point where the railway (now Ontario Northland) crossed the Montreal River on its way to the Little Clay Belt, it was renamed in honour of Francis Robert Latchford (1856-1938), Ontario's Commissioner of Public Works. The first bridge crossed the river in 1904, and the town was surveyed in 1905, the same year the Empire Lumber Company launched the community's first sawmill. The discovery of silver at Cobalt

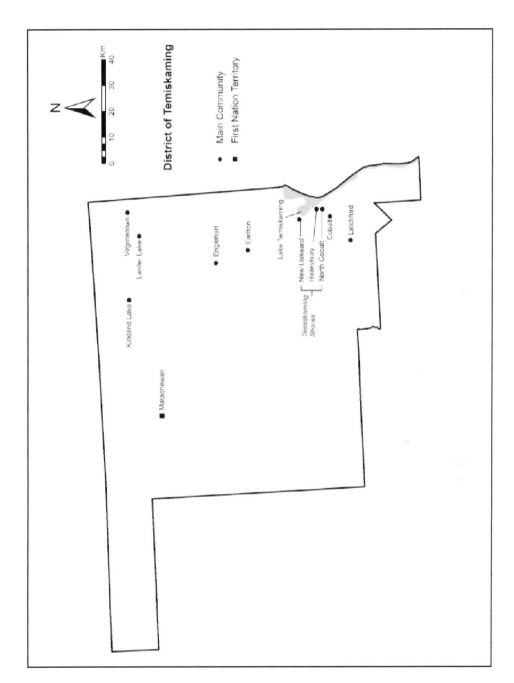

District of Temiskaming

sparked a boom, and Latchford became a provisioning point for prospectors. Incorporation followed in 1907 and the Census of 1911 reported a population of 429. With the depletion of the silver mines, timber and pulp mills enabled the community to survive, even if its nicknames are "Sawdust City" and "the best little town by a dam site."

Latchford's tourist attractions include Montreal River Heritage Tours, the world's shortest covered bridge (fewer than three metres in length), the overfilled House of Memories Museum and the Ontario Loggers' Hall of Fame. In 1986 the bridge over the river was named in honour of Aubrey Cosens who won the Victoria Cross during World War II. The bridge itself had to be reconstructed after it collapsed in 2003.

The museum, which opened in 1994, includes a bunkhouse, cookery and blacksmith shop. The Heritage Logging Days Festival recreates the lives of logging and sawmill employees during the 1930s. Latchford offers starting points for power boats, canoes, hiking trails, snowmobiling and cross-country skiing. Motels, a bed and breakfast and campsites provide overnight accommodation.

Earlton, population 600 in 2016 in the township of Armstrong (largely French-Canadian; population of 1,166 in 2016; 1,199 in 2021), south of Englehart on Highway 11, is best known as a weather station. Its airport serves Temiskaming Shores to the south and Kirkland Lake to the northwest. Located at the halfway point between North Bay and Cochrane (200 kilometres from each) amid dairy farms, its principal attraction used to be the Temiskaming Wildlife Centre (formerly the Earlton Zoo), which had a reputation as the only place in Ontario north of Toronto with African animals. The centre became home to injured creatures. The nearby Hilliardton Marsh has more than 600 species of birds, fish and plants, some of which can be viewed from a boardwalk. A five-kilometre trail (one way) leads through three marshes. On the third weekend in July, the town hosts the Earlton Steam and Antique Show. In 2009, Earlton was the site of the International Ploughing Match, an event which until then had never been held at such a northerly latitude. NHL player Wilf Paiement, formerly of the Toronto Maple Leafs, is one of Earlton's famous sons.

Near Earlton is the cheese producing community of Thornloe, named for a pioneer Anglican bishop. The farmers' cooperative which produces the cheese is south of Highway 11, but their shop on the highway offered a great variety of their special products. The shop suddenly closed in 2023. Just south of Earlton, a former bison farm had a huge model erected to commemorate the animal.

Englehart, population 1494 in 2006, 1,479 in 2016, and 1,588 in 2022, is 15 kilometres north of Temiskaming Shores on Highway 11. It is the site of the world's largest wafer board manufacturing factory, owned by Grant Forest Products, but bought by Georgia-Pacific after bankruptcy protection and being restructured. The surrounding area offers many hiking trails, and the Kap Kig Iwan Provincial Park (Ojibwe for "running water over the edge") has a waterfall that can be crossed via a suspension bridge.

Like Latchford, Englehart resulted from the building of the Temiskaming and Northern Ontario Railway. The railways stockpiled equipment at Mile 138 on the Blanche, now the Englehart River. In 1906, Englehart became a divisional point,

World's Shortest Covered Bridge, Latchford

with repair shops and an engine roundhouse. A post office, churches and schools followed. Incorporated as a town in 1908, the first municipal council was elected that same year. Englehart takes its name from Jacob Lewis Englehart, then the top official of the Temiskaming and Northern Ontario Railway Commission.

Matachewan First Nation (Ojibwe and Cree) promoted itself on a website with the phrase "Where the road ends, the adventure begins." Located at the end of Highway 66, it is on the Montreal River near High Falls. The band signed a treaty for land sharing in 1906 when still engaged in the fur trade. The Hudson's Bay post was eight kilometres north. In the early twentieth century gold and copper were found, and the small town had the usual boom and bust cycle of mining centres. Its population has declined (1991 at 453, 2001 at 308, 2006 at 375, 2016 at 61, and 268 in 2021). The First Nations group is involved in mining ventures and offers training for youth.

Northeast of Kirkland Lake is the territory of Beaverhouse First Nation, population around 200 in 2022. It is an old settlement on the banks of the Misema River, known as Maasseema Queesh in Algonquin. It has its own Roman Catholic Church, rebuilt in 2004, but depends upon Kirkland Lake for ambulance, fire and judicial services. The band did not receive recognition in the early 20th century treaties, but as of 2022 the Canadian government acknowledged it as a First Nation collectivity and provided some compensation for previous years.

Larder Lake (population 745 in 2021, 730 in 2016, 700 in 2006; 1,000 in 1991;

one-third French) is 30 kilometres east of Kirkland Lake on Highway 66 (leading to Quebec). There, the first major gold find of Northeastern Ontario was discovered in 1906. That led to some 4,000 prospectors swarming the area and resulted in the Kirkland Lake gold rush. Larder Lake still relies on mining and forestry, but tourism is very important. With its attractive setting on a large lake the community offers great fishing, swimming and boating. It also boasts trails and a ski hill, but numerous fishing derbies involve efforts to catch trout, catfish, pickerel and pike. Bears, moose and small game are quite abundant. The tourist centre includes displays about the region's rich history. Eighteen large stones encircle the lake with some matching sunrises and sunsets at summer and winter solstices. Some Indigenous consider the site sacred. Does the large trout statue at this northeastern entry to Northeastern Ontario match the more famous Wawa goose in the west?

The Virginiatown area (mainly French speaking) stretches along Highway 66 from Kearns, within walking distance of the Quebec border, to Virginiatown and North Virginiatown, about 10 kilometres to the west. Like other communities on either side of the provincial boundary, its raison d'être was gold production, but since the Kerr Addison Mine ceased production late in the twentieth century, its population has been declining till recently, sharply from 1100 in 2001 to 700 in 2006 and 609 in 2016, but 745 in 2021. Like other communities, it once had a significant English-speaking population. Yet, Virginiatown continues to provide fishing and hiking opportunities, even a base for climbing the odd-shaped Mount Cheminis on the border with Quebec. The Virginiatown Heritage House is a historical museum, and the Heritage Gold Trail offers displays of mining equipment. The town has basic stores and accommodation, as well as a curling club.

Resources
Ontario Heritage Trust, *Founding of the Town of Latchford* (Toronto: Ontario Heritage, 2009).
Herb Kruger, *A Place Called Krugerdorf* (Barrie: Barrie Press, 1994).

Temiskaming Shores

Temiskaming Shores (population 12,904 in 2011; 9,634 in 2021) is one of Ontario's smallest cities. It dates from a 2004 amalgamation of the towns of Haileybury and New Liskeard with Dymond Township. Located about 150 kilometres north of North Bay on Highway 11 and on the Ontario Northland Railway, it sits on the western shore of Lake Temiskaming. Roughly two-thirds of the people have English as a mother tongue, and one-third French. The economy depends on agriculture, education and tourism, although some who work in the mining industry of nearby Cobalt live in Temiskaming Shores. Agriculture is possible because of the Lesser Clay Belt, which straddles the boundary between Ontario and Quebec. Both the Lesser Clay Belt around northern Temiskaming Shores and the more northerly Great Clay Belt in the Districts of Cochrane (Ontario) and Abitibi (Quebec), 29 million acres in total, resulted from the draining of Glacial Lake Ojibwe after the most recent Ice Age.

The Temiskaming area, especially the rivers, lakes and their shorelines have been inhabited by Indigenous people for centuries. They had trade routes to James Bay and to Lake Nipissing. The Algonquin, Ojibwe and Cree hunted, fished and engaged in some agriculture, frequently changing their domicile.

In 1795, the Montreal based North West Company (NWC) established a fur trading post on the shore of Lake Temiskaming. Later, the NWC merged with the Hudson's Bay Company (HBC), and that led in 1889 to the arrival of Haileybury's first settler, Charles Cobbold Farr, an HBC employee. At that time, travellers reached the area by water, upstream from Mattawa on the Ottawa River. With the discovery of silver in Cobalt, food from the Haileybury area found a market, and the arrival of the Temiskaming and Northern Ontario Railway (now Ontario Northland) after 1903 made Haileybury more accessible. In 1904 it became a town, and in 1912 the District Seat of Temiskaming. That same year, the Haileybury School of Mines, which has a global clientele, opened its doors. By 1910, Haileybury had hotels, and even a National Hockey Association team, the Haileybury Comets. Haileybury's electric streetcar service, The Nipissing Central Railway, transported some 2,000 residents of Haileybury, New Liskeard and North Cobalt to and from their workplace in Cobalt each day.

In June 1978, Haileybury experienced a devastating tragedy when when twelve boys from St. John's School of Claremont (northeast of Toronto) died of hypothermia after capsizing on Lake Temiskaming while on a canoe trip.

Visitors can enjoy and gain knowledge from the Haileybury Heritage Museum at 575 Main Street, uphill from Lake Temiskaming on the approach to Highway 11. Outside sits the *M.V. Beauchene*, a diesel-powered tugboat built in Owen Sound and named for the Beauchene River. *The Beauchene*'s owner, the Upper Ottawa Improvement Company, used it to tow log booms on lower Lake Temiskaming and the upper Mattawa River, where from 1882 until 1965 it was one of 50 working boats. Later the *Beauchene* linked the community of Temiskaming, Quebec, with Mattawa, Ontario.

The museum highlights the fire of 4 October 1922. In six hours, the blaze destroyed 90% of Haileybury's buildings, killed 11 people, left 3,000 homeless, and cost $2 million in property damage. 87 streetcars arrived from Toronto to provide temporary housing; one of those trams is on display.

A bit of infamy is attached to Haileybury because from 1929 to 1961 it was the hanging capital of the northeast. The museum provides some context: Nine prisoners were executed at this judicial seat though the crimes were committed in Cochrane, Hearst, Kirkland Lake or Timmins. With one exception, all were Caucasian males; one was an Asian male. Four were crimes of passion.

One section of the museum is devoted to ghost writer Leslie McFarlane, a Haileybury author best known by his pseudonym Franklin W. Dixon, "author" of *The Hardy Boys* series. While living in Haileybury from 1932 until 1936, McFarlane authored nine titles of the famed series. At the same time, he wrote four books in the less well-known *Dana Girls* series. McFarlane and his wife Amy, who later wrote one of *The Hardy Boys* books, rented the house at 580 Brewster Street. McFarlane memorabilia includes his typewriter and a picture taken with his class at Haileybury High School in 1917. His son Brian was one of the voices of the NHL hockey broadcasts during the 1970s and 1980s.

Not surprisingly, part of the Haileybury Heritage Museum deals with sports. Hockey player and native of Haileybury, Leo Labine (1931–2005), played with the Barrie Flyers when they won the Memorial Cup in 1951, after which he had a ten-year career with the NHL's Boston Bruins. A picture dated around 1941 shows the winners of the Northern Ontario Women's Golf Association championship: Haileybury's Grace McDonough, Margaret Atchison, Flora McFarlane and Mrs. E.G. Ryley. The Museum also houses exhibits on the Ontario Provincial Police, who have their district headquarters in Haileybury, on geology and on Haileybury's founder, Cobbold Farr. Born in Suffolk, England in 1851, Farr studied at Haileybury College in Hertfordshire, England. He arrived in Canada in 1871, and in 1873 became a clerk with the Hudson's Bay Company, with which he served until 1889. In 1883 he purchased 30 acres of land at Haileybury, and in 1896 he distributed pamphlets to recruit prospective immigrants to farm in the area. In 1906, two years after Haileybury's incorporation as a town, Farr became its mayor. He died in 1914.

Another tourist attraction is a walk along Haileybury's Brewster Street and Latchford Street, where prominent people used to live in mini mansions. When fire destroyed much of Haileybury in 1922, the homes on those streets managed to survive. Residents included Noah

Grant house, Haileybury. Allegedly Canada's largest.

Timmins of Hollinger Mines and Sir Harry Oakes of Kirkland Lake.

Lake Temiskaming—the source of the Ottawa River—offers many recreational opportunities. Near it is Haileybury's short nine-hole golf course. Temiskaming Shore's new City Hall is in Haileybury and houses a well-lit art gallery. Locals point out Haileybury's newest attraction: Canada's allegedly largest house at 65,000 square feet. Built by the Grant family, whose waferboard plants went bankrupt, it currently stands for sale unfinished, with its own breakwater and yacht facilities beneath the modernist villa. Full of garbage and covered by graffiti, in 2023 a project was initiated for it to be cleaned and renovated while making a tv documentary about the process.

New Liskeard, to the north of Haileybury, attracted veterans of the militia that had challenged Manitoba's Louis Riel during his second rebellion (1884-1885); they became the first settlers. They displaced some of the Timiskaming First Nation which continues to exist on the north end of the lake, mostly on the Quebec side. The territorial limits of their land remain in contention. The lumber industry also lured settlers to New Liskeard, which became a town in 1903. In 1905, a company which subsequently dominated telephone service through much of Northern Ontario, NorthernTel, began in New Liskeard. Over the next two decades, NorthernTel purchased smaller companies until in 1928 it became the Northern Telephone Company. It sold its assets to Bell Canada and Télébec in 1969 and 1976, respectively. In 2023, the community celebrated its 121st Fall Fair. The University of Guelph has an experimental farm at New Liskeard, and forest products are a mainstay of the local economy.

One cannot separate the history of New Liskeard from the activities of the prolific Shepherdson family, on display at New Liskeard's Little Claybelt Homesteaders' Museum on Highway 65. In 2010, the Museum celebrated a full century of the Shepherdsons' presence. Since their arrival in 1910, various family members have farmed, promoted hockey and music and held political offices. They have invented or manufactured water pumps, machinery to fabricate six-quart baskets, laundry hangers, and coffins,and operated a blacksmith shop. William Shepherdson invented and patented a mobile saw for milling logs in the United States in 1922 and in Canada in 1939. George Shepherdson is owner of Mid Canada Fiberglass, which manufactures fiberglass canoes, and designed and produced the spaceship outside Moonbeam, hundreds of kilometres to the northwest along Highway 11 in Cochrane District.

The Museum also features an exhibit about the Great Fire of 1922 and its effect on 18 townships at a cost of 43 lives. In addition to Haileybury, mentioned above, the Great Fire of 1922 destroyed lives and property in Englehart, Cobalt, North Cobalt, Charlton, Thornloe and Heaslip before a sleet storm on 5 October helped to extinguish the blaze. Outside the Museum stands an enormous cow, symbolic of the region's agriculture.

New Liskeard is also known for recreational facilities, such as the large arena that serves skaters and hockey players from the region. Like Haileybury, it has an extensive waterfront beach, as well as parks and marinas where boats can be launched inside a protective breakwater.

Dymond Township, incorporated in 1901, remains largely agricultural. Annual events include the Lioness Harvest Queen Festival and the Tri-Club Master Poker Run (for snowmobilers). Both Haileybury and New Liskeard have golf courses, and North Cobalt, also part of Temiskaming Shores, offers the Devil's Rock Hiking Trail and the North Cobalt Flea Market.

One of the most prominent residents of Temiskaming Shores is David Ramsay, MPP for Temiskaming. Ramsay initially won election to the Ontario Legislature in 1985 as a New Democrat, but he defected from that party and joined the Liberals. Unlike most defectors, he managed to win re-election in 1990 and 1995. Between 1987 and 1990, Ramsay served successively as Minister of Northern Development and Mines, Minister of Correctional Services, and Minister of Agriculture and Food in the Liberal cabinet of Premier David Peterson (1985-1990). When the Liberals returned to office in 2003 under the leadership of Premier Dalton McGuinty, Ramsay became Minister of Natural Resources (2003–2007), and from 2005, Minister of Aboriginal Affairs. Following the Liberal re-election victory of 2007, Ramsay became Parliamentary Assistant to the Premier of Ontario.

Resources

Michael Barnes, *The Tri-Towns: Cobalt, Haileybury, and New Liskeard* (2000).
Louis S. Kurowski, *The New Liskeard Story* (Cobalt: Highway Book Shop, 1991).
Leslie McFarlane, *The Ghost of the Hardy Boys* (1976).
Dave McLaren, *The Way It Was* (about Haileybury), (Cobalt: Highway Book Shop, 1996).

Thessalon

Water dominates Tesssalon: the town is on a peninsula jutting into Lake Huron and the Thessalon River runs through the town. Hence locals claim some of the best fishing, canoeing and boating in the country are close at hand. Numerous parks are located on water, its largest lakeside park has a nicely painted community centre and a large marina, which serves North Shore yachters and sailors.

Located at the junction of Highways 17 and 129, Thessalon (population 1,312 in 2011, 1,260 in 2021) is surrounded by, but not part of, the township of Huron Shores. It depends upon retirees, timber and tourism. A plywood and lumber mill as well as a hospital and retirement home provide employment. Affordable homes overlooking one of the Great Lakes are available here at better prices than at almost any other location in Ontario (though Elliot Lake and Massey too advertise retirement living at low cost). A large arena, curling rink and imposing community hall provide activities. Lake Huron's beaches are attractive to young people, and both the lake and its tributary, the Thessalon River, offer opportunities to fishermen. Hunting for moose, deer and grouse north of Highway 17 is popular; the Voyageur Hiking Trail passes just a little further north.

Thessalon was incorporated as a Township in 1887, when a branch line of the Canadian Pacific Railway, along the north shore of Lake Huron from Sudbury to Sault Ste. Marie, passed through the area. The name comes from a First Nations word meaning "something big above something small." Supposedly a native hunting party was on the peninsula and saw a big bear on a small limb, whereby one exclaimed "Thessalon."

The Anishnawbek have lived in the area for hundreds of years, engaged in fishing, hunting as well as crafts. According to the 1850 treaty the Indigenous thought they were to receive 144 square miles but the treaty itself was for 16, though surveyors laid out some 40. The Thessalon First Nation continues to claim the remaining 104 square miles.

According to local historian Edith Cameron, Nathaniel Dyment founded Thessalon, by establishing a mill there in 1877; it was the first steam driven mill and second sawmill on the North Shore. Dyment "bought the Township of Kirkwood from the McArthur Bros. who were square timber operators. In the same year, he purchased 300 acres on the east side and at the mouth of the Thessalon River, from the Department of Indian Affairs, for a mill and townsite. By 1884, there were about 200 permanent residents, 18 houses, eight shacks, a general store, a hotel, two churches and a one-room school. Mail came by boat during summer and by dog team in winter. The Soo extension of the Canadian Pacific Railway was built in 1887, but most of the commerce was carried by water, as about 14 boats docked there per week during the navigation season. By 1887 it had a newspaper which reported the disastrous fires of 1888:The paper of 20 July 1888 mentions a very bad fire which started in the Desert (probably Kirkwood) and burned very furiously. At other points, fire threatened the new railway and both trains and boats were delayed by dense smoke which covered the whole area. About 1 September, the Dyment sawmill was destroyed by fire starting in or near the boiler room. Mr. Dyment immediately ordered the erection of a new and larger mill, and most of the construction was done that same Fall. In the same year, 1888, the town was surveyed into lots and the first permanent bridge was built across the Thessalon River. In 1906, the population was 1,242—approximately the same as it is today."

A local tells a different story about an aspect of Thessalon: Mrs. Marjike Mahaffy recounts that a relative had to threaten Klu Klux Klan members who tried to burn a cross at their farm. The Klan was quite active during the 1920s and 1930s in parts of Northeastern Ontario near the U.S. border. The Klan died out in Thessalon during the 1940s but whether its racist attitudes remained is not known.

Resources
J. E. MacDonald, *This Point of Land: An Account of the Early History of Thessalon* (Sault Ste. Marie: Sault Star, 1972)

An informative website can be accessed by a search for "A Historical Journey: North of Huron".

Timmins

Timmins is more than a hundred years old (established 1909–1912, depending on the part), and it is big. Geographically it stretches twenty kilometres east-west over what is known as The Porcupine. It has also incorporated much territory to the north and south. Like Sudbury, all the outlying towns have been amalgamated into one urban centre, although some still retain their identity. Perhaps like all places affected by the boom-and-bust cycles typical of mining centres, the result is a city centre that is not uniform but a conglomeration of buildings from many eras with no identifiable style.

The City of Timmins uses the following land acknowledgment: "we are located on the traditional lands of Mattagami First Nation, Flying Post First Nation and Matachewan First Nation," all of whom signed treaties with the crown in 1905.

Timmins (population 46,500 in 2006; 41,145 in 2021), which calls itself "The City with a Heart of Gold," owes its existence to gold mines. The name comes from two merchants from Mattawa, Noah and Henry Timmins, who made a fortune from Cobalt's silver. The discovery of gold north of Cobalt in 1905 led to an immediate gold rush in the Porcupine area, in which the Timmins brothers were prominent as financiers. A barber from Cobalt, Benny Hollinger, struck gold south of Gillies Lake during 1909. The Timmins brothers created a syndicate with Hollinger and,

Hollinger Mine, Timmins

with others, incorporated the Hollinger Mine in 1910. By 1912 three large mining companies—Hollinger, McIntyre and Dome Mines—were operative.

During the twentieth century more than a hundred mines existed in the Timmins area, extracting copper, asbestos, silver and other minerals. Today Newmont Goldcorp is the main, near monopoly, gold producer, though Glencore at Kidd Creek, which mines copper, zinc and silver, has one of Canada's largest open pit mines. Goldcorp is among Timmins' largest employers with about one thousand employees and contractors; its mine shafts descend to over 9,000 feet. However, it has closed its refinery. As the price of gold increases, Goldcorp is reworking old claims and re-opening old mines. In the twenty-first century, Timmins has been booming, resulting in the usual overpriced accommodations because of increased prospecting and financial activities, though also bringing more employment opportunities. Lakeshore Gold is the new player, having made a substantial gold discovery on the westerly boundary of Timmins. Timmins is also the principal regional headquarters for de Beers which is extracting high quality diamonds from its site at Attawapiskat.

During the Porcupine gold rush, the Temiskaming and Northern Ontario Railway, which reached Cochrane in 1908, quickly built a branch line east towards the Mattagami River, on which Timmins is located. Motorists will find Timmins on Highway 101, west of Highway 11 from North Bay (350 kilometres), and east of Highway 144 from Sudbury (300 kilometres), though those road connections came only in the 1920s and 1970, respectively.

Despite a huge fire at South Porcupine (estimates start at 16 square kilometres burned) taking 71 lives in 1911, in 1912 Timmins became a town. Since the mining areas stretched from the Mattagami River east through Porcupine and smaller mining camps to Nighthawk Lake, the region developed haphazardly, based on the needs of the mining industry. To coordinate municipal services and to bring mining companies within municipal boundaries for tax purposes, in 1973 the government of Ontario amalgamated Timmins with surrounding communities, including Mountjoy

Township, Porcupine, South Porcupine and Schumacher, so that for more than two decades the Corporation of the City of Timmins was Canada's largest municipality in terms of surface area. Since 1995, three other cities, including Greater Sudbury, have relegated Timmins to fourth place, though the oddity of driving through 30 kilometres of bush from the city limits to the suburbs of Timmins remains.

Timmins is a regional economic, health and religious hub. It is the site of the Anglican cathedral of the Diocese of Moosonee, which extends from the Arctic-Atlantic Watershed (100 kilometres south) to Moosonee. It is also the seat for the Roman Catholic Diocese of Timmins. Lumbering, the other early pillar of the local economy, continues with one major mill, but has lost its relative importance. Education (Northern College, Collège Boréal, Laurentian University extension courses, Collège de Hearst satellite campus), health services to the surrounding area and tourism are considered the potential growth areas.

About half the population of Timmins is French Canadian, but only about 35% continue to claim French as their primary language while nearly half are bilingual. The strength of French is reflected in the large Centre Culturel La Ronde, a Francophone community centre housed in a renovated school with reception halls, workshop space, bar and crafts. Finns, Italians, Croatians and Poles too had their own halls, but European ethnic silos or separateness have declined due to intermarriage since most of the European workers came early in the twentieth century or just after World War II. Until the 1950s, 38 ethnic and union halls had dances with live orchestras, nearly all of which have been displaced by integration and electronic technology. The First Nations Friendship Centre seeks to help the increasing number of First Nations youth joining the workforce adjust to urban life. Though the main office of the United Steelworkers has been centralized to Sudbury, the union continues to recruit and to monitor work conditions, as do the Canadian Auto Workers (formerly Mine Mill) at Glencorp.

Timmins has had some tragic moments. A fire at Hollinger in 1928 cost 39 lives; another less disastrous fire in 1965 inspired singer/songwriter Stompin' Tom Connors to compose the song, "Fire in the Mine." In 1953, a strike lasting 230 days at Hollinger and McIntyre devastated the economy to the point where challengers withdrew from the municipal elections of that year to allow incumbents to return by acclamation and thereby spare Timmins the expense of a race. However, out of the 1928 disaster came the creation of Ontario's system of mine safety and rescue, including fire drills and refuge stations underground. Recently, the rising price of gold has helped Timmins survive the downsizing of the forest industry.

Among the cultural entrepots is the Timmins Museum National Exhibition Centre, situated in a renovated building near the public library since 2011. It provides the history of the Timmins area through photos, newspapers, artifacts and displays. A permanent exhibit "Where We Stand – Stories of the land" explores the over 5,000-year-old history of the area, including First Nations. The Hollinger House, representing company housing for mine workers, is located at the Timmins Museum. The Aboveground Art Gallery and the museum's temporary art gallery are also in a renovated Hollinger building and have very well-lit spaces to display the work of national-level exhibits and local artists.

An attraction is the Cedar Meadows resort and spa, namely a motel complex

Hollinger House Timmins Museum (Credit: City of Timmins)

combined with a large area to display animals of the northeast (bison, moose, elk, deer). Some of the animals approach wagons transporting viewers at feeding time.

Timmins has some older buildings such as the Airport Hotel in South Porcupine where a bush pilot's club existed in the 1940s, and the McIntyre Lodge (now a bed and breakfast), which provided accommodation for mining executives. Downtown along Algonquin, on the main street, the boom town years are represented by the Old Public Library (originally a post office in the 1930s), the Empire Complex (seniors' residence; formerly the Empire Hotel, built in 1928 and recognized at the time as one of the North's best hotels—it even had a fountain in the Fountain Court Lounge!), and the New Goldfields Theatre.

Timmins has produced more than its share of entertainers and other celebrities. Singer Shania Twain, who spent her formative years in Timmins, was honoured by a museum but it closed in 2013 for lack of attendance. Charlie Angus utilized his fame as a singer and social activist to win election as an NDP member of the Canadian Parliament in 2004 and continues as a strong voice for the north. Stompin' Tom Connors launched his career in 1965 as a guitar player and singer at Timmins' Maple Leaf Hotel. Because he was a nickel short, the bartender allowed him to pay for beer by performing, and then the hotel offered him a contract. Singer Dave Carroll gained fame in 2009 after United Airlines mangled his guitar and refused to accept responsibility until Carroll posted a song about the incident on YouTube. He and his brother Don perform in the band Sons of Maxwell. Valerie Poxleitner (a.k.a. "Lights"), a native of Timmins like the Carroll brothers and Charlie Angus, has won a Juno award. Comedian Paul Bellini writes for the CBC television programme *This Hour*

Has 22 Minutes. Timmins-born Derek Edwards is the only Canadian to win the Vail Colorado Invitational Comedy Competition. Timmins-born Lola Lemire Tostevin has written multiple novels and books of poetry. Timmins-born Bruce Watson plays the guitar with a Scottish rock band, Big Country. Comedian Maurice LaMarche moved to Timmins as a child but by the age of 19 was performing in New York and shortly thereafter in Los Angeles.

Offstage as well, Timmins has produced famous people. Media magnate Roy Thomson's first newspaper was the *Timmins Daily Press*, purchased in 1934; he already operated a radio station in North Bay. Gordon Thiessen (Governor of the Bank of Canada 1994-2001) was born in Timmins, as was Myron Scholes, co-author of the Black-Scholes equation, for which in 1997 he won the Nobel Memorial Prize in Economic Sciences. Alfred Aho, a computer scientist, gained many honours for his programming and textbooks.

Noteworthy politicians include Wilfred Spooner, Mayor of Timmins at the time of the 1953 strike and subsequently a provincial cabinet minister; Alan Pope, a cabinet minister from 1979–1985; and Jamie Lim, the first woman to become Mayor of Timmins (2000—2003). Lim's defeat in the municipal election of 2003 may have been attributable to her preference for a new library over a new police station.

Timmins offers a wide choice of recreational opportunities, including many parks and conservation areas within city limits, that allow for pleasant walks and waterfront strolls. Endless possibilities exist for canoeing and kayaking expeditions, boating, fishing and swimming because of the multitude of rivers and lakes in the region, including nearby Kettle Lakes Provincial Park. Many hiking and cross-country ski trails are being developed on the edges of the urban landscape as the huge hills made of mine tailings are covered and reclaimed. 15 kilometres to the west of the city, a downhill ski resort is at Kamiskotia, where 1976 Olympic Gold medalist Kathy Kreiner learned how to ski. However, snowmobiling is probably the most popular sport, with very extensive trail systems running for hundreds of kilometres in all directions. Timmins continues to supply its share of hockey players to the NHL, and for years after World War II, McIntyre sponsored one of Canada's few indoor skating rinks, where figure skaters could practice throughout summer. The arena was built in 1938 for the company's employees but the McIntyre Community Centre has added a curling club and ballrooms open to the public. The Big Band dances continue an earlier tradition of public dances by various European ethnic groups. Summer concerts are held weekly in Holinger Park. Festivals or major events include ice fishing derbies, winter carnival, drama, curling, ringette, summer and rib fests with the Porquis Blues Fest going for three days and the Great Canadian Kayak Challenge competitions drawing large audiences.

Resources

Kerry M. Abel, *Changing Places: History, Community and Identity in Northeastern Ontario* (Kingston: McGill-Queens Press, 2006).

Karen Bachmann, *Porcupine Gold Fields, 1920–1935* (St. Catherines: Looking Back, 2004).

Eau Claire Falls

Waterfalls

Northeastern Ontario is rich in waterfalls. Rivers and lakes situated on the Canadian Shield must find cracks or weak points to descend to the next level on their way to Hudson Bay or the Great Lakes. The results are frequently spectacular drops, though some become small cascades during dry years or in late summer. Only major falls are highlighted here, but smaller ones can be delightful finds near major and minor roads.

Manitoulin Island has two notable falls, one in the hamlet of Kagawong and one near Manitowaning. The former, Bridal Veil Falls, is true to its name and offers an even sweep of water which is best viewed in spring or early summer, though charming in winter. The other is on the east side of the road just south of the fine lookout at Ten Mile Point on the way to Manitowaning from Little Current. The rustic viewing area has picnic tables. The falls, known as High Falls, can become a mere trickle during dry summers, but are worth viewing for the way the slabs of fossil-laden rock have been exposed by the water's action. Rattlesnakes sometimes sun on the north side.

High Falls is a name often given to waterfalls, and Northeastern Ontario has several. One, also known as Onaping Falls, is just north of Chelmsford, northwest of Sudbury on Highway 144 to Timmins. A.Y. Jackson of the Group of Seven did paintings of the falls, hence the parking, picnic and viewing area is named A.Y. Jackson Lookout. A hiking trail follows the west side of the falls over special rock formations that are part of a marked geological tour of the area; part of it is wheelchair accessible. Three kilometres of trails wind through diverse tree stands, going over a footbridge above the falls from which a very different perspective is offered. The falls are a special experience during the autumn when leaves turn to orange, yellow and crimson. Nearby, following the road north to Windy Lake, then Ministic and Armstrong Lakes, and cross country to Fairbanks Provincial Park, provides some of the best shows of fall colours in Ontario.

To the northeast of Sudbury and southwest of Temagami is Lady Evelyn-Smoothwater Provincial Park with rugged terrain and many waterfalls. They are not easily reached except by strenuous hikes or canoe. Most are on the Lady Evelyn River, which offers numerous whitewater possibilities. Nearer to Sudbury or other towns along Highway 17 many waterfalls have been partially blocked by power dams as at Sturgeon Falls or Nairn Centre (a village on the Spanish River). Seen only from the picnic site off Highway 6 are the Whitefish Falls about 25 kilometres south of Highway 17 on the way to Manitoulin Island. Especially impressive is the larger setting of the village park and La Cloche Mountains. Lorne Falls on the Vermillion River is 40 kilometres west of Sudbury, along Lorne Falls Road to its end. The best view is from a canoe.

Duchesnay Falls is just west of North Bay, easy to access by a two-minute walk from a parking stop on Highway 17. The identification is Duchesnay Creek, which becomes small during dry years. This cascade is a series of jumps dropping over eight metres. In fall, bright colours highlight the white churning water.

Forty kilometres east of North Bay off Highway 17, following Highway 630 seven kilometres, then off Peddler's Drive, is Eau Claire Falls in the Eau Claire Gorge Conservation Area. The parking area has a trail map. The falls, just off a scenic, easy trail in a well-forested gorge, drops about 12 metres and is about half that width. This has been termed "a first-class, sizeable waterfall hidden in the wilderness," by Mark Harris in Waterfalls of Ontario. Large red pines line the trail.

Aubrey Falls, in the small provincial park of the same name, is 80 kilometres north of Thessalon. A short trail leads from Highway 129 to the falls with good views from a bridge over the gorge. The water drops nearly 50 metres in a series of cascades going in different directions, but sometimes the flow is reduced by the impressive power dam at the end of the trail. The bridge over the river and rough landscape around the falls make for an experience, as one negotiates the terrain.

Also, near Thessalon, just 3.5 kilometres north of Highway 17 on Highway 129, are the Little Thessalon Falls. Though small, they are quite pretty.

A kilometre north of Massey at Chutes Provincial Park, a trail north of the campgrounds leads to a series of cascades that twist and wind through interesting rock formations. It contrasts sharply with the lower broad and calm river running through town.

Chippewa Falls, on the river of the same name, 30 kilometres north of Sault Ste. Marie on Highway 17, has a path leading to both the Lower and Upper falls. Closer to the Sault at the Kinsmen Park (two kilometres north of Sixth Line) are the impressive Crystal Falls. One can walk and climb right beside the cascading

Michipicoten Falls

water on a circular trail of about two kilometres. Hiawatha Falls, just north of the Sault has a set of stairs leading ever higher right beside the twisting falls.

Silver Falls on the Michipicoten River and Scenic High Falls on the Magpie River are near Wawa, west off Highway 17, and are among the many waterfalls on rivers dropping into Lake Superior. The picnic area of the former is a bit primitive, but the latter has good interpretive signage about logging and power development. Both falls with their 15 metre drops are worth the few kilometer trips off the main road.

Agawa Falls near Frater just off Highway 17 is large and very impressive with its double plume. Among the small waterfalls between Wawa and Sault Ste. Marie are Batchewana Falls, at the river and bay of the same name, and Montreal Falls, also named after its river, just south of Lake Superior Park. Many falls are in that park, including the large Sand River Falls which is readily accessible at the north end, although Gargantua and Bald Head are only reached by hiking a couple of hours.

A spectacular waterfall, New Post, at the Abitibi River gorge, is near Fraserdale (from Highway 11 just east of Smooth Rock Falls on Highway 634 about 80 kilometres north). It may be threatened by hydro expansion.

Resources
Mark Harris, *Waterfalls of Ontario*, accessible at http://www.start.ca/users/

Wawa

The town name comes from the Ojibwe word for "wild geese" and has been used since 1899. The community celebrates that origin with a huge goose monument just off Highway 17 at the south entrance to the town. The first goose was erected in September 1960 to mark the completion of the last link of the Trans-Canada Highway. In 1963, the original plaster sculpture was replaced by a steel one that was claimed to be "the largest of its kind in Canada" (28 feet tall, 19 wide). In 2017, due to the disintegration of the steel, a new bronze goose of the same size was unveiled. The tourist information centre directly behind the goose has local history and walking-tour brochures and provides an excellent introduction to the outdoor offerings of the town and hinterlands.

Michipicoten First Nation lived at the mouth of the Michipicoten River for centuries. The word Michipicoten means "high bluff", though the Indigenous have been displaced to the west away from the hills.

The town has many visitors because the Trans-Canada highway and Highway 101, that link northern communities on Highway 11, join near the airport after 101 crosses through the town centre. The distances from major centres make Wawa a natural stopping point. Sault Ste. Marie is 230 kilometres south; Timmins is 330 kilometres east.

Some 2,700 (in 2021) people reside in the town, but its population shifts with fishing derbies, hunting season and snowmobilers. The town has an ideal location on

The Wawa Goose

the hill overlooking Lake Superior and beside the Magpie and Michipicoten rivers, making it a scenic stopping point and a gateway to outdoor adventure. The large Wawa Lake on the east side of town offers a Boreal Gateway Boardwalk with benches, picnic area and markers that provide information in English, French and Ojibwe on the natural and cultural heritage of Wawa's rich boreal landscape. Many motels serve the seasonal clientele who join the locals in skiing, ice fishing, snowshoeing, golfing, hunting, hiking, canoeing, gem-panning, four-wheeling, flying into remote camps and swimming. The Annual Ice Fishing Derby in March offers large prizes and draws some 4,000 people; a Salmon Fishing Derby is held in July. Naturally Superior Adventures offers group outings in a 36-foot replica of a voyageur canoe as well as other guided outings to showcase the area.

The town on the hill emerged much later than the Michipicoten River Village on Lake Superior about 10 kilometres down the Magpie River. The village was first the site of a First Nation settlement, next a missionary encampment (hence still called "the Mission") and Hudson's Bay post, then the docks from which ores were shipped to Sault Ste. Marie and is now the local marina for access to Lake Superior. The Michipicoten First Nation is located northwest around the bay at Michipicoten Harbour. On that road is the Sandy Beach Ecological Interpretive Centre with information on native life and vegetation patterns. The beach with dunes is about a kilometre long. The Voyageur Hiking Trail can be followed between Wawa and the River Village; the trail also runs to Lake Superior Park. Two major waterfalls (Silver and Magpie High) are just off Highway 17.

The early settlement history of the area is associated with the fur trade and then with logging. In 1896, a gold rush that followed a find on Wawa Lake pushed the population from a few loggers to a thousand. By 1906 production slowed but some small enterprises continue to the present. The search for gold led to the discovery of iron ore in 1897 and it soon was shipped from the Helen Mine to Sault Ste. Marie to fuel Clergue's steel mill. From 1900 to 1918 it was the most productive iron mine in Canada. To support the mining, by 1912 Superior Power generated electricity at High Falls on the Magpie River. But between 1911 and 1921 the population sank from 1,001 to 101. In the late 1930s a recovery started as different mining technologies were employed, but boom and bust cycles continued to plague the industry and town. In 1998 the mine closed. Similarly pulp and paper—the mill 30 kilometres east of town closed in 2007—and lumbering have suffered market declines. Yet, Wawa exudes a local pride and determination to survive through tourism and presenting itself as a healthy outdoor paradise.

Resources
Florence Clarke, *Magpie Memoirs.* Edited by Johanna Rowe (Wawa, n.d.).
Johanna (Morrison) Rowe, *Heart of a Mountain, Soul of a Town: The Story of Algoma Ore and the Town of Wawa* (Wawa, 1999).
Johanna Rowe, *Signs of a Town* (Wawa, 1999)

West Nipissing

West of North Bay, Highway 17 offers magnificent views of Lake Nipissing and then flat agricultural lands. As the water retreated from the last Ice Age, it left fertile regions. Nipissing First Nation utilized the land and lakeshore for some centuries as archeological finds have confirmed. Fur traders and loggers were the first settlers. Once the Canadian Pacific Railway provided a link with Montreal in the 1880s, settlers from Quebec proceeded to displace the Indigenous. The CPR and the later highway, usually within sight of each other, hug the north shore of Lake Nipissing. West Nipissing is to the west of the Nipissing First Nation Reserve.

Since early exploration took place under the French regime, Lake Nipissing originally had the name Lac des Sorciers (Magicians) and the river running into it from the north de Champlain. When the English took over, they termed that river Nipissing, the same as the lake.

Although European settlement in what is now West Nipissing pre-dates the CPR, the actual Town of West Nipissing was born in 1999, with the amalgamation of Sturgeon Falls and surrounding communities. West Nipissing's core remains the former Sturgeon Falls, located where the Sturgeon River enters Lake Nipissing. It was named for the large sturgeon which made its way upstream through the rapids of the Sturgeon River to spawn. From 1888, Sturgeon Falls had a commercial fishery, which ended in the late twentieth century when the fish faced extinction. A recovery plan, in place since 1991, has proven successful, but there is no longer a commercial fishery. Tourists may well begin their tour of Sturgeon Falls with a visit to the Welcome Centre (which contains a small art gallery), on the south side of Highway 17 toward the east part of the community. On one wall is an 85-pound (roughly 40 kilo) sturgeon from Lake Nipissing. Until the supply neared the point of exhaustion, the sturgeon also provided caviar.

More than half West Nipissing's population (13,410 in 2011; 14,583 in 2021) lives in the former Sturgeon Falls. Residents of Sturgeon Falls claim to have Canada's highest proportion of bilingual people (73.4%), easily able to speak both English and French. Lumber has provided the economic backbone of Sturgeon Falls, although that community has an assortment of restaurants, motels and garages. It also offers the most varied shopping opportunities between North Bay and Sudbury.

The first Canadians of European extraction to live north of Lake Nipissing resided in what is now West Nipissing. Fur traders established a post on an island in Lake Nipissing as early as 1790, almost a century before the arrival of the CPR. The fort moved to the mouth of the LaVase Creek in what is now North Bay, where it remained until 1848. From 1848 until 1879, it operated as an outpost of the Hudson's Bay Company on the site of the present Musée Sturgeon River House, on the lower Sturgeon River just west of Sturgeon Falls, five kilometres south of Highway 17. The Musée began as a centennial project in 1967, and its ground floor is devoted to the fur trade. There, tourists can see the kinds of buildings and tools that fur traders used along with an exhibit of stuffed fur-bearing animals from the area: beaver, bobcat, fox, mink, muskrat, wolverine. The exhibit includes a dire warning from one-time trapper Carl Monk: "If you take a muskrat from a marsh, you reduce the population by one. If you take away the marsh, you reduce the muskrat population to zero forever." Whether his ecological advice impacted patterns of trapping is unknown. Hiking trails radiate from the Musée Sturgeon River House and include access to the Wetlands Park.

Upstairs, the museum displays an exhibit on the French-Canadian pioneers who settled West Nipissing, encompassing Cache Bay, Crystal Falls, Desaulniers, Field, Lavigne, River Valley, Sturgeon Falls and Verner. The exhibit includes a reconstructed school classroom and other aspects of pioneer life. With the arrival of the CPR, Québecois in search of farmland settled and provided homes to families whose surnames remain prominent. Unfortunately, as the growing season was short and the farms were small, many of the men had to work as loggers from November through April. Living conditions, as a video about the life of a lumberjack in 1932 indicates, were rough. For $150 pay per season, the men lived in bunkhouses, without privacy amid odours from dirty socks to tobacco. They quickly learned to eat their breakfast—then considered "the most important meal of the day"—in silence. Given that they had only 15 minutes at the table, the more they talked the less they could eat. Except for on Sundays, they worked for 10 hours each day, and the death toll was atrocious.

Throughout the year, the Musée Sturgeon River House hosts a range of activities: winter guided snowshoe tours, the Annual Northern Pike Tournament (late in June), Canada Day (1 July) celebrations, day camp for children throughout summer, a Cranberry Festival (the first weekend of October), the Traditional Family Christmas Dinner (early in December). Canada Day celebrations in 2010 included music, canoe rides, a dog agility show, face painting, a blacksmith at work and guided tours of the museum. In August, West Nipissing hosts the Sturgeon Falls Annual Step Dance and Fiddle Festival.

Ten kilometres to the west—where Highway 64 veers south from Highway 17—is Verner, named for the wife of CPR superintendent Archie Baker who oversaw the track laying. The arrival of the rails created job opportunities for French Canadians who had migrated to Michigan but feared that they would lose their language if they remained in the United States. At one point, more than 6,000 people attended

Musée Sturgeon River House Museum

Verner's St. Jean-Baptiste celebrations, French Canada's day to commemorate the arrival of explorer Jacques Cartier in what is now Quebec on 4 June 1534. Once a lumbering centre, today Verner is primarily an agricultural supply depot, with credit unions and coops. The Quebec influence can be seen in the upswept roof lines of some houses.

South of Sturgeon Falls on the shore of Lake Nipissing is Cache Bay, once the site of activity in the fur trade, logging and pulp and paper industries, even the site of a hospital. Now it is little more than a residence for people who work elsewhere.

Field, north of Sturgeon Falls on Highway 64, is primarily a logging town. In 1958, it was the site of a violent strike when members of the International Woodworkers of America voted to down their tools but some workers at the Field Lumber Company regarded voting procedures as unfair and tried to keep working. The Field Lumber Company dates from 1914, and one of its owners was Zodique Mageau, who moved to what is now West Nipissing in 1892. For more than a decade Mageau served as Mayor of Sturgeon Falls and then won elections as a Liberal Member of the Provincial Parliament in 1911, 1914, 1919 and 1923. Near Field is River Valley (northwest on Highway 539) where an annual country music festival draws large crowds on a summer weekend.

Among other personalities of West Nipissing whom residents consider prominent, and again illustrating the French and Roman Catholic Church predominance, have been Abbé (Abbot) Thomas Ferron, who founded Sturgeon Falls' Sacré Coeur parish in 1892;

239

Quebec-style house near Verner

the Filles de la Sagesse (Daughters of Wisdom), nuns who reached Sturgeon Falls in 1904 to teach and to launch both a boarding house, Notre-Dame de Lourdes, which survived until 1969, and an orphanage, which lasted from 1937 until 1946; Abbé Charles Langois, who arrived in 1902, founded Sacré Coeur Church and the convent Notre-Dame de Lourdes at Sturgeon Falls and who helped establish Sudbury's Collège du Sacré Coeur; Alphonse Legendre, who arrived from Michigan in 1897 and became an avid proponent of the French language; the Rev. Charles Alfred-Marie Paradis (1846-1926) who managed to persuade French Canadians who had migrated to Michigan to move to Verner; and Mgr. J. Oscar Racette, who arrived in 1914 and served 50 years as parish priest.

Resources
Wayne Labelle, *Sturgeon Falls, 1895–1995* (Field: W.F.L. Communications, 1995)

Zinger Lake

Yes, there is a Z: Zinger Lake, near Little Abitibi Provincial Park. You can fish for pickerel, trout, pike and burbot...so, Come On Over!

Afterword:
Thoughts on National Historic Sites

Northeastern Ontario deserves to have more National Historic Sites. Canada has a system which has identified over 2,200 places, people and events of national historic significance. Most are identified by roadside plaques. The designations of many are under review to create more regional and gender balance and to adjust outdated perspectives. Parks Canada operates the system, including the nearly 200 that have interpretive centres detailing the historic importance with artifacts, evidence and explanations.

Though Northeastern Ontario is central to Canada's history, it has only three such sites (Fort St. Joseph, Sault State Marie Canal, Ermatinger Clergue Houses) with interpretive centres. Only two are fully supported by the federal government through Parks Canada, which operates many across the country. For a region with so many important historical areas and events, this gap is a large oversight.

Though some Northeastern places have been given National Historic Site designation, such as mining in Sudbury-Timmins-Cobalt, archeological finds in Sheguiandah, residential schools such as Shingwauk in Sault St. Marie, or early settlement at Moose Factory, none have interpretive centres, though Shingwauk offers a tour. By comparison, the Niagara region has over 23 centres while Eastern Ontario has 42! Newfoundland, with the same population as Northeastern Ontario, has 160 designations with seven fully funded interpretive centres. Yukon, with a population of 42,000 (compared to Northeastern Ontario's 500,000) has 73 designations with six interpretive centres. One of the sites in Northeastern Ontario, Fort St. Joseph, finally has signage on Highway 17 (the Trans-Canada Highway, from which such signs were removed in the 1990s), but its budget is insufficient for extensive advertising. Furthermore, Newfoundland has a World Heritage Site at L'Anse-aux-Meadows, whereas on the same issue regarding early contact by Europeans, James Bay and Moose Factory are just as significant, but not acknowledged. Arguably, Cobalt's history is as exciting as that of Dawson City, and its silver rush led to the Porcupine gold rush which was far more important than the Yukon's. In all, the Porcupine Camp has produced over 120 million ounces of gold (by 2020) and continues to add to that total while the Klondike produced only 12 million ounces in total. Yet, Cobalt has received only a National Historic Site designation, not an interpretive centre. A similar argument about historical importance could be made for the LaVase portage east of North Bay that was crucial to the fur trade, and to east-west travel before the railway. Again, LaVase and the Mattawa River route have received designation but no centre.

Another potential national historic site is Algoma Mills. A side trip on the six kilometres of Highway 538 off Highway 17, about midway between Sudbury and Sault Ste. Marie, leads to a railway underpass and bridges at Algoma Mills. Here, at a siding off the railway, originally an extension of the Sudbury CPR line, is the typical North Shore beautiful scenery: rocky shoreline, islands and many pines. Nestled among the latter is a large cemetery. However, no town is nearby, only a scattered set of houses. A small incongruously bright locomotive, accompanied by two figures with the symbolic names "Spencer" and "Fillion" driving railway spikes, stands near a causeway and park. A set of large plastic-covered plaques announces the meaning of the locale. Here was once a commercial fishing industry, a huge lumber mill, a wharf for steamers, a trans-shipping location for coal and a planned hotel with 300 rooms for what would be a resort town. Algoma Mills is one of Northeastern Ontario's most historic places, but aside from the plaques and the nearly hidden cemetery, it is hard to guess that this was once a busy depot and industrial site, or that it once supported Indigenous hunting and fishing. A historical summary notes "As many as six passenger trains arrived daily in the early days of the Canadian Pacific Railway. In those days, Algoma Mills had an immigration and customs officer, a post office, three general stores, a bakery and two hotels with a population twice that of Blind River, the nearest town. The complete complex of Algoma Mills changed in 1910 when the Canadian Pacific Railway moved its coaling facilities to Byng Inlet, later changed to Britt." The tourists have come, but in small numbers and they usually zip by on the main highway, unless they stop to buy some smoked fish beside that road, or to go fishing on the opposite side of the road, at Lauzon Lake.

Algoma Mills may represent more than the boom and bust of early development, seen also in ghost towns like Worthington, Creighton, or Victoria Mine near Sudbury. It may embody the lackadaisical attitude of the federal and provincial governments towards an important past and potential present.

Perhaps related to the potential for historic tourism would be to suggest a different kind of travel: instead of the usual fast-food franchise or mall stops, why not try the foods and offerings of First Nations? If one started at Nipissing First Nation west of North Bay one could experience various meats, fish and many crafts, including carvings and leather goods at shops right on Highway 17. Or just south of West Nipissing (Sturgeon Falls), Garden Village would provide fare equal to that found on the main highway. The terrain at Whitefish Falls on the way to Manitoulin leads to more crafts, smoked fish and great picnic places. Near Massey the Sagamok First Nation lands offer hiking while at Serpent River a very large trading post has tasty food. Woodland paintings are for sale at a large building by a local park facing Lake Huron, and just up the hill, teepees from movie sets are on display. The circular community centres at nearly every First Nation community are usually architectural as well as symbolic statements, while the cultural centres offer historic and lifestyle information. Just east of Sault Ste. Marie, Garden River's fast-food places are just as good as any of the franchises but have the advantage of parks and lookouts over the St. Mary's River. By stopping at such territories, the diversity of life and work among First Nations is readily seen, and often opportunities arise to exchange views with locals. Should one add that not one of the places mentioned—including many where important encounters occurred during the fur trade, the lumber booms, the mining rushes—has become a National Historic Site?

Another unrecognized element prevalent in the Northeast is mercantile history. Though much is made of the fur trade and the voyageurs, that it was a trade is sometimes difficult to discern in all the excitement of shooting rapids, portaging and overcoming distances. The small businessperson, often an itinerant migrant, but just as readily the stable base for many new communities, has hardly received recognition. For instance, a review of the many businesses that comprised a small community such as Little Current on Manitoulin Island shows that the McGilverys, Sims or Turners provided continuity for communities. That rich history of the era of steamers and early railroads, the creation of small hydro plants, of telephone exchanges and telegraph offices, even local printing presses, too has not been registered for Northeastern Ontario.

Historical display at Algoma Mills

Acknowledgements

I am indebted to many helpful people. Foremost is Lisa J. Buse, who edited much of the text in both editions. Lisa Lafromboise posed many helpful questions for the first edition; Alex Yau and Matthew Foti for the second. Laurentian University's retirees' research fund helped defray the cost of some travel for the original edition. Laurentian's Department of History, through chair Sara MacDonald, made available a collection of materials gathered to create a large encyclopedia of Northeastern Ontario. The listeners of CBC Morning North responded to requests for stories, some of which are included. Special thanks go to Morning North's host, Markus Schwabe and its principal technical operator, Roger Corriveau, with whom I did numerous broadcasts. Matthew Foti, who designed the interior of the second edition. Publisher Laurence Steven provided insights on the area and the book's contents for the first edition while Heather Campbell took the risk of a second edition as well as of the two-volume military history of the region.

Eileen Goltz, Darrel Manitowabi, Alan Corbiere, David Bell, Andre Laferriere and David Pearson contributed articles, or parts of articles. In the first edition Graeme S. Mount wrote numerous texts, shared research travels and presentations about our findings. He passed all book rights to me.

Many librarians, museum curators, welcome centre and economic development personnel, and other people gave advice, support and information. Some gave special tours. Some provided photos, others financial support. I hope none have been omitted in the following list: Christina McManus (Timmins), Doug Newman (North Bay), Sandy McGillivray (Little Current), Marion Gilmour (Sudbury), Sharon Cornett (Haileybury), Marjike Mahaffy (Sudbury), Mike Dacey (Sault Ste. Marie), Tracy Winn (Sudbury), Donna MacLeod and Debra McKnight (Sudbury), Sheila Jacques (Smooth Rock Falls), Chris Clark (Blind River), Diane Salo (Sudbury), Lois Weston-Bernstein (Temiskaming Shores, who taught us how to spell without an i), Tim Gallagher (Espanola), Deb and Jib Turner (Little Current), Chat Noir Books (Temiskaming Shores), Highway Book Shop (Cobalt),

Cecile Langlois and Michelle Lebel (Kapuskasing), William E. McLeod (Sudbury; re: Chapleau), Tony Galic (Sudbury), Rick Nelson (Kagawong), Gary Duhaime (Sudbury), Alexa Wollan (Iroquois Falls), Mark Gregorini (Sudbury), Ajith Perera and Marc Ouellette (Sault Ste. Marie), Michael J. Mulloy (Sudbury), Harriet Kideckel (Sudbury), Erika Westeroth (Sudbury), Ron Janser (Ministry of Natural Resources), Margaret Clipperton (Walford) and the students, many formerly at Laurentian University, encountered at welcome centres, on trains and as tour guides.

Some informed persons reviewed our texts: Karen Bachmann, Debbie Berthelot, Rod Carley, Gaétan Gervais, Frances Heath, Maya Holson, Rick McCutchen, Ardis Proulx-Chedore, Johanna Rowe, Ursula Stange, Paul Trussler, Melissa Vernier. David Bell created the website and offered use of his special bird photos (see http://neontario.webs.com).